A Spirited Life

BOOKS by BOB ANDELMAN

Stadium For Rent
Why Men Watch Football
*Bankers as Broker*s with Merlin Gackle
Mean Business with Albert J. Dunlap
The Profit Zone with Adrian J. Slywotsky
Built From Scratch with Bernie Marcus and Arthur Blank
The Corporate Athlete with Jack L. Groppel
Profit Drivers

Will Eisner
A Spirited Life

Bob Andelman

PRESS™

Milwaukie

M Press
10956 SE Main Street
Milwaukie, OR 97222

mpressbooks.com

Book Design by Debra Bailey with Amy Arendts
Index by Randall W. Scott

Library of Congress Cataloging-in-Publication Data
Andelman, Bob.
Will Eisner, a spirited life / Bob Andelman.—1st M Press ed.
 p. cm.
 ISBN 1-59582-011-6
1. Eisner, Will. 2. Cartoonists—United States—Biography.
I. Title: Will Eisner. II. Title: Spirited life. III. Title.
 PN6727.E4Z55 2005
 741.5092—dc22

                                        2005026326

ISBN 1-59582-011-6
First M Press Edition: October 2005
10 9 8 7 6 5 4 3 2 1
Printed in the United States of America
Distributed by Publishers Group West

For Mimi and Rachel

CONTENTS

BLACK & WHITE

APPENDIX

Acknowledgments

Writing the biography of a man whose professional career covered more than seventy years is a formidable task that calls for the assistance, cooperation, and direction of many good people. In researching this book, I interviewed more than seventy-five people, plus many more who sent me further down the right path when it came to finding details or corroborating stories.

In truth, this project started in 2002 as an autobiography, with me helping Will Eisner tell his stories and organize his experiences. After reading the first draft, however, Will threw up his hands, laughed, and said, "This is too much work! Why don't you just write it and I'll authorize it?"

That's exactly what we did. The people I'd like to thank first are Will and Ann Eisner, who welcomed me into their lives almost weekly for more than two years, told me things they never told any interviewer before, and trusted me not to keep their secrets so much as to tell their story well. I hope I succeeded.

Will's death following heart surgery on January 3, 2005, came at a time when this book was already written and in production. It was a great shock to many of us. Personally, I lost a friend, a mentor, and, in many ways, a protector, someone who always looked out for my interests and spoke vehemently on my behalf when he felt the need. I miss Will for so many reasons, personal and professional, but that is a big one.

I'd also like to acknowledge the assistance and friendship of Will's brother, Pete Eisner, for many years the official gatekeeper to all things Eisner, who was a pleasure to know and deal with. His passing in December 2003 saddened me greatly.

This book was conceived during the first conversation I ever had with Will's literary agent, Judy Hansen. We started talking about 5 P.M. one evening, introduced by a mutual friend, Kevin Lang, and, more than two hours later, *Will Eisner: A Spirited Life* and a new friendship were cemented.

Denis Kitchen, Judy's partner in the Kitchen & Hansen Literary Agency and a father of the underground and alternative comics publishing industry, was at my elbow through every step of the journey. He offered advice, information, anecdotes, his Rolodex, and even his home as resources. (Thanks also to Stacey Kitchen for technical assistance and delicious meals!)

Diana Schutz, my first editor at M Press/Dark Horse, is always so calm. How?

Victoria Blake cleaned and scrubbed the manuscript in the editing stages, offering an independent eye on content and style. Thanks to Amy Arendts and Debra Bailey for the Eisner-esque design elements. And to Randall W. Scott, comic art bibliographer at the Michigan State University Libraries, for providing the book with the valuble index.

During the 1970s, Catherine "Cat" Yronwode did groundbreaking research into Eisner's life and career as his assistant and editor of *The Art of Will Eisner* and *The Spirit Checklist*. I am grateful not just for the platform she created but also for her graciousness in reconstructing her time with the Eisners.

Among the elements I hope set this biography apart from any reporting that preceded it are the interviews. When people heard this was a book about Will, doors magically opened. My thanks to the following people for sharing their experiences and thoughts: Murphy Anderson, Paul Aratow, Tom Armstrong, Florian Bachleda, John Benson, Karen Berger, Ray Billingsley, Chris Browne, Charles Brownstein, Nick Cardy, Mike Carlin, Gary Chaloner, Bob Chapman, Mark Chiarello, John Coates, Jon B. Cooke, Jerry Craft, Dale Crain, Howard Cruse, Jack Davis, Jim Davis, Steven E. de Souza, Jackie Estrada, Mark Evanier, Jules Feiffer, Al Feldstein, Neil Gaiman, Lorraine Garland, Steve Geppi, Dave Gibbons, Mike Gold, Jerry Grandenetti, Bob "R. C." Harvey, Irwin Hasen, Stuart Henderson, Benjamin Herzberg, John Holmstrom, Arthur Iger, Robert Iger, Carmine Infantino, Jack Jackson, Jim Keefe, Joe Kubert, Adele Kurtzman, Batton Lash, Stan Lee, Paul Levitz, Bob Lubbers, Jay Lynch,

Scott McCloud, Patrick McDonnell, Jim McLauchlin, Legs McNeil, Angie Meyer, Bill Mohalley, Alan Moore, Geoff Notkin, Denny O'Neil, Robert Overstreet, Mike Ploog, Byron Preiss, Joe Quesada, Seymour Reitman, Jerry Robinson, Diana Schutz, Julius Schwartz, Garb Shamus, Jim Shooter, Dave Sim, Joe Simon, Ralph Smith, David Steiling, Roy Thomas, Kim Thompson, Maggie Thompson, Rick and Karen Trepp, Rick Veitch, Frank von Zerneck, Mort Walker, Jim Warren, and Marv Wolfman.

Marc Svensson provided me with videotapes of Eisner and *Blackhawk* artist Chuck Cuidera participating in a 1999 Comic-Con International in San Diego, as well as a 2002 panel on "The Eisner Shop." And special thanks to Marisa Furtado de Oliveira, for making her Eisner documentary, *Will Eisner—Profession: Cartoonist*, available and providing a translation of the Portuguese narration.

Among the many online resources I found enormously useful were: AbeBooks.de; WildwoodCemetary.com; Eisner-L, the Will Eisner List-Serv on Yahoo! Groups (http://groups.yahoo.com/group/eisner-l); Jerry Stratton's "The Annotated Dreamer" (http://www.hoboes.com/html/Fire-Blade/Fluff/Comics/dreamer.shtml); Ken Quattro's "Rare Eisner: Making of a Genius" (http://www.comicartville.com/rareeisner.htm); Lambiek Comiclopedia (http://www.lambiek.net); and Tom Spurgeon's index of Eisner-related sites (http://www.comicsreporter.com/index.php/briefings/commentary/674/).

Lucy Shelton Caswell, curator, and Dennis Toth, librarian, were extremely generous with their time and resources during my work at The Ohio State University Cartoon Research Library.

I am also indebted to the timeline created by N. C. Christopher Couch and Stephen Weiner for their book, *The Will Eisner Companion*, and their willingness to share information. Any fan of Eisner will find the *Companion* a must.

And a great big thank you to Michael Chabon and Neal Adams for adding their personal thoughts about Will Eisner with an introduction and appreciation, respectively.

An enduring personal support group has had my back for years. Thanks to Bruce Kessler, Allen Solomon, Steve Goldin, Jim Doten, Tony Doris, Steve Bonett, Bob Pinaha, Jeff Chabon, Sean Wood, Michael Bourret, Wayne Garcia, and Dean Hendrix.

Finally, my family always endures my being away for many hours—sometimes days—during the research and writing of a book. Special thanks go to: my niece and nephew, Chris and Tony White who housed and fed me while I did research at Ohio State University; to my wife, Mimi, who (correctly) never believes me when I say the book will be done next week at the latest; and to my daughter, Rachel, who broke the ice at my first meeting with Will by drawing him a picture of a snowman ... in a snowstorm.

Author's Note

Will Eisner: A Spirited Life is the culmination of more than two years of interviews with its subject, as well as dozens of the men and women who intersected with his personal life and professional career during his eighty-seven years. His life is related through what, I hope, are fresh, untold stories from his colorful and vast experiences—shared with me by both Will and his friends. What you won't read here is an art critic's approach to Will Eisner's work; that credential is not in my résumé. This is not a critique of his brush style or wordsmithing; it is the story of Will Eisner's life and the way he lived it.

Introduction
by Michael Chabon

Back when I was learning to love comic books, Will Eisner was God. Not God as in Eric Clapton—to be bowed down before, forehead to the ground, in a haze of dry ice and laser light. Gustave Flaubert once wrote in a letter that "An author in his book must be like God in the universe, present everywhere and visible nowhere." In 1975 Will Eisner was God like that to me. Some of the artists and writers of the day whose work I liked most—Neal Adams, Jim Steranko, Steve Gerber, Steve Ditko— had been directly influenced by Eisner, but I didn't know that. All I knew about Will Eisner was what I had read in Jules Feiffer's *The Great Comic Book Heroes*. In that book by one of Eisner's protégés—a key work on the history of comics—Feiffer passionately instructed the reader that Will Eisner was a genius and a pioneer, the one from whom all others stole; and so forth. And I believed him. But I pretty much had to take Jules Feiffer's word for it. The eight-page Spirit story that Feiffer reprinted in his book—"The Jewel of Death"—remained for a long time the only full example of Eisner's work that I had seen. Eisner was out of print, out of comics. As a publisher, a packager, a talent scout, an impresario, and as an artist and writer, Will Eisner had created the world of comics as I knew it. But until I saw some of the later Warren (or maybe it was the Kitchen Sink) reprints, I really had no idea who he was or what he had done.

By the time I sat down to interview Will, in 1996, I was better educated. I had just started to write the novel that became *The Amazing Adventures of Kavalier & Clay*. A crucial part of my preparatory research was getting hold of all the Eisner I could find—the Spirit, the graphic novels, the books of comics theory—and the truth of Jules Feiffer's claims was obvious. Eisner brought radical technical innovations to the comics page—some borrowed from the movies, some from the theater, some from the fine art tradition—and that was impressive and important. But the amazing thing about his Spirit work—all of Eisner's tricks and technical bravado, his wild angles and striking use of shadow—was how fresh and new it still looked, even after fifty years of constant imitation by peers, inferiors, and successors. It was like *Citizen Kane* in that regard. And to a certain extent Will Eisner and Orson Welles stand as parallel figures in their respective media. Both of them were prodigiously gifted and managed at a young age to get their hands on a vehicle—a Hollywood studio, a newspaper syndicate—that would allow them to put on a dazzling display of those gifts. Both had a phenomenally sharp eye for talent in others, and the knack for yoking it to the service of their own schemes and ambitions. Both of them served as the secret and open inspiration, as touchstone and mark of comparison, for the generations of directors and comic book artists who followed them.

But Will Eisner had something—was something—that Orson Welles never quite managed, or permitted himself, or possessed a head hard enough to be: Will Eisner was a businessman. He was a Welles and a David O. Selznick, a Brian Wilson and a Clive Davis. He was labor and management. He was the talent and the guy who had to fire the talent. Sometimes he signed the paychecks, and sometimes he was hanging on, himself, until the next one came. He started companies, negotiated contracts, acquired rights, packaged material for sale. At the same time that he was practicing all that capitalism, he was dreaming and writing and drawing. He revolutionized an artistic medium, opened it up and theorized it and made it a superb vehicle for his memories, his emotions, his way of looking at the world. He had his failures, as an artist and as a businessman, because he took risks, as an artist and as a businessman.

Sometimes it's hard, trying to make art you know you can sell without feeling that you are selling it out. And then sometimes it's hard to sell the art that you have made honestly without regard to whether or not anyone will ever want to buy it. You hope to spend your life doing what you love, and need, and have been fitted by nature or God or your protein-package to do: write, draw, sing, tell stories. But you have to eat. Will Eisner knew that. He knew what it felt like to be hungry, to feel your foot graze against the cold hard bottom. He knew how lucky you were to be born with a talent that people would pay you to share. But he was also graced with the willingness (and when he was lucky, the ability) to get people to pay a little bit more, to drive the price a little bit higher, to hold out for a better deal or a lower price from his suppliers.

Will Eisner was a great artist and a skilled businessman, inextricably both. I loved that about him. More than fifty years after the first issues of *Blackhawk* and *Doll Man* and the other titles that he and his partner Jerry Iger packaged for Quality Comics had hit the newsstands, he still remembered the sales figures, the distributors' names, the dime-and-dollar details of hits and flops. And I sensed that all that stuff was every bit as interesting—every bit as important—to him as the nuance of an inked line, the meaning that could be compressed into and sprung from three square panels in a row. There may be many routes to happiness for a man; there may be only a few. But in his artistry and acumen—in the way that he moved so comfortably through the world as an artist who worked for money and a businessman who worked for art, I think he came awfully close to finding one of those routes. He was lucky like that.

Will Eisner: An Appreciation
by Neal Adams

I was born in 1941; I grew up as a teen in Brooklyn in the 1950s. I never saw *The Spirit* comic section in New York. None of the four big papers carried it. Will Eisner did not exist in Brooklyn.

Then, in 1953, my family moved to Germany for two years as part of the occupied forces there. When we returned, I became aware that something had happened in my absence. Comics had changed. Frederic Wertham and his book, *Seduction of the Innocent,* happened. There was no longer an EC Comics. I couldn't believe Captain Marvel was gone! Joe Kubert was no longer doing *Tor.* And Will Eisner—although he was not yet on my radar—essentially disappeared from comics. All that was left was DC doing these awful comics. And the Comics Code Authority was in place, calling the shots.

How was I to run into Will Eisner? He didn't exist in comic books when I broke into the business at Archie Comics in 1959 and was still invisible to the industry as I moved on to Warren Publishing's *Creepy* and *Eerie* before landing at DC in 1968.

Suddenly, in the hallways and around the water cooler at DC, Will Eisner's name would come up in conversation. "He created all these innovations!" someone would say. I knew by then that he created *The Spirit,* a guy with a mask, but I didn't get the reverence with which his name was spoken. Over time, people showed me bits and pieces of his work. And I'd look and listen.

After a while, as my comic book career advanced, the impact of Will's work began to slowly crush in on my head. It got to be a community. People would bring stuff in, making their arguments for his influence. We'd get together at the DC Comics lunchroom and exchange tidbits about what was going on in the industry. More and more people brought in Will Eisner's work and we became reawakened. "Where is Will Eisner? Did he go away? To Europe?" Then somebody threw *PS Magazine* on the table. "This is what Will Eisner is doing?" I said. "Holy shit!"

Then guys started to imitate Eisner's style. Mike Ploog did it first. Of course, he worked for Eisner, but we didn't know that then. When I met Ploog, he told me about Will, and, for the first time, he became real.

Time went by, and at some convention, I was introduced to "Commissioner Dolan." He shook my hand—it was Will Eisner! He was the Spirit and Dolan coming together! It was really cool. And he was such a nice guy.

By this point, I realized it was not just that Will Eisner did comic books, he did revolutionary things.

In my own life, I was setting another revolution in motion, trying to get artists and writers together to fight for better rates and reprint rights. I also led a much-publicized battle to get royalties paid to Superman's creators, Jerry Siegel and Joe Shuster. I had decided, if I was going to stay in, then I had to change the business to suit my way. Because the way it was sucked. Somebody like I was then would naturally be drawn to Will Eisner because he changed his corner of comic books to conform to something no one else would do.

When everyone was going to superheroes, he conceded to the marketplace and put a mask on his guy. But the Spirit was no superhero. Will never fell for the superhero thing. Then he took comic books to a new arena, *PS Magazine*, where you could contribute to your country and still do comics.

He did well because he had a brain. And he used it and continued using it. That's something you don't usually see in comic book artists. That's not an insult. But they don't tend to step forward and do many new things.

So here was Neal Adams in 1977 trying to shake up the world, and here was Will Eisner, who had already done it.

I could talk to him about a new idea or approach and he wouldn't say, "You can't do that." He would say, "That's possible." Now I'm the one telling a new generation of artists, "Don't start your sentences with the word 'No.' Start with 'Yes' and see what can be done."

I used to be on the board of the Academy of Comic Book Arts. I pushed them long and hard about demanding the return of original art from comic book publishers to artists. "We should at least say we believe in that," I insisted. And I would hear from the very artists who would benefit from this, "Oh, Neal! You're gonna get us fired! Why would they give it back? It's theirs."

But I knew if I told Will that I believed artists were entitled to own their art, this man who kept all of his own work over six decades would say, "How would you implement that?"

What I got from Will Eisner was a like mind. He was nothing like me, but in the areas of processing thought, moving forward, and taking a chance, we were absolutely like thinkers. If I were scratching around for an idea or I needed someone to bounce something off of, Will was the guy.

Several years back, my company, Continuity Studios, was approached about supplying the art and comic book stories for *PS Magazine*. I sat down and thought about it. But then I had a better idea. Joe Kubert has this school, The Joe Kubert School of Cartoon and Graphic Art in Dover, New Jersey, and he has eager, talented students there in need of practical work experience. It seemed to me that projects out of that school, done for the U.S. Army and controlled by Joe, would be a perfect fit.

I called up Will and outlined the idea to him. His response was, "That's a great idea, let's try to do it. Anything you need to know, Neal, I will give it to you. Have Joe call me; I'll give it to him." It was like calling a brother.

Take all those examples back to the earliest days of *The Spirit* and multiply by the thousands of people he touched in a long and sustained career, and that's why people love Will Eisner. Will is not a Michelangelo. He has his own style—it's semi-cartoony. But he tells a fuckin' story! That's why people are drawn to Will.

When people ask, "Who do you like in comics?" the two people I mention are Will Eisner and Joe Kubert. Everyone else is a skilled artisan. When it comes to human beings, it's Will Eisner and Joe Kubert, and then it's hard to keep counting.

Will Eisner and Al Hirschfeld
(Courtesy Will and Ann Eisner)

Al Hirschfeld, age 99:
"You still working?"

Will Eisner, age 85:
"Yeah. You?"

Hirschfeld:
"Yeah."

Eisner:
"How many hours you working?"

Hirschfeld:
"I quit at 7 P.M. You?"

Eisner:
"I quit at five. My wife won't let me work any later."

A Spirited Life

Four-Color

ONE
The Eisner & Iger Studio

Sam Eisner was impressed the first time he saw his sixteen-year-old son Billy's byline—"by William Eisner"—on an original comic strip in his DeWitt Clinton High School newspaper, *The Clintonian*, in 1933.

"It looks like you really want to do this," he said.

Billy smiled and nodded.

Inspired, Sam told Billy about a cousin of his who ran a large boxing gym in New York City, Stillman's. It was the "in" place where well-known boxers trained. Sam called Lou Stillman and told him about his eldest son's desire to be a professional cartoonist and asked if he knew any other cartoonists.

Stillman said, "I know one; he hangs around the gym a lot. He does a comic strip about a boxer. Let me get you an appointment, maybe Billy can get a job with him."

The cartoonist was Ham Fisher, creator of *Joe Palooka*.

One day, Billy carried his big black portfolio up the stairs of an old, yet posh Tudor building. He went up the elevator, knocked on the outsize oak doors, and who should open the door but James Montgomery Flagg. Flagg, whose early published work appeared in *Judge*, *Life*, *Scribner's* Magazine, and *Harper's Weekly*, was the painter of perhaps the most famous piece of American propaganda in the twentieth century, the World War I poster of Uncle Sam pointing his finger above the slogan, "I Want YOU For U.S. Army." Eisner would have recognized Flagg anywhere—he looked like his famous character.

Eisner was awestruck. All he could say to the legendary artist was, "Uh, what pen do you use?"

"290 Gillette," Flagg said.

"I went out and bought 290 Gillette pens," Eisner said later. "But I couldn't draw like him." Startled by meeting one of his idols in that way, Eisner replayed the scene many times in his mind. Retelling the anecdote to art students sixty years later, he said, "I always wished I could redo that moment."

Ham Fisher—his full name was Hammond Edmond Fisher, in his fifth year of producing *Joe Palooka* at the time Eisner met him—appeared a few seconds later and Flagg introduced their young guest. But Fisher didn't even want to look at Eisner's work. Instead, he railed about someone Eisner had not yet heard of, Fisher's "goddamn, rotten assistant who cheated me and stole my characters"—a fellow by the name of Alfred Gerald Caplin, better known a year later as Al Capp, creator of *Li'l Abner,* one of the most beloved strips in comics history. (Capp quit Fisher in 1933, complaining of poor pay, and allegedly lifted several hillbillies for his own use. They fought like cats and dogs through the '30s and '40s. In the early 1950s, Fisher took Capp to the National Cartoonists Society and tried to get him exposed and kicked out. Fisher himself was eventually banned from the National Cartoonists Society for allegedly manufacturing fake evidence against Capp.)

"That son of a gun is a dirty crook!" Fisher snapped. "I am fed up with assistants!"

Since meeting Ham Fisher was not the big break Billy imagined, he finished high school and applied for jobs at advertising agencies. College was not a financial option. His struggling parents needed whatever income he could bring home to the family. He made the rounds with his big black portfolio and was turned down over and over again. In New York City, that is a lot of rejection. Then as now, there were more agencies in Manhattan than in any other city in the world.

Finally, he was hired on the cheap by the advertising department of the *New York American* newspaper. Assigned a night shift, Billy worked from nine at night until five in the morning, creating spot illustrations for little advertisements that were known as pimple ads. A typical evening started in the newspaper's writing department on the fourth floor, where he was given his assignments. After lunch—which was at midnight—Billy went down to the third-floor art department and worked on whatever drawings were ordered.

That job lasted only a couple of months, because Billy ran into his high school friend Bob Kahn, who changed his name to Bob Kane.

Later, with the help of Bill Finger and Jerry Robinson, Kane created the character of Batman. Kane was taller and skinnier than Billy; he fancied that he looked a lot like the handsome crooners sweeping the nation's radio waves and making teenage girls swoon. He never played sports and often complained about lingering cold symptoms, although his friends thought he was a hypochondriac.

Billy Eisner and his family lived one block off the Concourse, the main avenue running through the Bronx; Kane, whose father was a successful insurance agent, lived in a big apartment farther down the same street.

Eisner and Kane, who were often together in art classes at DeWitt Clinton High School, got along largely because Eisner envied Kane's way with the ladies, while Kane admired Eisner's talent. Kane's art was not the best, but he was spirited, ambitious, and gifted with a sense of humor. "Quite honestly," Eisner said later, "he was a poor artist. But he was an aggressive guy. He was always able to get two things. I was a much better artist and cartoonist than Bob at the time, but he got jobs and girls, so I hung around with him."

Most Saturday nights they went out together. Eisner was so preoccupied with cartooning that he never made time to develop a social life that would enable him to meet girls. But Kane would call him up and say, "I have a date for you." Their double dates usually involved dancing at

Undated photo of a teenage Will Eisner
(Will Eisner Collection, The Ohio State University Cartoon Research Library)

places such as the old Glen Island Casino, way at the end of Pelham Parkway.

It was 1935, the golden age of big bands such as the Dorsey Brothers and Benny Goodman, and the young artists liked to dance with the girls at the Casino. "The trouble with Bob," Eisner said, "was that the girls he brought were always pretty but utterly stupid. *Really* stupid, what Al Capp referred to as 'stupid American beauty.'"

Kane's nightclub behavior was predictable—he ran out of money a lot and Billy wound up paying the check. Another typical element for them on a night out was showing off their cartooning talents for the girls. Whatever Kane drew, Eisner drew better. It was a competitive artist thing; the girls couldn't care less. They liked the music, they wanted to dance, and that was it.

On the way back one particular night, Kane asked Eisner, "How did ya do?"

"Well," Eisner said, "I got a feel."

That was pretty good for a high school senior in those days. Too good, in fact. The ever-competitive Kane never double-dated with Eisner again.

━━━━━━━━━

Kane had many interesting quirks as an artist and person. One of them was a matter of vanity: he claimed to be four years younger than Eisner, despite attending DeWitt Clinton High School as classmates.

"Bob had enormous pride in the fact that in high school he got more attention for his art than Will did," said Mark Evanier, a comic book writer, animation scriptwriter, and comics historian (*Mad Art : A Visual Celebration of the Art of MAD magazine and the Idiots Who Create It; Comic Books and Other Necessities of Life; Wertham Was Right!*). "And he thought Will was a genius. Bob used to tell me that he became an artist for two reasons, and both were girls. He would draw a picture and girls flocked around him. The other reason was that there were art classes where you could draw naked women. Where else, at that age, could you see naked women?"

As well as Evanier knew and liked Kane, he said that whatever stories Eisner might tell about Kane, they were probably all true.

"There was always something sleazy about Bob," Evanier said. "Bob was a hustler, always getting a deal. He did as little work as possible. Bob, whatever else he was, was a guy who figured out how to make it pay. His role models were newspaper strip guys. They thought it was delightful that you sold your strip, got successful, and hired people to do it while you stayed in a hammock. Ham Fisher never drew *Joe Palooka*. Bob got Batman sold, got a franchise going, and let other people do the work (most notably writer Bill Finger and artist Jerry Robinson). He thought Will was amazing because Will kept drawing. Will did more art in his eighties than Bob did in his entire life."

Whatever Kane thought about Eisner, he didn't share it with readers of his 1989 autobiography, *Batman & Me*. Kane and his cowriter, Tom Andrae, made just two mentions of Eisner in that book, each vague (they were competitors on their high school newspaper) and about a sentence long. And one was just wrong: Kane credited Eisner with co-creating *Wow! What a Magazine!*, but Eisner always credited Kane with telling *him* about the magazine, which is where Eisner met his future partner, Jerry Iger.

That same year, the first modern-era Batman movie came out, and Kane made an appearance at the Comic-Con International in San Diego doing promotion for signed and numbered prints that he drew. "Will was making an appearance at my booth at the same time Bob was next door pushing his prints," recalled Kitchen Sink Press Publisher Denis Kitchen. "Both were besieged by fans. When there was a momentary lull, Kane leaned over the dividing curtain and insisted that he and Will get together for drinks when the convention closed, which I recall being 5 P.M. Will nodded his head in agreement. Before Will departed with Bob at 5:00 he whispered to me, 'I have a very important call at 5:15.'

"At a quarter after, I dutifully went to the nearby bar," Kitchen continued. "I apologized profusely for interrupting the two and told Will that he had an urgent call that he had to return right away at his hotel. He shook Kane's hand and we left.

"'Fifteen minutes with that man is all I can bear,' Will explained to me outside."

A year and a half after finishing high school, Eisner and Kane had a chance encounter on the streets of Manhattan. After exchanging pleasantries, they got down to business.

"What are you doing these days?" Eisner asked.

"Selling cartoons to *Wow, What a Magazine!*" Kane replied.

"Do you think *I* could sell them any?"

"Bill, they buy from *everybody*," Kane said. "Go up there and see."

Wow!'s office was in the front end of a loft on 4th Avenue. The owner was John Henle, whose real business was the shirt-manufacturing factory in the back. Henle had literary ambitions and wanted to be a publisher; his magazine was based on the format of British boys' magazines that featured stories and cartoons. It presaged the advent of comic books.

As Eisner was showing his work to Sam "Jerry" Iger, the *Wow!* editor, Iger received a phone call and said abruptly, "I have to go now. I can't look at your portfolio. We have an emergency and I have to go up to the engraver's plant."

"Can I walk with you?" Eisner asked desperately. "Let me show you my work while we walk."

Eisner knew that if he came back another day, the opportunity might not be waiting. So he accompanied Iger and showed him his work as they walked up the street. Even on the sidewalks of New York, it was quite a sales pitch. Iger feigned interest in a few pieces and asked an occasional, distracted question. When they arrived at the engraver's shop, there was a big problem. For some reason, the printing plates were being punched through.

"We aren't getting a clean repro here," the engraver said.

Several puzzled men stood around a big stone table, scratching their chins and shaking their heads in frustration. Eisner stood by silently.

Fortunately for them, Eisner handled design and production for his high school yearbook and literary magazine, and knew about burnishing tools and printing because he also worked after school in a print shop cleaning presses for $3 a week—one of the most valuable learning experiences he ever had. In those days, you maintained or repaired your equipment yourself; if you didn't, you were out of a job. So he knew a few printer's tricks.

Eisner cleared his throat.

"Do you have a burnishing tool?" he asked.

"Yeah, sure," the engraver said dismissively. "Here."

Eisner brushed and rubbed the burrs in the plates. When printers
make engravi͟n͟g͟   es leaves burrs on the edges where it
                         l the burrs down. Problem solved.
                         d said, "Who is this guy?"
                         ly new production man."

                         vays found a way of capitalizing on a
                         ow! office and Iger grabbed Eisner's
                         e look. In earnest, he said, "What do
                         r's first adventure story, "Capt. Scott
                         s popular *Doc Savage* pulp stories.
                         eatured on the August 1936 cover of
                         cover. Two months later, after only its
                         oke.
                         for Eisner.
                         product was called a comic magazine
                         issue of *Famous Funnies* in May 1934.
                         h color reprints of Sunday strips such
                         eff," "Tailspin Tommy," and others.
                         ge comic published by Eastern Color
                         Eastern Color produced the color
                         day newspapers around the country,
                         et size and folding them in half to a

                         geoning new American industry at
                         Funnies sold like hot cakes on the
                         on to reprinting daily newspaper
strips such as Chester Gould's *Dick Tracy,* compiling a complete new
adventure every six weeks. All the adventure continuity strips followed
a similar reprint pattern.

But sudden success meant new challenges. Publishers soon exhausted
the supply of daily and Sunday strips available to the new comic magazines. There were only so many newspaper strips in the country at the

time, of which maybe ten or twenty were adventure strips that could be reprinted as serials. (Humorous, non-serial strips were also reprinted.) Simultaneously, the once invincible pulp magazines were declining in circulation. But while the pulps faltered, their distribution system held great value. American News Company and Union News dominated the newsstands in America. Both distribution companies were looking for a suitable replacement for those pulp racks. Comics were ideal.

Where pulp publishers saw an economic hammer coming down, the inexperienced Eisner, then nineteen years old, saw a golden opportunity. He was living with his parents in the Bronx, unemployed after the collapse of *Wow!*, thinking about all this. Though his instinctual silver-lining insight would one day become the hallmark of his career, in 1937 Eisner was motivated only by a hunger to establish himself and prove his talent. Gathering his courage, he called Jerry Iger. It was a gutsy thing to do, considering that two months earlier Eisner was a novice cartoonist begging Iger for a chance to get published professionally.

"Jerry, can you meet me downtown?" Eisner asked. "I have a proposition for you."

Iger was out of work after his position at *Wow!* came to an end, and he agreed to meet Eisner. They rendezvoused at a little restaurant on 43rd Street, across the street from the printing plant of the *New York Daily News*. Eisner had all of $1.95 to his name.

"Jerry," he said, "I want to start a company and I want you to be my partner."

Iger, for some reason—probably his own desperation—didn't laugh in the young man's face. (Eisner had told Iger he was twenty-five, not nineteen.)

"The new comic magazine publishers will need original material," Eisner said, barreling forward. "Let's create complete new stories for them. I would like to start a comics studio."

"Aw, kid," Iger said, "that's going to take money."

Iger had just resolved his second divorce. It was the middle of the Great Depression and he was damned near penniless himself and already owed future alimony. That's probably why he didn't blow Eisner off. What other options did he have? "I don't have any money left," he said, "maybe a couple hundred bucks. And my ex-wife is getting half of that."

"*I* will put up the money," Eisner said.

Iger knew how little Eisner made while working at *Wow!*, but he agreed to the plan anyway. "If you will put up the money, okay, I will go along with it," Iger said.

Eisner approached Iger because Iger was thirteen years older and he possessed the real-world business experience that Eisner lacked. Iger was also a good salesman. And he bore characteristics not great for human beings but perfect for a salesmen—he was feisty and aggressive. Iger had no hesitation in cold-calling, and just because someone said no the first time didn't stop him from asking again. And again.

Eisner was just nineteen years old and very much an artist. He couldn't go out and sell his own stuff, couldn't handle the inevitable rejection.

He told Iger about a building at 43rd Street and Madison Avenue where the landlord rented no-lease rooms (to bookies, mostly), charging just $15 a month. For that price, lessees got a roughly ten-by-ten room— enough space, Eisner guessed, for a desk and a drawing board.

Eisner had just done a commercial job for a printer on Varick Street. The printer paid him $15 for a cartoon promoting Gre-Solvent, a hand-washing soap. It was Eisner's first commercial comic sale; he titled it "Sketched from Life." He also could borrow $15 from his father for the second month, so he had enough cash on hand for two months' rent.

Iger and Eisner shook hands on the deal. Since Eisner was the financier, Iger let him pay for lunch. The bill came to $1.90, leaving Eisner a single nickel to return him to the Bronx on the subway. Iger didn't know that, of course, and, as they were leaving the restaurant, Iger chided Eisner for being too cheap to leave a tip for the waitress.

"You didn't leave a tip."

"Oh, I didn't? I forgot."

The Eisner & Iger Studio—Eisner's name was first because he put up all the money—created adventure-, science fiction-, and jungle story-themed comics. The two young men didn't know it then, but they'd opened a packaging house. They put together ideas with writers and artists, selling the finished work to publishers rather than

Will Eisner's first paying job as an artist and writer was this pamphlet for Gre-Solvent.
He used the proceeds to pay the rent on the first Eisner & Iger Studio

(Will Eisner Collection, The Ohio State University Cartoon Research Library)

publishing it themselves. One of their first publisher clients, Fiction House, hired the duo to do adaptations of mid-nineteenth century Irish novelist Charles Lever's adventure stories. Fiction House also published a line of pulp magazines that included *Planet Stories,* which was science fiction, and *Jungle Stories.* Eisner had created "Sheena, Queen of the Jungle" as a Tarzan-like character for their *Jungle Comics* title.

In the beginning, when it was just the two of them, Eisner wrote all the scripts and drew the studio's first five comics under five different names including Willis B. Rensie ("Eisner" spelled backwards), W. Morgan Thomas, Erwin Willis, Wm. Erwin, and Will Eisner. When Iger wasn't out on the street selling their services to comic book publishers, he did the lettering for most of the books, putting the spoken words in balloons next to a character or narrative above or beside them.

As the workload rapidly increased—Eisner & Iger created the Universal Phoenix Feature Syndicate to distribute their creations globally—they hired other artists and parceled out the assignments to a young but immensely talented (and fast) stable of artists. The bull-pen continued the books in whatever style Eisner established. Comic book studios were operated like galley ships in those days; Eisner & Iger hired about fifteen staff people, and together they quickly rowed into bigger offices.

One of the first people Eisner hired was his high school chum and date magnet Bob Kane. "I must confess, I was pleased to do that," Eisner said. "He worked for me for a short time before he quit to create Batman for *Detective Comics*." Kane's first original comic for Eisner & Iger was *Peter Pupp*. It was a deliberate imitation of the charming new funny-animal characters being created by an animator named Walt Disney.

In 1938 Eisner hired Jacob Kurtzberg, whose name Eisner changed to "Jack Curtis." Later on, Kurtzberg changed it again to "Jack Kirby." Kirby—who later in his career became known as the "King" of comics—came to Eisner & Iger at the age of seventeen from Max Fleischer's animation studios, producer of *Ko-Ko, Betty Boop,* and *Popeye the Sailor* cartoons. His most noteworthy work for Eisner was the production of features such as *The Count of Monte Cristo*.

Then there was George Tuska, Bob Powell (who was born Stanislaus Koslowsky), and Lou Fine, who, just out of the Pratt Institute, was already a recognized illustrator. They were all good men and top-notch illustrators who were later recognized as fathers of the industry. Artists Bernard Baily (later the cocreator, with Jerry Siegel, of "The Spectre") and Mort Meskin (he did "Sheena" for Eisner and later worked on "Vigilante," "Starman," "Wildcat," and "Johnny Quick") also were employed at the studio.

Eisner & Iger often advertised for artist/illustrators. There weren't many career comic book people floating around in those days, because the field was so new. As a result, most of the recruiting was done from the related fields such as the pulps, or book and magazine illustration. In fact, many recruits came from the fine art field—people like artist Alex Blum (*Spy Fighter, Shark Brodie, Kayo Kirby*) and letterer Martin DeMuth.

The studio initially started selling comic book art to publishers at $5 a page and ultimately pushed the price up to $20 a page. Comic books were sixty-four pages then, twice the length of today's typical comic, and Eisner & Iger produced them in assembly-line fashion, the way Henry Ford revolutionized and standardized automobile production. Eisner had an instinct for creating efficient systems. He hired everyone on salary because it was more practical, kept talent in place, and gave Eisner better control over quality than if he paid for work by the piece.

In addition, hiring his staff gave Eisner immediate oversight and control over the direction of the stories. In contrast to staff artists, freelancers worked at home, delivered their work, moved on, and rarely looked back. But staff artists did what they were told. And in those late-Depression days, a salary was a lot harder to come by—and more desirable—than freelance work. Even though their salaries gave them less than their aggregate work was worth on the riskier freelance market, Eisner & Iger artists were paid enough to keep them steadily eating and working.

Party invitation designed by Eisner for Fiction House publisher Thurman Scott
(Will Eisner Collection, The Ohio State University Cartoon Research Library)

During this time, Eisner created a remarkable roster of original second-tier strips including "Yarko the Great" (the forebear of "Mr. Mystic") and a buccaneer comic called "Hawks of the Seas," which was inspired by Rafael Sabatini's pirate stories. "Hawks" was actually the strip's second incarnation, having first appeared—for four episodes—in *Wow!* as a feature called "The Flame."

One of the legendary stories of the Eisner & Iger bullpen was George Tuska's unrequited love for Toni Blum, a staff writer and daughter of artist Alex Blum. Tuska was one of those men that every woman wanted to sleep with—muscular, strong, and yet gentle. It would have been just as reasonable to see him as a lifeguard at a pool instead of drawing comics.

Referring to Blum's daughter, Bob Powell once told Will—in front of the entire studio—"I could fuck her anytime." Incensed, Tuska slowly cleaned off his brush, placed it on his desk, and decked Powell. Then he walked back to his table and calmly returned to drawing.

Eisner's telling of the Tuska story in his 1986 graphic novel *The Dreamer* left out many details. For example, he himself had an unfulfilled crush on Toni Blum.

─────────

One day Eisner received a letter and sample art from two Cleveland kids, Jerry Siegel and Joe Shuster. They were peddling two comic strips, one called "Spy," the other "Superman." Eisner wrote back and told them they weren't ready yet and suggested they study their craft at the Cleveland Art Institute for another year.

"The truth of the matter is that when I saw their stuff, I didn't think that any of our customers would buy it, and I was right," Eisner said. "They sent their work all over New York, and none of the publishers bought it until Harry Donenfeld, publisher of National Comics (now known as DC Comics) got it from Maxwell Charles "M. C." Gaines (publisher of the first comic book, *Famous Funnies*) as part of feature material for his new *Action Comics* series."

Siegel and Shuster, of course, went on to great fame, if not great fortune, and Superman became one of the world's greatest cultural icons. Eisner shrugged off the missed opportunity because virtually everyone else in the industry missed it, too.

─────────

A National Comics accountant named Victor Fox played a strange and unpleasant role in Eisner's early comics career. Privy to National's financial books, Fox saw how much money the company made on its *Superman* and *Action* comic books. He quit working for Donenfeld and started his own company, hiring the Eisner & Iger Studio to produce his books at $7 a page.

"What I want," Fox told Eisner at a meeting, "is a guy with a red, tight-fitting costume, and a red cape."

Wonder Comics No. 1
(Courtesy Gemstone Publishing)

By the time Eisner returned to his studio, he was more than a little dubious about Eisner & Iger's new assignment.

"Hey, Jerry," Eisner said, "this sounds just like Superman."

"Don't ask me any questions," Iger said. "Just do it. He's paying us well for it."

Eisner tried arguing with Iger, but it went nowhere. A paying customer with deep pockets was like a newly crowned head of state as far as Iger was concerned. Bow, scrape, and collect your money on the way out the door was his attitude.

"Just do it," Iger said.

So Eisner did it. The character he created was called Wonder Man.

Shortly thereafter, Fox Features Syndicate published *Wonder Comics* number one featuring Wonder Man and was promptly sued by Donenfeld. It was the only issue published, although Eisner did produce a second, unpublished story for the character, who in "real life" was mere mortal Fred Carson, a "timid radio engineer and inventor." Carson received his powers from a magic ring given to him in Tibet by a yogi.

As Wonder Man's creator, Eisner was subpoenaed. He felt the weight of a great dilemma. Iger, however, didn't see what the big deal was, and couldn't understand his partner's angst. "It's simple. Go into court and say you thought up the idea, and that's it," Iger said. "They can't sue *you* because you were paid for it."

"I can't *do* that," Eisner said. "It's not true. Victor described the character exactly the way he wanted him in a handwritten memo. Obviously, a complete imitation of Superman."

"Will, the guy owes us $3,000. We need that money."

And Fox was no better. Worse, actually. "This guy was a little Edward G. Robinson type of a guy," Eisner said. "He looked me straight in the eye and said, 'Kid, you go into court and you tell them it was your idea. Try anything else and you will never see the money I owe you.'"

Iger, meanwhile, told Eisner, "We're dead in the water without that dough." The studio was growing and thriving due to its reputation as a reliable source of quality art and stories, and Fox was a major contributor of that success, at least on paper. The money he owed Eisner & Iger was the difference between profit and barely staying afloat.

Eisner agonized about what he'd say at the trial. Finally, he decided that he couldn't commit perjury and, when called to the witness stand, he testified that Fox literally instructed Eisner & Iger to copy Superman. That was all it took. National won its case, a landmark which gave National dominance in the field. (The decision's effects didn't stop there: Fox's Batman-like rip-off "The Moth" was dropped from *Mystery Men Comics,* eventually finding a home with Fawcett Publications' long-running and best-selling "Captain Marvel" family of comics.)

Fox was furious with Eisner. Iger was fed up with him, too. "We ain't gonna get anywhere with you acting like this, Will!" he scolded. "This is not high school, you know!"

Needless to say, the studio didn't collect the $3,000 Fox owed it. That was a huge amount of money to be out, and the partners struggled for some time after that to catch up.

The trial's aftermath also cost them the continuing services of the future "King" of comics, Jack Kirby. Without Fox's business, the studio couldn't afford to keep Kirby (who went on to create or co-create Captain America, Boy Commandos, Fantastic Four, The Hulk, The X-Men, Thor and the Silver Surfer), among others, on staff. Fox hired Kirby to work for him directly.

In many ways, Eisner was a role model for Jack Kirby. "Jack never spoke in less than glowing terms about Will. Will was beyond reproach," Mark Evanier said.

Before joining the Eisner & Iger Studio, Kirby worked for a number of syndicates that sold strips to smaller newspapers, drawing several under pseudonyms. He was at that stage in his career when he should have been learning on the job, but there was no one there to teach him.

When Kirby went to work for Eisner in 1936, he was nineteen and it was the first time he was surrounded by talent. Finally, he could see how real cartoonists worked and grew. It was a learning experience not only about art but also about business. "Jack looked at his time with Will as a major point in his career," Evanier said. Kirby saw what Eisner had and he wanted an office and employees of his own. For poor young Jewish kids, having a job and hiring other people were signs of status. What Eisner did didn't seem so out of reach to Kirby.

The record of his career showed that Kirby never cultivated Eisner's business acumen. Of course, when it came to negotiating rates or contracts and talking to accountants, neither did most people in comics. While Kirby and Joe Simon formed one of comics' most enduring partnerships in 1940, and even operated their own studio for a time, it became clear that business administration was not their forte. (Simon didn't come to terms with Marvel Comics on rights to a char-acter he created in 1941, Captain America, until late in 2003, long after Bob Kane settled with DC on Batman and Siegel & Shuster—with the help of Neal Adams—worked a charitable deal as compensation for their creation of Superman.)

One of the most famous stories about the Eisner & Iger Studio stars Kirby, not Eisner. "The Towel Story," recounted by Eisner and Kirby on the lecture circuit and by Eisner in *The Dreamer,* was actually about towels, not coffee, as many people believed. It didn't ring true sixty years later because who thinks of towel service in an art studio today? But at the time, the Eisner & Iger bullpen employed fifteen artists and was in the market for a cheaper source of clean, laundered linen towels for the office washroom. Services brought fresh towels in the morning and took away dirty ones, much as the milkman once delivered fresh bottles to American porches and removed empties every morning.

Eisner called the company's provider and warned that the studio was looking for a new towel service. The following Monday morning, a goon straight out of Hollywood-gangster casting—broken nose, black hat, white tie, and black shirt—showed up at the office.

"We own the towel service," the goon said. "We wondered, 'Why you are unhappy?' Please, don't make no trouble."

"Well, there are other people we can call," Eisner said.

"No, that's where you're wrong," he said. "We have this building."

While Eisner talked with him, Iger became feisty and the conversation got a little hot. Out of the back of the studio walked Jack Kirby. He went right up to the goon.

"You get the hell outta here," Kirby said in his most threatening Brooklynese. "We don't want to deal with you. We won't take any fucking shit from you. Get out."

As the goon walked out, he turned and said, "Let's not make any trouble; let's be nice."

When the man was gone, Eisner called another service to solicit a bid. When Eisner told them the studio's address, they said, as predicted, "We can't service it."

"I heard the story from Jack and from Will and they pretty much match up," Evanier said. "It was basically true. Jack came out of a tough neighborhood. He was a short guy but a tough guy. In a fight with someone a foot taller, I'd bet on Jack. Jack was never afraid of a fight. And that showed in his drawing—he drew like a tough guy. When his characters threw a punch, I think he felt it in his own body."

Eisner also envied the circulation of Kirby's work, especially *Young Romance*, which sold about one million monthly copies at its height. But Eisner managed a nice career without going hat-in-hand begging Timely/ Marvel Comics founding publisher Martin Goodman for work.

"Jack felt that an awful lot of people were talented the way that Will was, that comic books were full of geniuses that could do something people wanted to read," Evanier said. "Will was the only one who made it pay. He never had that reduction to subservience that Jack's peers did. All the other artists and writers were prisoners of the mediocre men who ran comic books. You ran into this wall at DC and Marvel, where no matter how well your work sold, the best you could get was a $2-a-page raise. Will got out of that trap."

Kirby wasn't well paid most of his career, despite creating or cocreating many of the industry's most successful characters. Even during his prominence in the 1960s, following the cocreation of the Fantastic Four, the Incredible Hulk, and other concepts, he was unable to turn that fame into anything substantive. "What am I doing wrong that I'm not rich?" Evanier quoted Kirby as saying to himself over and over again. Even if he went from Marvel to DC and back, he was still in this little box.

Iger and Eisner got along, but Iger was a difficult guy.

Most Saturday nights Iger made the rounds of New York's night-clubs. Every once in a while on a Monday a girl wearing black fishnet stockings and a tight dress would sashay into the office and say, "I'm your new writer."

"*You're* writing for *us*? Writing *what*? Who hired you?" Eisner would ask.

"Jerry hired me on Saturday night."

"Saturday night?"

"I met him at a nightclub. Cute little guy. Said he draws funny books."

Iger wasn't all bad, of course. In a charitable mood one Friday after-noon, Iger said, "You work all the time. You need a break, so I set up a date for you tonight."

"You really have?" Eisner was stunned.

"Come on," Iger said, "it will do you good."

They went up to a house that Iger knew well in Hastings-on-Hudson. Eisner spent the night with a girl who Jerry introduced him to. It was a welcome break for a guy who stayed at the office from the crack of dawn until long after the sun went down.

On Monday morning, Iger came into the studio and said, "Did you have a good time Friday night?"

"I sure did. Thanks, Jerry!"

"So how much did you leave her?"

"I didn't leave her anything," Eisner said. "Why?"

"You *shmuck*!" Iger said. "These girls make their living this way."

"You mean they … were … *prostitutes*?"

"What did you expect? You think a guy like you's gonna get that lucky without paying for it? *Kerrrrist,* Will! I'm going to have to pay her myself."

Eisner said, "I'll mail her the money. Tell me how much."

"No," Iger said in frustration with his partner's utter naiveté, "I'll take care of it."

When their partnership began, Iger lived in a small room in Manhattan's George Washington Hotel on 23rd Street. As his income rose, he moved uptown into a larger apartment where he hired a Japanese valet. Eisner, by contrast, still lived on Riverside Drive with his parents, helping with the family bills and conserving his money whenever possible.

Some staffers and associates simply didn't get along with Iger. Eisner often interceded in the arguments, and then Iger would say, "Why the hell did you do that? Are you trying to make out that you are the nice guy around here?"

Iger gave Eisner hell one day. He said, "I know what you said to the guy at the bank; you said, 'My partner—you have to *understand* him.'"

Eisner didn't lie. He said, "That's *exactly* what I said."

"Will, keep your goddamn nose out of my business. I don't need you to defend me!" Then Iger yelled and scolded him, as if he were talking to a child.

Still, Eisner learned a lot about business from Iger. Iger attracted overseas business for the studio by creating the Universal Phoenix Feature Syndicate, which sold reprint rights to the British and Australian editions of the comics tabloid *Wags*. When they started out, of course, Eisner was the "money" man. Iger went into the partnership without much initial enthusiasm—Eisner was the same age as everyone else in the shop, except Iger—but Iger had the contacts and he knew where comics were being bought; Eisner didn't know those practical aspects yet. Eisner didn't like his partner much personally, but he respected his savvy at the negotiating table and absorbed all he could. What he learned about business from Iger would serve him well for decades to come.

TWO
A Spirit (and Quality Comics)
is Raised

Everett M. "Busy" Arnold, publisher of Quality Comics, called Will Eisner in the fall of 1939. It was one of those fateful calls that less fortunate people never receive, or don't recognize the opportunity it presents until years later.

"I don't want to speak to your partner," Arnold said rather mysteriously. "I want to speak to you."

Most of the studio's customers didn't like Jerry Iger, particularly when it came to discussing creative matters, and it wasn't unusual for someone to seek Eisner out for a private conversation.

Arnold and Eisner met for lunch, which led to another secret rendezvous. As a guy who spent much of his life reading pulp magazines and creating comic books, there was nothing like a whiff of mystery and intrigue to keep Eisner interested. If nothing else, he could always use it later as a plot point in a story of his own.

At the second lunch, Arnold introduced Eisner to Henry Martin, sales manager of the Register & Tribune Syndicate. "We have an idea," Arnold said, "and we would like to see if you are interested."

Newspapers around the country were taking note of the explosive growth of comic books. They felt they were in danger of losing a segment of their readership to this new industry. Conversely, they thought comic books, properly presented, could be a magnet for new readers. Martin's idea was the production of a sixteen-page "ready-print," a freestanding insert similar to today's *Parade* magazine or the regional TV-listings magazine distributed in Sunday newspapers. What the newspaper syndicate needed was somebody like Eisner to put it together.

Arnold was at the meeting because he was the publisher of Quality Comics, as well as a printer. He could print the newspaper supplement for the syndicate.

Eisner said to Arnold, "Why come to me? You have all these guys working on comic books for you." Eisner discovered that the syndicate already tried the best guy on the Quality staff, but he proved not good enough. The medium was still in its infancy and not everybody understood it yet. Not only that, but the syndicate was afraid that this particular artist wouldn't meet deadlines because he drank heavily. In newspaper production, there is no margin for lateness. Newspapers come out at the same time every day, 365 days a year. Nobody would stop the presses because the comic book artist was on a bender the previous night and didn't finish the current installment. Eisner was reliable, and he respected an inflexible deadline structure. So much for art! But Eisner was also astute, and sophisticated enough to recognize that his reliability was his trump card to play.

Eisner took the assignment with the understanding that it meant leaving Eisner & Iger. The comic book newspaper supplement would be a full-time job. Seven or eight pages a week were a daily grind, not to mention supervising production of a second eight pages. Besides, Arnold said the only condition of the deal was that Eisner produce it independently of Iger. He wanted nothing to do with Iger. This obliged Eisner to make a decision.

The Eisner & Iger Studio was a corporation of which Eisner owned fifty percent of the stock. Iger owned the other fifty percent. The partners had agreed that the first person to leave the corporation would offer his stock to the remaining partner. This arrangement, common to partnerships, assured that, in the event of a separation, neither of them would be saddled with a partner he didn't know or like.

Eisner offered Iger the option to buy his stock and Iger agreed, with the proviso that Eisner would not raid their bullpen for talent. Eisner would be restricted to hiring no more than three or four people out of the Eisner & Iger Studio.

In the studio at that time there were more than a dozen artists and writers working full-time on salary. Eisner asked for Lou Fine, Bob Powell, and Chuck Mazoujian. Fortunately, they all wanted to come with him and Iger did not object.

Still, Iger couldn't resist telling Eisner that he was crazy to take the newspaper project on. It was 1939 and war was coming. Iger said, "You are going to be drafted, sure as hell, and you pick now as the time to start something new? You're crazy, Will! Who knows where it will go?"

At the time, Eisner was so eager to gain the larger, more diverse and respectable readership that the newspaper field promised that he sold Iger his share of the company for $20,000. It was probably worth much more, but compared with the $15 investment that started the company—and the fact that no one in the Eisner family had ever seen that much money in their lives—made it quite a windfall for a twenty-two-year-old.

In selling his half to Iger, Eisner sacrificed his financial interest in any and all the characters he had created or cocreated while at the studio, including "Sheena, Queen of the Jungle." It was a good business decision because it prevented Iger from obstructing anything Eisner did in the future. Eisner was initially afraid that the notoriously litigious Iger might come back and claim authorship for any ideas used in Eisner's new creations.

"That was a little bit of self-preservation business I no doubt learned from Jerry," Eisner said, amused by the irony.

=====

Decades later, long after Eisner sold Iger his share of the studio in 1940, Iger began taking credit for developing Sheena. By then there were few people alive who could argue otherwise. It was only the two of them, one man's word against the other's.

"Anybody who knew the company laughed (at his claim) because Iger never created anything," Eisner said. "He ran the business side of the company and his creative contribution was limited to the lettering of the books."

Iger tried to sound convincing. He told a comic book fanzine in 1985 that the name "Sheena" came from "Sheenie," an anti-Semitic phrase. Eisner maintained that none of the many Jewish artists who worked at

Eisner & Iger would have ever taken part in something so hypocritical, offensive, and crude.

The true origin of the character's name, according to Eisner, was from H. Rider Haggard's book *She,* one of the first fantasy-adventure novels. *She* was about a heroic woman, and Eisner freely admits that he used *She* as a basis for the naming of the jungle-adventure character.

═══════

Iger often boasted that his $20,000 buyout of Eisner's share of their company was a steal. It really didn't matter to Eisner; this was his big opportunity to climb out of the comic book ghetto. At least that's what Eisner thought. At the time, his literary nutrition was the pulp magazine. He was a big fan of O. Henry, Ambrose Bierce, and Guy de Maupassant, and religiously read all of their stories.

So Eisner made a deal with Busy Arnold and the Register & Tribune Syndicate. When the question of the character copyright came up, Eisner's partners wanted to own the rights, as was standard policy for syndicates. But Eisner firmly said, "That's a deal-breaker." Two years of partnership with Jerry Iger had taught him the full value of rights ownership. Even though 1940 was still early enough in the comics business that officially licensed spin-off products—movie serials, TV series, radio shows, Captain Midnight decoder rings, Superman pajamas, and Batman cowls—had not yet evolved into a lucrative ancillary industry, Eisner saw enough potential to want full ownership of his rights.

"We can't do a deal like this," Arnold said. "The newspapers will not accept a comic strip that is copyrighted by the cartoonist himself. They are afraid that the artist will abruptly walk off the job and stop production, leaving them high and dry. If this should get popular, and you leave, we'll have a serious problem."

So Eisner proposed an unprecedented solution, which they accepted.

"I'll let you register my work in your name," Eisner told Arnold. "But our contract will state clearly that if there is any dissolution of our agreement, the property reverts to me."

As a result, the first few issues of *The Spirit* newspaper supplement were published bearing the copyright "Everett M. Arnold."

For such a young man—Eisner was barely twenty-three—he struck a tough business deal and became one of the very first cartoonists to own his own creations. Eisner's high school chum Bob Kane never owned Batman (although he did later tell Eisner that he negotiated a handsome annual stipend); Joe Shuster and Jerry Siegel literally signed away the rights to Superman, as was customary then, and years of litigation failed to recover them. Even Stan Lee, the modern father of Marvel Comics, has no copyright claims on the X-Men, Spider-Man, the Fantastic Four, or the Hulk. Ownership was vitally important to Eisner because he felt it would guarantee creative control.

===

At the start of his new venture, Eisner rented a fifth-floor, two-room apartment in Manhattan's Tudor City neighborhood and converted it into a studio/office for himself, Lou Fine, Bob Powell, and Chuck Mazoujian.

As he began noodling over new character concepts, Eisner's first idea for the newspaper supplement was to do a weekly Ring Lardner-style story in comic book form with no hero, just a slice-of-life short story every week. It was a highly literate idea, but not a commercial one.

Busy Arnold said no.

"We need a costumed character," he insisted.

"How about a detective?" Eisner countered.

It was raining outside of Eisner's studio as they discussed this by telephone, a future trademark scene right out of *The Spirit*. (Artist Harvey Kurtzman later created a Yiddish-sounding name for the rain that frequently pelted Eisner's panels. He called it an *Eisenshpritz*.) Arnold was not in his office but called Eisner from a nightclub or bar; Eisner could hear the jukebox playing. Arnold had already had several drinks and he was slurring his words.

"What's *thish* detective of *yoursh* look like?" Arnold asked.

"He is tall, and he is good looking, sophisticated—kind of like Cary Grant."

"But what's *hish* costume like?"

"Costume?" Eisner said innocently. He had no interest in drawing costumed heroes.

"*He'sh gotta* have a costume," Arnold said. "Can't sell *thish* thing to the newspapers without a costume! They're expecting a costumed hero."

"He wears a mask," Eisner said. "Like, *um,* the Lone Ranger." Eisner was drawing him even as they spoke, so he quickly drew in a mask that covered the detective's eyes.

"That *thoundth* good," Arnold said.

"He wears gloves, too!"

"Okay, *thash* great; *lesh* go with that," Arnold said. And he hung up.

Arnold was happy, but a masked detective character really wasn't what Eisner had in mind. First of all, Eisner had no intention of creating a superhero. (The word "superhero" wasn't used in those days; the industry called them "costumed guys.")

Incidentally, the Spirit's hat should have especially pleased Arnold—it was the same style as the one he always wore. It was an "in" joke for Eisner, one his partner never got.

———————

Batman's base of operations was an elaborately designed cave beneath stately Wayne Manor. Superman changed his clothes in alleys and telephone booths, and later got away from it all in his Fortress of Solitude at the North Pole.

Eisner gave The Spirit an underground home beneath Wildwood Cemetery in Central City.

"I don't know whether it really occurred to me, a Jew," Eisner said, "that the Spirit's origin was a Christlike idea, like the Resurrection. I think it was more of an instinctive solution. It was just that I needed a place to show where he went after he 'died.' I was fascinated with suspended animation after reading an article somewhere about somebody who died—supposedly died—after going into cardiac arrest. He came back to life shortly afterward, and I thought, *gee, this is a great idea. I'll use that.* I had private investigator Denny Colt come back—after everyone presumed him dead—as The Spirit. Only his sidekick Ebony and Police Commissioner Dolan knew the truth. I didn't want him to be supernatural. I didn't want him to be a superhero. Over the years, I tried so hard to get rid of his mask; he wore dark glasses for a while, and he even went blind once."

Eisner designed the cemetery, or at least what he thought one would look like. "My whole idea was absolutely absurd, of course," he said. "*The Spirit* dug a hole in a cemetery and constructed a secret headquarters and home underground. It even had air conditioning! Then there was the Autoplane, which either the Spirit or his sidekick, Ebony, could drive or fly. I quickly abandoned it after Bob Kane gave Batman a Batmobile. It just wasn't necessary in the stories that I wanted to tell."

In addition to *The Spirit,* Eisner needed two additional features to fill the Sunday supplement's weekly sixteen pages.

He added "Lady Luck" (created by Klaus Nordling) and his own creation, "Mr. Mystic" (itself a remaking of an earlier Eisner character, "Yarko the Great"), and turned them over to the veteran artists he brought with him from the Eisner & Iger Studio, Mazoujian and Powell, respectively. Powell offered the extra bonus of being able to write his own scripts. (Nick Viscardi took over "Lady Luck" when Mazoujian moved on to create advertising art. Viscardi was, in turn, followed by Klaus Nordling.)

As for Lou Fine, the third man in the new bullpen, he came with Eisner because he wanted the freedom to work in his own way on features of his own making. As part of his deal with Busy Arnold, Eisner was to create several traditional newsstand comic books. In fact, Eisner had aspirations of becoming a publisher himself.

Unlike the packaging operation of Eisner & Iger, Eisner made a deal with Busy Arnold to publish two more magazines as equal partners, plus *The Spirit.* One of the magazines was *Hit Comics;* the other was *Police Comics.* He created new features for them, including *Doll Man, Uncle Sam, Blackhawk, The Black Condor,* and *Espionage.*

In addition to the three artists who came over from Eisner & Iger, Eisner hired artist Phillip "Tex" Blaisdell. Dave Berg and Al Jaffee—who both later became famous at *MAD* magazine for their distinctive humor and strange characters—eventually joined the shop as steady freelancers, with Berg drawing *Death Patrol,* a predecessor to *Blackhawk.*

Back in the Eisner & Iger days, Eisner laid out pages for storytelling, and he had developed generally agreed-upon production standards. Like the Walt Disney Studios or any other, there was a creative philosophy characteristic of Eisner's shop. Eisner insisted on stories that made sense—even in a comic book reality—and had a beginning, middle, and end. He believed in continuity of characters and their features, as well as keeping them similar to real people in speech and behavior when appropriate. His love of adventure and short stories gave him a grounding that less well-read competitors lacked.

The Spirit made its first appearance on June 2, 1940, in five Sunday newspapers with a total national circulation of one and a half million. *The Philadelphia Record,* one of the section's charter newspapers, reported a ten percent increase in circulation after *The Spirit* began to be distributed. At the height of *The Spirit*'s success in the mid-1940s, the strip appeared in twenty newspapers and was available to five million readers.

Adults were drawn to *The Spirit* because of Eisner's ability to produce and tell a noir "B" movie every week in just seven pages. And his opening splash pages were amazing and consistently innovative. Unlike other artists, Eisner didn't rely on a set logo every time, a practice that was unheard of in comic books, newspapers, or magazines. To put what he did in context, imagine the *New York Times* changing its front-page logo every day. Not likely. The Old Gray Lady is known for her moribund consistency. Because of Eisner's gutsy originality, *The Spirit* became universally recognized for the proud inconsistency of its brand mark.

Despite his character's instant popularity, Eisner always worried that someone else would come along with a competitive newspaper supplement. And, indeed, the Hearst Syndicate tried producing one. Will Gould created a detective hero called "Red Barry." It didn't last long. Hearst abandoned the product after about six months, and no one ever challenged Eisner again.

"On the other hand," Eisner said, "competition is something that you really don't worry about because it opens up the marketplace; it lends a legitimacy for your own product. The amazing thing—astonishing, really—is that *The Spirit* was the first of its kind and the last of its kind. Stan Lee (creator of Spider-Man, Fantastic Four, X-Men, Silver Surfer) told me that he was going to try to start one at Marvel Comics in 1980 but he never got anywhere with it."

The new Eisner studio at 5 Tudor City consisted of one large room, a bedroom, and a small kitchen that was nothing more than a wall. Eisner used the bedroom as his private office. (Staffers frequently borrowed the key on weekends as a place to bring their dates. There was no bed, but the couch was extremely popular.)

Front page of *The Spirit* Sunday section, *Newark Star-Ledger*, December 29, 1940
(Will Eisner Collection, The Ohio State University Cartoon Research Library)

Only Bob Powell was given his own key to the Tudor City studio apartment. If Eisner wasn't there, he could count on Powell to open up in the morning or close up at night. By his own description— confirmed by those who knew him at the time—Eisner led a monastic life during those days. While guys like Powell were leading wonderful, colorful lives, Will was the outsider, drawing the lives he thought other people were having.

One Friday evening, Will took a dinner break, planning to return and spend a quiet night drawing. But when he opened the door to his private studio, he discovered Powell with twin redheads. Embarrassed, Will quickly closed the door and waited in the outer room for them to finish.

Eisner drew beautiful women, but Powell—like Iger—actually got the women.

In one famous example, Eisner gave the character Sheena the looks of one of Powell's girlfriends. But what Eisner introduced to the pages,

Powell sometimes took away. In *Mr. Mystic,* a backup feature in the weekly *Spirit* comics, there was a character called the "Shadowman of Death." Every time Powell dumped a girlfriend, the Shadowman took her away.

Powell horrified Eisner because he was so casual with women. Powell would sometimes start a conversation with, "I picked up a couple of whores ..."

The main room in the Tudor City studio was the bullpen, the production shop where Powell, Fine, Blaisdell, and Mazoujian worked on *The Spirit* newspaper insert and the comic magazines Eisner created for Busy Arnold's Quality Comics imprint.

Fine worked on the studio's superheroes, The Ray and The Flame. He was a good artist, but Eisner found he needed better writers to carry out his concepts. He hired Blaisdell's brother-in-law, Dick French, to be a full-time writer.

(Fine sometimes slept overnight on the couch at the Tudor City apartment. He had polio as a child, which left him with one leg shorter than the other, and he couldn't walk well.)

Unlike Fine, Powell wrote and drew his own stories. Like Eisner, he also wrote scripts for other artists in the bullpen. He wrote an Eisner-created feature called *Death Patrol,* which later became *Blackhawk* (and became a fifteen-episode, 242-minute, 1952 movie serial titled *Blackhawk: Fearless Champion of Freedom,* starring Kirk Alyn, who also played Superman on the silver screen in the serials).

Another thing Powell was known for was being anti-Semitic.

He made snide remarks about Jews from time to time, which Eisner usually let slide, not feeling like it was worth making it into an issue. But when the war started and the world realized that the focus of Hitler's wrath was the Jewish race, Powell's complaining and nastiness became bolder.

Busy Arnold offered Powell a sizable raise to leave Eisner's shop and join the Quality Comics staff in Connecticut. Powell told Eisner about the offer, thinking he would get his boss's blessing and be on his way. But Eisner was incensed. He called Arnold and let him have it.

"Do you want a lawsuit?" Eisner asked. "This is terrible, stealing talent out of my shop! We're partners!"

Arnold backed down. He called Powell and apologized. "I'm sorry, Bob," he said. "I have to cancel the deal because Will Eisner is threatening to sue me if you come up here."

To Powell, Eisner's actions confirmed everything he always believed about Jews. In a rage, he stormed into Eisner's office.

"That's some kind of a cheap Jew trick!" he said. "You are intentionally hurting my career."

Despite his animosity toward the boss, Powell remained in Eisner's studio after the incident. When Eisner later turned the studio's operations over to Arnold and entered the Army, he received an unexpected letter from Powell. It read, in part:

> *Dear Bill,*
>
> *... I don't want to get sickly sentimental but as I probably wont (sic) get to see you before you go, I'd like you to know that all my best wishes go with you. I don't know what you think, but believe this. I never had anything against you personally whatever differences we might have had were because of business reasons, on my part anyway ... I might have said some nasty things when we were having our little trouble— which Tex probably told you—but they were said because I was boiling mad. Mostly, I find now, because of the fact that I'm much better suited to work by myself ... Now I'm sorry if I was hasty. You're a pretty okay guy, and it's too bad that we'll never be able to be real friends again ...*
>
> *So again, guy, the best of luck, show 'em how to do it, and give 'em hell ... and God bless you ...*
>
> *Sincerely*
> *Bob*

According to Eisner, the guy who really ran his Tudor City studio was an artist named Chuck Cuidera, whom he referred to as the shop steward.

One day, Cuidera stuck his head in Eisner's door.

"Hey boss," he said. "I gotta talk to you about something."

When Cuidera called Eisner "boss," it wasn't a sign of respect, it was an accusation, Eisner joked.

"We need a good inker around here," Cuidera said. "I've got a name—he's good."

"Good," Eisner said. "Tell him come in on Monday."

"He's here," Cuidera said. "He's got to start right *now*."

"Now?"

"He's working for (rival comics producer) Harry A. Chesler. Sit him down at my table and start him on something now. I'll be right back."

Eisner stepped into the bullpen and found a young man sitting there, trembling. He had no idea where Cuidera went, and no idea why he was hiring this nervous kid.

"What's your name?" Eisner asked.

"Alex Kotzky."

Cuidera's instincts were right; the kid had talent and made his mark over the next decade, drawing *The Spirit, Plastic Man, Doll Man, Espionage, Kid Eternity, Manhunter,* and *Blackhawk.* Cuidera, incidentally, left the studio that day to smuggle Kotzky's pencils and personal belongings out of Chesler's shop before their competitor knew the kid was gone.

Cuidera was on hand when another famous character of that era came into existence—Blackhawk. Blackhawk was the star of *Military Comics,* produced by Eisner and published by Quality Comics. The parentage of the war veteran was never an issue during the 1940s, 1950s, or 1960s. But in the 1970s, when comic book fandom took on a life of its own and fans sought out more details about creators and their creations, a schism developed between Cuidera and Eisner.

"Chuck claimed *he* created Blackhawk," Mark Evanier said. "And he was mad at Will for claiming *he* created it. Will never says Chuck created Blackhawk."

In recent years, Eisner, not wanting to upset Cuidera, whose only claim to fame in comics was his early involvement with *Blackhawk,* stopped claiming credit for creating it. He didn't deny it, but he didn't claim it, either.

Murphy Anderson worked alongside Cuidera at DC Comics during the early 1960s and for Will Eisner in the late 1960s. Thirty years later, Anderson was instrumental in getting Cuidera invited to the San Diego Comic-Con where he was recognized for his contribution to Blackhawk and appeared in a panel discussion with Eisner.

"Chuck had felt he wasn't getting enough credit for it, but Will just shrugged his shoulders and said, 'Well, what can I say?'" Anderson recounted. "Chuck had deep feelings about Will, and I think he felt a little guilty about him, too. I have heard a lot of stories about the shop that Will had back in those days, but most of them were just anecdotes. And there are always a lot of people working for someone, for anybody, for a corporation or whatever, who gripe about the work, and I think that is all it was, because everything I have ever heard is that Will was fair."

During a panel discussion at the San Diego Comic-Con in 1999, Eisner and Cuidera were reunited for the first time in decades. Evanier was the moderator and Eisner lost no time in setting the tone.

"I've been wanting to say this for a long time," Eisner said, "because there's been a lot of talk about who created what. *It does not matter.* It's not important who created it. It's the guy who kept it going, who made something out of it! Whether or not Chuck Cuidera created or thought of *Blackhawk* is irrelevant. The fact that Chuck Cuidera made it what it was is important; that's where he should get credit."

"Will was careful on that panel to not take anything away from Chuck but not concede anything, either," Evanier said. "My theory is that the notion of who created Blackhawk was very casual. Will probably said to Chuck, 'Let's do a book about so-and-so. Chuck then drew the first story. Chuck said Bob Powell wrote the first; Will said he did the first. I think Will believed he created it, but there was no harm in letting Chuck take some bows for it. Besides, nobody remembered Chuck's work after (later *Blackhawk* artist) Reed Crandall got it."

Comics historian R. C. "Bob" Harvey agreed with Evanier's assessment of the duo's San Diego appearance. "Will handled that panel with his typical grace," he said. "He said it didn't matter *who* created

Blackhawk. It's who *perpetuated* it. Chuck created the ambience; if any-one should get credit, Will said, it's Chuck. He gave credit to the man who needed it. It was a marvelous bit of diplomatic maneuvering."

After his comic book-industry historical novel *The Amazing Adventures of Kavalier & Clay* was published, Michael Chabon found himself pulled into the controversy over the creation of the "Blackhawk" character. Chabon had off-handedly credited the title to Eisner in an interview, inadvertently stirring up a sensitive topic.

Eisner took him aside at a convention and said, "I didn't create it, that was Chuck Cuidera." He wasn't upset that Chabon had said it, but he wanted to make sure that in the future, if the issue came up, Chabon didn't cite him as the creator.

Chabon believed that it was more a measure of Eisner being gracious to Cuidera, who was closely identified with the title, than actually resist-ing the credit for himself.

"There's a great epigraph at the beginning of the first volume of Gabriel Garcia Marquez's memoirs, *Living to Tell the Tale,*" Chabon said. "It reads: 'Life is not what one lived, but what one remembers and how one remembers it in order to recount it.'"

Eisner artist Tex Blaisdell brought a real kid into the studio one day in 1939. "The idea," Eisner said, "was that this kid would sweep up and at the same time have the opportunity to look at the artwork. For a twelve-year-old kid, that was quite an experience."

The kid's name was Joe Kubert.

"Even the twelve-year-old kid who swept the floors in our office had talent," Eisner said. Kubert went on to draw *Tor, Hawkman, Sgt. Rock,* and *Tarzan.* Later he also became a brand name in the industry as an educator, founding The Joe Kubert School of Cartoon and Graphic Art in Dover, New Jersey, and as a graphic novelist, producing *Fax From Sarajevo* and *Yossel: April 19, 1943.*

"I was just starting high school," Kubert said. "I had been going from pub to pub, playing hooky from school with my partner, Norm. We went to the High School of Music and Art in Manhattan, uptown.

I lived in Brooklyn. It took me an hour and a half each way to get to school. When we'd got out of school, Norm and I would go to visit comic book publishers.

"I met Jerry Iger first," he said. "Iger said, 'Yeah, kid, go up and see Will, maybe he'd have something for you.'"

During Kubert's summer holiday from school, Eisner gave him a job pushing a broom.

Eisner was the boss at Tudor City. He was physically removed from what was going on in the fifteen-by-fifteen production room where the staff artists worked. Kubert only visited the boss's office once or twice; the notion that they were the only Jews in the place did nothing to spark a friendship.

Will Eisner at work, undated photograph
(Will Eisner Collection, The Ohio State University Cartoon Research Library)

Kubert remembered being struck by Eisner as a handsome, dashing figure.

"First of all, he had a lush head of black curly hair," Kubert recalled. "He was a good looking guy, trim, slim, and a head of hair. He always gave me the impression that he was in control of everything going on. Not throwing his weight around or having to prove he was the boss. But you *knew*. Even as a kid, I recognized that. I could talk to the other guys pretty well. But not Will. He was laid back, but you knew he was the boss. He had been dealing with adults in areas most people feared to tread. One of the lessons he taught me was that it's as important for an artist to know what he's doing business-wise as well as art-wise. We're not just responsible for drawing pictures and telling stories, but also finding out what happens to our art after it leaves our hands. What happens when the engraver gets it? Nobody saw our original art. Everyone gauges your work when it's printed. But if we put quality into our work, everybody who touched it afterward would take that same care because they would have a sense of it."

There were half a dozen drawing tables set up in the main room. Bob Powell, whom Kubert remembered as being rather intense, worked by the window next to Nick Viscardi (who later changed his name to Nick Cardy). Fine worked upstairs at Tudor City, apart from the others; Kubert didn't meet him until much later. Tex Blaisdell's table was by the wall. Kubert's station was off to the side, away from the artists.

"Tex said, 'Sit there, kid,'" Kubert said. "The guy I probably got closest to was Tex. He was lettering and running the shop. During lunch hour, we'd play handball. There was a schoolyard downstairs with courts set up."

In time, Kubert's responsibilities increased to include erasing pencil marks from the finished boards and doing cleanup work, using white paint where he couldn't erase the pencil. "The great thing about where I was positioned was that I could see what they were all doing," he said. "Going over their work was a tremendous learning experience for me. It was important to me to get the information, seeing where the guys worked, the kind of tools they used. The real value was seeing what went on in the business. I got paid $12.50 a week. To me, that was a fortune. It went a long way; I couldn't have asked for more.

"I remember a cover that Chuck Cuidera did. It was a good example of the work done at that time. Blackhawk was climbing down a hemp rope and there was a spotlight circle behind him. I got this on a thirteen-by-eighteen board. I started whiting out the whole thing and I got involved in the rope. I was putting more hair in it, taking it out. When the drawing was done, I was putting in more lines, taking out other lines. When I finished, Chuck looked at it and said, 'All you're supposed to do is *erase* and *clean*. Don't draw on my stuff!' He wasn't mean, but he wanted to make it clear he didn't want anyone to change or alter his drawing once he was done with it."

Kubert remembered meeting Dave Berg in the studio. "He was doing similar things, but was more advanced than I," he said. "Dave didn't have a full-time job in the place. He would do some work, drop it, and then leave. I don't remember him working on *The Spirit* itself. The work I remember that he did were half-page inserts in the back of *The Spirit*. In the back, sometimes they'd need a half page of drawings, nothing related to the main strip. It wasn't something steady. Will let me do that and I think Dave had the opportunity to do that as well, to write as well as draw."

When Eisner was in the Army, Kubert officially joined the Quality Comics staff. He is credited with inking many *Spirit* sections from November 1942 through August 1943, and with often drawing the strip from August 1943 through December 1943.

───────────────

Nick Cardy joined an ad agency after high school in 1939 and shortly thereafter showed up at the Eisner & Iger offices—post-Eisner—looking for work. Iger sent Cardy's samples to Eisner at the new Tudor City offices. Only when Eisner approved of his work did Iger hire Cardy on.

Why did Eisner's opinion matter to Iger after their partnership ended? Because Eisner couldn't produce all the comics that he owed Quality with just his own studio.

Few people know, even now, that Eisner subcontracted a great deal of work to Iger. It was a marriage of convenience, not choice. And as correspondence in the Will Eisner Archives at The Ohio State University Cartoon Research Library demonstrates, the relationship between Eisner, Iger, and Arnold was rarely less than contentious. And it's worth noting that all of Iger's letters were written on "Eisner & Iger, Ltd." stationery—long after Eisner left his partner.

Here's a sample of the back and forth:

> *December 26, 1941*
> *Dear Jerry,*
> *... In closing may I take a crack at the statement in your letter of December 4th where you say "Maybe I'm a fool, but I've turned down considerable business so that I may better serve you in your books. What do I get in return?" Are you trying to be funny or do you think I am a bit simple? You never turned down any business because of me and grabbed off all of the accounts you could get from such magazines as* Pocket Comics, Champ Comics, *and* Speed Comics. *And aren't you the same Jerry Iger who started* Great

Comics *and* Choice Comics *with Fred Fiore even though you were supposed to be concentrating on producing extra-good work for E. M. Arnold and Thurman Scott? Don't make me laugh, Jerry.*

And please don't tell me again that you personally developed every top-notcher in this business including Bill Eisner. He was largely responsible for the success of Eisner & Iger as you well know. Bill always was a swell artist with a flair for writing interesting plots and nobody helped develop him except Wm. E. Eisner, a lot of natural ability and plenty of good hard work.

In regards the $10,000 you paid Bill for his share of the business, may I remind you that I had nothing to do with this and it was a matter entirely between Wm. E. Eisner and S. M. Iger. We paid you several thousands (sic) dollars as a split on the first ten issues of Hit Comics *and* National Comics *after Bill sold out to you and you got plenty more from Scottie about the same time. So I guess the deal you made with Bill was pretty fair to you both ...*

Sincerely yours,

E. M. Arnold

(In copying the above letter to Eisner, Arnold handwrote at the top: "Maybe you better send Jerry some smelling salts and flowers. Is paragraph #5 on page 3 okay or did Jerry really develop W. E. Eisner?")

(Arnold got the amount of Iger's buyout of Eisner wrong, incidentally. It was $20,000, not $10,000.)

April 3, 1942

Dear Jerry,

It was nice seeing you again in New York. When I reached Stamford, I really looked over "X of the Underground." On the level, this stuff is almost as bad as the work done on this unfortunate feature heretofore. Busy may be a little more lenient in purchasing B material than I, for after all, he has more books than I have …

I would like to repeat that I am one of the boys and I think I know good stuff when I see it … and I don't see it in "X of the Underground."

Cordially yours,
Bill

April 4, 1942
Dear Bill,

While I don't agree with you that the feature "X of the Underground" is bad, I'll put another man on it … What in 'ell has come over you? Making cracks about "B" features and "being one of the boys" and "factory jobs." As far as this office is concerned, we consider all features important.

If you don't think I can handle this feature to your satisfaction than (sic) perhaps you'd better forget it.

Sincerely,
Jerry

April 6, 1942
Dear Jerry,

Come, come, come, Mr. Iger, since when did I have to pull punches and kowtow or even worry about supersensitive feelings with you. I thought at least to YOU I could speak my mind (what there is of it).

As for the quality of that feature, Busy agrees with me that it wasn't the best I could have gotten for the money. In fact, he doubts whether it was done by the "Kid Patrol" artist …

Believe me, Jerry, it is very important to me to have Military Comics the best-published book I could turn out. For I am not selling pages—I make my money as, if, and when, the public buys the magazine. So if I am a little cranky about that, please understand.

Re. your last paragraph—I DO think you can handle this feature to my satisfaction and I have no intention of forgetting it.

Sincerely yours,

Bill

April 6, 1942

Dear Bill,

This is a letter to end all letters, except cordial ones! Is it a deal? Must I send you an affidavit or get a Philadelphia lawyer to convince you that "X of the Underground" was done by the artist who does "Kid Patrol"!

It is also vital to me that all features leaving this office produce readers, for obvious reasons.

Kindest regards,

Jerry

April 8, 1942

Dear Jerry,

It was nice to see you again despite our "hot" correspondence which I think has cooled off and will be very placid in the future. I liked the artist you proposed for "X of the Underground" and after talking to Mr. Smith (who is obviously a very intelligent young man), I am sure that "X of the Underground" now has a happy future ...

Thanks for being so helpful and tolerant.

As ever,

Bill

Without Eisner, the Eisner & Iger Studio was run on an even tighter budget, according to new hire Nick Cardy.

"Iger said, 'Nick, we're expecting taborets," recalled the artist. "'Meanwhile, you go to the grocery store on 3rd Avenue and get yourself an orange crate.' When I started work in the studio, all the artists had orange crates with spilt ink all over them. These guys—and their crates— had been there a long time! I realized that there were no taborets coming. The crates were twenty-eight inches high with cheap slatted wood on the outside and a little divider inside for shipping oranges."

Cardy was paid $18 a week by Iger. Some months later, the boss called him over, smiling.

"*Pssst!* Nick!" Iger said, wiggling his finger. "Look in your pay envelope. There will be a surprise."

And there was: a fifty-cent raise!

"Iger used to have these tall, sexy girls come parading around the office," Cardy recalled. "And here was Jerry, five-foot-five, thin, with a puffed lower lip that affected the way he spoke."

The other thing Iger did on a regular basis was get the bullpen's attention. "Around three o'clock every afternoon, when guys were falling asleep, he'd drop a metal basket on the cement floor and would laugh as they woke up. It was like a bolt of lightning," Cardy said. To get even with Iger, one of the artists dropped a firecracker in Iger's wastebasket while he was asleep in his office. "I hated working with these guys after a while because if you had one practical joker, you never got any work done," Cardy said.

Around 1940, after Chuck Mazoujian was drafted, Cardy moved to Eisner's Tudor Studio where he took over the art chores on "Lady Luck" in *The Spirit* supplement.

———————

Comic book fans often romanticize the Tudor City bullpen. Chuck Mazoujian, Bob Powell, and Tex Blaisdell were there when Cardy arrived, although he didn't remember Lou Fine or George Tuska working with Eisner at the same time he did. Freelance writers periodically dropped off scripts but rarely hung around the office.

"My mother used to work in a sweatshop making pants," Cardy said. "Well, we made comics."

Powell, who sat at a drawing table behind Cardy in the bullpen, was the new kid's protector, much as Blaisdell helped Kubert along. "If I didn't know the ropes, Powell would say, 'Do it this way.' Or he'd say, 'Let's go eat here,'" Cardy said.

Powell even wrote Cardy's name into a "Lady Luck" story in which the characters were looking for the "Viscardi Diamond." But Cardy's time at Eisner's Tudor City office was brief; he moved on in 1943, shortly before Eisner himself left to fulfill his Army service. Many people shuffled around between studios and freelancing. There was a huge difference in what publishers such as Busy Arnold at Quality Comics and T. T. Scott at Fiction House paid the studios per page and what actually filtered down to the creative talent. Cardy, for example, tripled his pay rate when he left Eisner for a higher-paying staff art job at Fiction House. And, at the end of 1942, he was paid a $400 Christmas bonus on top of that.

═══════════

Busy Arnold was never shy—or diplomatic—about offering his two cents about the quality of the material that Eisner's studio provided. Here are excerpts from Arnold's many letters to Eisner:

> *July 11, 1941*
> *Here is another example of the terrible work your staff is doing.*
> *In one panel of "Lady Luck," Lady Luck and another man are in a rowboat. In the next panel, there are two men in the boat with Lady Luck.*
> *How about checking more carefully?*
>
> *July 15, 1941*
> *Ed Cronin has just called my attention to the fact that in the issue of the weekly comic book which you sent up today, both Lady Luck and Mr. Mystic have the same stories. They are both built around kidnappings aboard yachts and, of course, this is very bad.*

July 17, 1941

I am sending you proofs of the first Uncle Sam Quarterly. *I agree with you that this is certainly a very punk job and I am afraid that it is going to "lay an egg" on us. So try and start working on the second issue right now and make this a better book in every way ...*

Not only was Uncle Sam Quarterly *a very punk job but it was certainly not checked at all. There were at least 200 mistakes in spelling in the entire book and the same applies to* The Doll Man Quarterly. *In this book, your boys didn't even spell a word the same twice in a row. Sometimes Darrel Dane was spelled "Darrel" and at other times it was spelled "Darrell." Sometimes The Doll Man had a "The" before it and at other times there was no "The" before this word. Sometimes Doll Man was two words and other times it was one word, Dollman.*

Until we got these issues of Uncle Sam Quarterly *and* The Doll Man Quarterly, *both Ed Cronin and I thought Jerry Iger took the prize for sloppy work. But we are now convinced that your boys are way ahead of anyone in the business.*

August 20, 1941

The present installment of "Blackhawk" (Military Comics No. 5) was not a good art job and it looked as though Cuidera had not done enough of the work on this himself. In fact, this feature was also the worst to date.

The episode of "Death Patrol" was atrocious and this artist is very much of a "ham." Features like this certainly will kill Military Comics if they are not improved immediately. Cut out Tex Blaisdell's gag pages in the future as these are awful.

Eisner himself was not spared Arnold's sharp words:

October 3, 1941

I think that the October 19 issue of The Spirit *was absolutely the worst you have done to date and I don't think you should run any stories in this groove. This particular episode was altogether too heavy and profound. It is on the philosophical side and will not interest most readers.*

But the all-time classic complaint from Arnold to Eisner about the quality of his shop's work has to be this handwritten post script at the bottom of a typewritten January 13, 1942, letter:

P.S.—"Lady Luck" for the past couple of months has been awful—not even comic book quality.

━━━━━━━━━━

Joe Simon, cocreator of "Captain America" and longtime partner of Jack Kirby, was a contemporary of Eisner's from the earliest days of comic books. They knew each other, but never worked together.

"I met him through an engraving salesman named Arthur Weiss," Simon said. "When I was doing *Captain America,* Will had just left Victor Fox and Arthur married Will's secretary, Libby. She had a crush on Will; I guess he knew it. The marriage only lasted a year or so."

"Will Eisner was idolized by the people working in the field," Simon said. "He was right up there at the top, well respected. He had a different type of storytelling, more literate than a lot of the other guys ... that a lot of people tried to copy. The guy was only twenty-two years old and he was a legend among his peers."

THREE
Joe Dope Saves the U.S. Army
(From Itself)

Will Eisner's impending draft notice was like having the Sword of
Damocles held over his head.

From the day he walked out of the Eisner & Iger Studio, Eisner kept
telling himself, *You are crazy! You will be drafted, and this whole thing will
fall apart on you!*

> *July 30, 1941*
>
> *Dear Busy,*
>
> *I was interviewed by the Board last night and I
> feel that they looked favorably upon the sheaf of stuff
> in my dossier. What they want is proof, in the form of
> an affidavit, from the Syndicate, stating in effect that
> without me there would be nothing, and that this
> section is a new innovation and, consequently, in my
> absence, men in the engraving and printing plants
> would be without employment. The Syndicate might
> also state that, inasmuch as a great deal of the feature
> is my style of writing, artwork, mind, and personality
> and is unique, they feel sure that newspaper editors
> might refuse to accept substitution and, possibly, cancel
> present contracts, which they are permitted to do. You
> might also add that a daily strip is now in preparation*

*for distribution in the fall, which will give my features
an even greater daily circulation.*

*It might not be amiss if you, too, in the official capac-
ity of publisher, state that you depend upon me to guide
the policies and edit* Military, *and that my services in
that capacity are unique and cannot be duplicated.
Besides, the only reason you invested in a publication
was because of my personal services. I think it best to
keep my position that of a nucleous* (sic)—*out of which
things come, rather than that of a bottleneck.*

w

Busy Arnold tried getting Eisner deferred as a "journalist" via the
Register & Tribune Syndicate, which possessed some credible political
power. But his attempt went nowhere. He did that not so much out of
friendship, but as a matter of self-defense, because if Eisner was gone,
Arnold was contractually bound to maintain *The Spirit* property.

When a deferment didn't arise, Arnold wrote Eisner of another idea
in this handwritten, undated letter: "P.S.—Just got a brain storm (*sic*) to
write Wood in Washington and see if he could use his drag to get you in
the Army on a soft job with plenty of spare time."

When notice was finally served on him in late 1941, Eisner was at
first quite dismayed. *There goes my career*, he thought. But, after Eisner
absorbed the first sobering shock, the draft notice provided him with a
feeling of immense relief.

At the age of twenty-four, Eisner had spent his entire adult life work-
ing alone in one studio or the other, day and night. Work was his mis-
tress; the Tudor City studio was his home. Suddenly Eisner felt like
Uncle Sam offered a chance to find out what the real world was about.
And, like other Americans, he was imbued with a sense of patriotism.
America was at war. "The horrible, despicable Nazis were slaughtering
Jews—my people—and I was given the opportunity to kill some of them
for what they were doing to the Jews.

"All of those feelings were in effect for me," Eisner said. "But to be perfectly honest, I was overwhelmed by a secret feeling—and I remember it so clearly—that, wow, this is my opportunity to really see the world."

―――――――

While Eisner's professional position didn't exempt him from the draft, it did give him a little special status. Because he was a businessman with responsibilities for the livelihoods of at least five men, the draft board gave Eisner three months to put his business affairs in order. He immediately set to work on organizing the team that would continue in his absence.

He visited Busy Arnold in Connecticut and talked about the problem of going into the Army. Arnold suggested moving Eisner's studio to the Gurley Building in Stamford, alongside Arnold's own operation. Eisner agreed and, effective March 28, 1942, leased space right next door to Arnold's office, on the same floor. He even established a fund to help artists who wanted to move up there, generously offering each of them enough for a down payment on home mortgages.

Promotional materials for the daily "Spirit" comic strip
(Will Eisner Collection, The Ohio State University Cartoon Research Library)

Arnold's own on-site staff included editor Gill Fox, who had long admired Lou Fine's work on "The Ray" in *Smash Comics*. Fox, Fine, and their wives soon became close, lifelong friends.

Because of his success in maintaining copyright ownership, the value of that clause in Eisner's contract with the syndicate came into play at this point. Eisner retained silent ownership of the property because the work would be continued while he was away.

In addition to producing *The Spirit* Sunday supplement, Eisner started a daily newspaper version featuring his reborn detective. Arnold and the syndicate—led by the *Philadelphia Record*—pushed him into it, but Eisner wasn't ready.

"To this day," he said, "I don't think I'd enjoy doing a daily. To me, it's like trying to conduct an orchestra in a telephone booth." He didn't get any satisfaction from it. But the Register & Tribune Syndicate wanted a daily strip almost immediately because they thought it would be a natural tie-in.

The daily "Spirit" debuted on October 13, 1941. Eisner only did six weeks of dailies before he went into the service. The dailies didn't do well because he tried all sorts of weird ideas, such as a whole daily strip without dialogue and with nothing but footprints in the snow. Criticism came from some of the Sunday *Spirit*'s strongest supporters:

> *"I think the daily* Spirit *is hard to follow from one day to another because of the complicated plots,"* wrote Bill Hawkes, editor of the *Philadelphia Record*, on October 28, 1941.

> *"I think it advisable to do away with most of the fancy angle shots in the daily strip,"* wrote Henry P. Martin, Jr., the *Register & Tribune Syndicate* manager on March 23, 1942. *"Too many times they are confusing and apt to slow down a reader. The simpler the strip, the easier it is to read."*

After Eisner was drafted, he continued writing the strip for a while with Lou Fine drawing it. But Fine, for all his brilliance, couldn't accurately draw a fedora on a head—kind of important when the title character wears a hat everywhere he goes.

"And I'll tell you something else he did," Eisner said. "When I said to Lou, 'Let's make this guy stand in a funny pose'—say, Ebony, for example—the result was weird. Lou's idea of funny was to put a big ass on the character, with him kind of bent over. Look back over his *Spirit* stuff, and you'll see what I mean. He thought this was funnier than hell."

Jack Cole (pre-*Plastic Man*) followed Eisner as writer/artist before giving way to writer William Woolfolk and back to artist Lou Fine. The strip limped along until it was canceled on March 11, 1944.

Quality Comics Editor Gill Fox (who died in 2004) once said the strip was before its time. To which Eisner later said, "maybe, but more likely it was thirty years *after* its time."

———————

Joe Kubert commuted from Brooklyn to Stamford five days a week during his high school summer vacations—he never stayed over—to ink Fine's pencils on *The Spirit* while Eisner was in the Army.

Kubert worked in the shop for two years, even when Busy Arnold relocated the studio to Connecticut. But while the staff artists all moved north, Kubert commuted every day by train from Brooklyn. "I'm Jewish and it was the first time I ever ate a non-kosher meal—ham and eggs. My mother kept a kosher home; my father was a kosher butcher. Lobsters and ham and eggs were foreign and exotic to us," Kubert said. "This was when Lou Fine took over *The Spirit*. Alex Kotzky and I inked over Lou's pencils. (Kotzky later created his own comic strip, "Apt. 3-G.") It was an experience that I loved. I loved every minute working with Lou Fine. It was another tremendous learning experience."

There were some benefits to Eisner keeping *The Spirit* in production while he served his country, not least among them the regular monthly check from the sales of *The Spirit* and the other comics his studio produced on top of his modest Army pay. Eisner used part of the money to support his parents and two younger siblings, who were by then living in an apartment on Riverside Drive, in Manhattan. His father had survived two heart attacks and could no longer work. Sam Eisner spent his time painting at an art gallery, but technically he was retired.

<hr>

Eisner military portrait, undated
(Will Eisner Collection, The Ohio State University Cartoon Research Library)

Eisner was inducted in May 1942. He went to the Army Recruitment Center at Camp Dix in New Jersey, and from there he was assigned to the Ordnance Department at Aberdeen Proving Ground in Maryland. When Eisner got in, he tried hard to get a correspondent's job. Unfortunately, fate decreed that he remain stateside. An ordnance corps was decimated at Kasserine Pass in Africa just before his induction, and the Army literally needed more warm bodies to fill its ranks.

"I arrived at Aberdeen with several other raw recruits and began by living in a tent with other guys taking basic training," Eisner said. "Basic training consisted of learning to go through barbed wire and using a rifle. They discovered that ordnance troops needed fighting know-how because when a fighting unit was occasionally overrun, the ordnance troops needed to defend themselves."

One evening when Eisner was in his tent resting, two men showed up to see him. One was an enlisted man, the other a sergeant, Bob Lamar. They were editors of the camp newspaper.

The Spirit was distributed in the *Baltimore Sun* and Aberdeen Proving Ground was near Baltimore; the newspaper was widely read on the post and everyone seemed to know about *The Spirit* insert. Putting his name on the strip from day one started to seem smarter and smarter.

"We need a cartoonist on the newspaper," Lamar said. "Would you be interested in doing it?"

Eisner jumped at the opportunity to join the base's Public Relations Office; any soldier in the midst of the physical filth and mental degradation of Army basic training would take any office job if they could get it. He immediately began drawing editorial cartoons and a weekly humor strip, "Pvt. Otis Dog Tag," for the camp newspaper, *The Flaming Bomb*. When they discovered Eisner could write, too, he penned articles as well.

The officer in charge of the newspaper, Lt. Colonel Rifkin, told Eisner that the ordnance department had undertaken a British idea called "preventive maintenance," which would change the entire concept of maintaining equipment. It's hard to believe today, but sixty years ago, preventive mainte-nance was primarily a volun-tary task; back then it resulted from a voluntary request on the part of the soldiers.

Eisner, center, looks at latest issue of the Army newsletter *The Flaming Bomb*
(Will Eisner Collection, The Ohio State University Cartoon Research Library)

"Look," Eisner said to Rifkin, "this means asking these soldiers to do something voluntarily; you can't order high morale any more." Up to this point, preventive maintenance involved maintaining the condition of your equipment by putting oil in it—at the very least. It required marketing the idea to the troops.

"The way to teach that," Eisner said, "would be to use comics."

Rifkin came back a couple of weeks later. "Hey," he said, "remember that thing we were talking about? The people who are running maintain-ance are interested. Could you do a couple of comic posters?"

Eisner did sample instructional posters and his work was chosen over the competition because it had a rugged GI-look to it. It was the kind of handling and voice that made Bill Mauldin's "Willie and Joe" strip so successful. The same humor done by somebody else probably would not have come across as well.

Then Eisner heard from Rifkin again.

"Get prepared to move out," he said. "You are being transferred. There is even talk about giving you a field commission."

"Wow," was all Eisner could say. "I won't have to go to OCS (Officer Candidate School)."

They were *about* to give him a field commission. Unfortunately, President Roosevelt's sons each received a gratuitous field commission at the same time that Eisner was up for his, an event which generated a press uproar. So while Eisner was in Baltimore awaiting his field commission, the Army abandoned the concept. Instead, Eisner was told, "If you take a test in administration, we could make you a warrant officer, which would enable you to work on this material and you'd be *like* an officer."

And so Eisner became a warrant officer, junior grade. The Army used warrant officerships as a way of retaining talented people whose specialties they wanted to use. The Army tried using civilians for certain jobs, but found that civilians couldn't do the things that an officer could. For example, a civilian couldn't eat at the same places that an officer could. And the Army couldn't pay much or order the civilians from one place to another at will. So they created a rank called a warrant officer—someone who is made an officer by warrant.

Eisner was sent to Holabird Ordnance Motor Base in Baltimore. There, he was assigned to design posters illustrating the importance of preventive maintenance for the Maintenance Engineering Unit. An article in the November 5, 1942, *Holabird Exhaust* newsletter trumpeted Eisner's arrival on base with a front page sketch of the Spirit and a story that notes:

> *You can see him, if you're lucky, in Room #310 of the Det., polishing his shoes or dreaming up a scenario for his famed* Spirit *strip ... A large staff in Stamford, Conn., keep* The Spirit *going while Artist Eisner is in the Army, but {he} still plans these comic adventures, does most of the art and all the editing ... by mail.*

At the start of his military service, Eisner tried serving both Uncle Sam and Busy Arnold. He wrote *Spirit* stories during basic training and smuggled them out of camp to someone Arnold had waiting outside the gates. Literally. But after a while, he simply couldn't do both jobs, and he reluctantly let go of *The Spirit*.

It didn't take long for the quality to fall off, while Eisner stood by and watched helplessly.

"By the time I read it, it was already published," he said. "For a while, Busy thought about sending me the scripts in advance, but that didn't work out because I was more interested in seeing the artwork than the script. If I read a script, I envisioned it the way I would do it. I wasn't so concerned about the dialogue as I was about the visualization of the story."

On a leave one weekend, Eisner met Arnold in New York and complained about the artwork in *The Spirit* section.

"You really ought to talk to Lou Fine," he said. "He has the Spirit hat on kind of a cockeyed way."

"Lou Fine's a very good artist," Arnold said.

"Yeah, I know, but you ought to talk to him about it."

Later on, Eisner complained about the way Fine drew Ebony, giving him a large ass that wasn't there before. Eisner felt it crossed the line of even acceptable stereotyping for the day.

———

Preventive maintenance was a new concept in 1942. Two civilians at Holabird, Norman Colton and Bernard Miller, produced a mimeographed instruction sheet called *Army Motors* that was distributed to maintenance soldiers. It was full of field fixes and equipment maintenance ideas. Eisner—entrepreneurial despite the uniform—suggested that what they were doing could be more effective as a proper magazine, with cartoons demonstrating the right way to do things.

"I designed the magazine; I laid it out," Eisner said. "They were technically the creators of the concept, but I increased the concept and changed it and made a package of it. I was more responsible at that moment for the packaging than I was for the editorial content, which they really were in charge of."

In its new format, and with Eisner as art director, the magazine grew rapidly; at its height, it reached a distribution of one and a half million copies per issue. Eisner created a comic strip for the magazine featuring a character called "Pvt. Joe Dope—M-1." Joe was a guy who always did things wrong. His mission, as reported in the September 23, 1944, edition of the *Washington Post,* was "to sell preventive maintenance to cut down on necessities for repairs or requisitioning new articles ... In the field, officers say his accomplishments are far above conservative estimates."

Army Motors became extremely popular. There were two million men in the Army at that time, and the newsletter went to every shop involved in vehicle and weapon maintainence.

(When Nick Cardy was drafted—on April Fool's Day 1943—he contacted Eisner through *Army Motors* to see if he might join him there. But there were no positions available and they never worked together again.)

Before long, Eisner was transferred to the Pentagon in Washington and joined the Chief of Ordnance's staff. His new job was providing visual materials for General Levin H. Campbell, World War II's Chief of Ordnance.

Eisner's first assignment was an unintentionally funny one. As he sat at his desk one Friday, the general called him into his office in the Pentagon's E Ring. The general held a stack of mimeographed sheets in his hand. He said, "Senator Truman's oversight committee is complaining about the Garand rifle because we are still paying the same price even after we bought a million units." Then he pushed a stack of papers, full of statistics, toward Eisner. "I want you to develop a bunch of charts for me. We will go into a meeting on Monday morning, and I'll speak while you will flip the charts."

Eisner spent that weekend developing charts and "learning how to lie with statistics," he said. He learned that "if you run a line graph from zero to ten and spread it out, it looks like a very slight increase, but if you press it and put the one to ten very close, it's a spike." With thinking like that, the charts were a success and the general was immediately indebted to his new assistant.

Next, Eisner helped start another magazine, *Firepower* ("The Ordnance Man's Journal"). Strangely, it was not financed by the Army, but by the civilian Army Ordnance Association. It published inspirational stories rather than specific instructional stories, something the Army felt it could not finance with tax dollars.

Meanwhile, as *Army Motors* grew, Colton and Miller built a large and influential staff, which eventually was moved out to Detroit, closer to the nation's automakers. Eisner continued doing all the cartoons, but he stayed at the Pentagon. Eisner created or developed several new characters who kept Pvt. Joe Dope company, including Sgt. Half-mast, the half-assed mechanic, and Connie Rodd, a pretty member of the Women's Army Corps or WAC.

He also introduced the use of instructional comic strips to *TMs*, the Army technical manual. "It fit the pattern that I have always enjoyed," Eisner said, "which is to find a hole in the woods and go through it before anybody else did it. I believed that comics were a valid teaching medium which had a future in this environment."

Once more, recognizing opportunity was a major motivating force in his career.

The irony of his situation was that Eisner made fun of Army SOP (standard operating procedure) from the inside-out and it was acceptable, even embraced, because he wrote, drew, and talked to GIs in a language they understood. There were some people who complained that Eisner hurt morale because he often showed officers as not being quite as efficient as they all thought they were. But he created publications with a different tone. When the technical manuals said, "Remove all foreign matter from the walls of the engine," Eisner would present it in Queens English: "Clean the crud out of the engine." GIs loved the conversational method, the plain talk, and the visualized instruction. It was quick and easy.

In the early 1940s, America was not the sophisticated, skeptical, and media-savvy nation it would become by the time of the Vietnam War. Military recruits came from all over the country. There were guys from Philadelphia who knew all the hip lingo from Fred Allen and Bob Hope, and still others from Kentucky who hadn't experienced indoor plumbing before they were inducted. All these soldiers needed a common language.

Early in his Army career, Eisner met a sergeant in Aberdeen whose entire unit was composed of illiterate American soldiers from West Virginia. This sergeant wrote letters for them to their girlfriends and parents because they couldn't themselves write; after work, he taught several of them to read. Eisner learned from that the importance of teaching at the reader's level. The magazines Eisner did were designed for people whose literary level was a little lower than the high vocabulary, hard-to-read technical manuals the Army tended to produce.

There were, naturally, people above Eisner who were not thrilled with his approach.

The adjutant general's department in charge of producing technical manuals tried to kill Eisner's use of comics for serious technical projects. Comics were only deemed acceptable for propaganda or attitude conditioning. The only way the adjutant general felt he could stop Eisner was through an efficiency competition. He persuaded the University of Chicago to run a test between the standard technical manual and Eisner's graphic journals on the same subject material. Eisner won because the readability and retention level of his material was greater than that of the precise but dry and pedantic technical manuals.

The results reinforced what Eisner believed to be characteristic of the comic strip: the ease with which images demonstrated process. As compared to a military language that worked overtime at obfuscating an issue, comics reduced any concept to a series of images which made a concept crystal clear to the reader.

For example, an engineer would say, "You *may* substitute this bolt ..." and Eisner would say, "You *can* substitute the bolt from the ..." "May" and "can," in his mind, were synonymous. Eisner couldn't see any difference. The engineers screamed and yelled; "There is a *big* difference!" The Army manual was extremely limited in terms of what it could graphically demonstrate; when it showed photographs, the images were stilted and limited. Eisner, however, had license to make dramatic drawings that emanated from the reader's position, showing and explaining precisely how to put a bolt on a piece of equipment. He showed readers the action from their view; a camera couldn't always get in on the same angle, or provide the visual clarity.

Ironically, no matter how many of these do-it-yourself mechanicals Eisner drew, he himself learned nothing about the subject. Eisner was good at explaining something, "probably because I was so stupid about mechanics," he said. "I explained the twenty-four-volt electrical system, visualized the whole thing, without personally absorbing how the hell it worked."

==================

Eisner's lanky younger brother, Pete, was drafted into military service in 1942, inducted in Long Island, staged at Fort Dix, and sent to Miami Beach, where he was assigned to the Air Force. He trained first as a belly gunner on a B-51, "until they got me into the plane," he said. "I could not fit into the turret, so they figured I wasn't going to be any help to them."

When that didn't work he was reassigned to an ordnance depot unit that was sent to Mobile, Alabama and San Francisco. On a firing range, Pete won an award for sharp shooting—"the worst mistake of my life," he said. "I should not have hit the target."

This time he was assigned as turret gunner on a troop ship—a better fit, apparently. But, as it traveled from New Guinea to the Philippines, the ship broke down, became separated from its convoy, and was left a sitting duck for a week, alone in the South Pacific. The crew eventually tried disembarking on an island in the Philippines, but the Japanese kept shooting at them.

Back in the United States, Eisner was looking out for Pete's welfare. He arranged a duty change for his brother as Pete left New Guinea for the Philippines. An order came through from the Pentagon giving him a detached service assignment. He became an intelligence NCO, a noncommissioned officer. Nobody in the field knew about the change but Pete and his commanding officer. He had a code name and was directed to report potentially subversive activities.

"Every second or third day, I went to the post office to post a morning report," Pete said. "I was spying on our own guys; in particular, one or two questionable people in command. One guy was born and raised in Germany. We used to censor his mail. I knew it; he didn't. The guy didn't get close or talk to anyone. That made him more suspicious. But I never found anything questionable."

More suspicious to Pete was his CO.

"My commanding officer became a captain because his original commanding officer didn't go overseas," Pete said. "This guy should have been a private. He had no qualifications. Back home, he was a meter reader for Campbell Soups, checking the heat on the soup vats. That was his background. He was always suspicious that people were after him. So when intelligence information was sent to me, he was nervous as a cat. Real neurotic. But with me, he couldn't do anything about it. Fortunately he had regular officers under him who were more the GI type."

If Pete resented his brother taking charge of his military career the way he did, he never said so.

"I didn't feel I was a hero then," Eisner said. "I got my brother a new post when he was in New Guinea because I didn't want him to get shot. Then he begged me to cool it because his company commander thought *he* was a spy."

Pete wasn't the only GI who benefited from Will's natural instinct to be everyone's big brother. He pulled several guys he knew out of camp and got them safe jobs before they went overseas. When a friend, Bernard Miller, was at Holabird, he told Eisner he was being sent overseas. "He had a wife and a kid, so I jumped," Eisner said. "I was at the Pentagon and I had a little muscle. I went up to personnel and got him transferred to *Army Motors*, where he eventually became editor."

———

Can anyone develop a reputation as an artist within the vast, face-less bureaucracy of the U.S. Army? Did people truly take notice of Will Eisner's work and actually attribute it to him?

As anonymous as the Army strives to be for most everything short of Purple Heart winners, it did help Eisner carve out a niche for his work. Partly because of this, some of that work survives until this day.

Army Motors was novel within the military ranks and it enjoyed imme-diate popularity with the troops. While the GIs and officers devoured every issue, they couldn't help but learn Eisner's name because, surpris-ingly, he was permitted to sign everything he did. "I let them know who I was in a very non-Army way," Eisner said. "Because beneath this smil-ing bloke of a guy is a businessman. Even in the midst of WWII."

Bill Mauldin became famous through his bylined "Willie and Joe" car-toons for *Stars and Stripes*. Eisner enjoyed doing something that nobody else had done before him, but he still *really* wanted to be a traveling correspondent. "I wanted to be a Bill Mauldin," he said, "but once I established a certain competency, the Army never would let me out of my post."

Eisner badly desired an overseas posting. His younger brother, Pete, was overseas; that's what Eisner dreamed of. He tried *everything*.

Once, Eisner was sent on temporary duty to develop educational materials for the Army Ordnance Department in Texas, which was still doing aircraft maintenance. Eisner became friendly with an officer he met and they went out to a bar and had a few drinks. Some time around midnight, they were drunk and swearing eternal fealty to each other. They were now blood brothers, they vowed. The officer told Eisner that he was actually stationed in Casablanca. "By God, Will," he said, "you gotta come out and see what I am doing there; bring some of your talent out there."

"Yeah, sure," Eisner said in his own stupor. "I'd love that." Of course, Eisner put it out of his mind when he returned to the Pentagon.

Three weeks later, Eisner got a call to immediately report to the general. He rushed to his office, saluted, and said, "Yes, sir!"

"I have here a telegram from an officer in Casablanca," the general said. Surprise registered on Eisner's face. "They want you to come out for temporary duty—a month or so—to do maintenance and educational materials."

Eisner said, "Really, sir?"

"Really."

The general then dramatically tore up the telegram. He said, "I am not letting you out of here. You know who wrote that goddamn telegram? It was that sonuvabitch George Patton! Once he gets you in there, he is not going to let you out!"

He turned out to be right. A colleague of Eisner's, Don Brennan, subsequently was promoted to major and was ordered to Casablanca on an ordnance assignment and Patton imprisoned him, so to speak, to write a history of his unit.

———————

Washington was a town in which there were few men during World War II and lots of women, so getting dates was pretty easy.

Eisner lived in the Wardman Park Hotel. *The Spirit* generated extra money, so he could afford to live off-base for $30 a month. "I wanted to live in the Wardman because it was a lot easier to get girls up to your room there than the apartment I briefly rented near the zoo," he said.

The first few months that Eisner was in Washington, he dated whenever he could. He even fell in love with Leona, an *Army Motors* staff writer he met while working on assignment in Detroit. "She caught my eye because she was one of the staff writers who would go out to the testing field and drive two-ton trucks around," Eisner explained. "She was very attractive, and it was a torrid romance after a while. You have to understand, during wartime these things go on with no concern about tomorrow."

The automobile companies were manufacturing military tanks and trucks, and Eisner frequently flew to Detroit to develop new educational materials. Assignment or not, he flew up there most weekends to be with Leona. He would hitch a ride at Bolling Field, which was the way a lot of officers got around stateside during the war.

"We usually went out nightclub dancing," Eisner said. "Leona was blonde, slim, and attractive, a gung-ho girl."

Leona was bright and well informed on the issues of the day, and Eisner enjoyed that they could not only dance but also talk about all kinds of things.

Their relationship continued until about a year after the war ended. But Leona and Eisner never lived in the same city. And she wasn't Jewish, which Will's domineering mother absolutely protested—her son could not marry a *goyim*! When Eisner finally accepted that he and Leona would not be walking down the aisle, he put an end to it.

FOUR
The Spirit Returns

Will Eisner was in the Army for almost four years. In many ways, they were the best four years of his life, a period during which the man matured into the talents that first surfaced in a boy on the sidewalks of Brooklyn. When he mustered out in 1945, he finally began telling the kind of *Spirit* stories he always intended to do. His first post-war *Spirit* was published on December 23, 1945. He wrote or pencilled or inked virtually every story from that day until August 12, 1951, when he would turn *The Spirit* over almost completely to his assistants.

"It was a wonderful time for me as a comic artist because I was free to do anything I wanted," he said. "There was no censorship, no editorial direction from the Des Moines Register & Tribune Syndicate at all because, as far as they were concerned, they didn't know anything about comic books, and I was the authority."

One of the few times Eisner got into any trouble with the syndicate was in the pre-war days when he wrote back-to-back stories about an ape that fell in love with a human girl ("Orang, The Ape Man" and "The Return of Orang, The Ape That is Human!"). "Busy Arnold called me at work and said that the San Antonio newspaper objected strenuously to what it felt was the promotion of racial mixing, miscegenation," he recalled.

And then there was the issue of the Spirit's black sidekick and taxi driver. One day, Eisner heard about Ebony from a high school classmate who was now a union organizer in Philadelphia. "He was ashamed of me for 'writing this Negro stuff' the way I did," Eisner said. The former classmate didn't appreciate the overt caricature of Ebony.

"This is *terrible*," the friend complained.

The same week, Eisner got a letter from the editor of an African-American newspaper in Baltimore who complimented him on the "nice" treatment of this character.

Eisner, who was never troubled by his portrayal of Ebony, had his own issues with the feature. "After about two years of doing *The Spirit*," he said, "I found it harder and harder to deal with a hero walking down the street, wearing a mask, dealing with real situations like standing in a subway train."

═══════════

Freed of his military obligations, Eisner nonetheless found himself as socially isolated as he was before being drafted. The Army changed him in many ways, forcing him out and about, and he discovered the fully formed, social animal within. He made a lot of friends during his service. But civilian life found him once again entrapped by his own creations, particularly the seven-page weekly *Spirit* comic. There was no studio to return to—everyone in his old Tudor City bullpen either moved to Connecticut with Busy Arnold or became a freelancer. Bob Powell was still in the service, Lou Fine was exiting the business, and Jack Cole was eager to move on from *The Spirit*. Not that Eisner ever socialized with those guys anyway; they were his employees, not his pals.

Needing a place to work, a leasing agent found him an office at 37 Wall Street.

"That was a very significant address," Eisner said. "When I walked into the building, I realized that I had sold newspapers in front of that building during the Depression."

Artist John Spranger, his first new staff hire, assumed responsibility for pencilling *The Spirit* as Eisner worked himself back into the rhythm of strip life.

═══════════

Jerry Grandenetti is another artist who received his first break in comics thanks to Eisner. Until he met Eisner, he was a junior drafts-man with a landscape architecture firm who daydreamed about drawing comic books.

One day in 1945, Grandenetti ducked out of work and, tucking a portfolio under his arm, paid a visit to Quality Comics. Busy Arnold, sufficiently impressed by the work he saw, said, "There's a guy named Will Eisner looking for an assistant." He gave him Eisner's new studio address in Lower Manhattan and set Grandenetti's career on a new path.

Eisner started Grandenetti as a background artist (he was a landscape architect, after all) until he learned the craft. And there were a few skills to pick up, such as inking, which he never tried before.

"He didn't give me any instructions at all," Grandenetti said. "Bill was busy writing his stories. He left it up to me. He was never critical. As I look back on it, it gave me an air of confidence."

The *Spirit* pages Grandenetti received from Eisner typically had the figures and heads already drawn and inked. In the background, Eisner left scribbled directions as to what should be filled in or left blank.

Soon after Grandenetti arrived, John Spranger left the studio to draw "The Saint," a syndicated comic strip. Letterer Abe Kanegson shared the load with Ben Oda, and a young Jules Feiffer—the future Pulitzer Prize-winning cartoonist joined the bullpen, which relocated to 90 West Street about a year after Grandenetti came aboard. Artists Klaus Nordling and Andre LeBlanc became regular contributors to *The Spirit* and other Eisner projects around this time.

Marilyn Mercer joined the staff as a secretary in 1946, but, like many people who started in menial jobs in an Eisner studio, it turned out she, too, could write. Here's how Mercer remembered those days in an article for the *Sunday New York Herald Tribune Magazine* ("The Only Real Middle-Class Crimefighter") from January 9, 1966:

> As I remember it, I was a writer and Jules was
> the office boy. As Jules remembers it, he was an artist
> and I was the secretary. Will can't really remember it
> very clearly. It is his recollection that Jules developed

into an excellent writer and I did a good job of keeping the books. Neither one of us could, by Eisner standards, draw.

Mercer later became a freelancer and, in the early 1960s, introduced her ex-boss to another up-and-comer, Gloria Steinem.

"Gloria Steinem was an editorial assistant at the time for Harvey Kurtzman's *Help!* magazine," Eisner recalled. "We talked for a few minutes, and Marilyn said, 'Maybe you should hire her.' Frankly, at the time I wasn't impressed with her. She seemed to be kind of a reclusive person, not at all the outgoing person that she later became. Good looking, very attractive, though—I noticed that."

The spring of 1949 saw the launch of one of Eisner's biggest miscues, the extremely short-lived Will Eisner Productions comics line. These included *Baseball Comics* featuring "Rube Rooky" (including art by Feiffer, Blaisdell, and Grandenetti) and *Kewpies*.

Yes, *Kewpies,* the cute little characters created in 1909 by artist Rose O'Neill for *Ladies Home Journal*. Kewpies were one of the first multi-media crossover stars, reproduced in everything from dolls and magazines to china and wallpaper.

"I wanted to publish my own comic books," Eisner explained. "The artwork was

Harvey Kurtzman's "Spirit" parody was originally published in *Lana* No. 2 (October 1948) and is taken from the Kitchen Sink Press "Hey Look!" Collection
(Copyright Harvey Kurtzman Estate. Used with permission.)

good and I thought there would be room for a Kewpies character. We animated the little characters. I tried building a publishing venture alongside *The Spirit*. But *Kewpies* and *Baseball Comics* were abject failures. I lost my shirt on them."

There is a playful, sometimes grouchy respect and admiration between Will Eisner and one of the most successful graduates of the post-World War II Eisner studio.

And, as became their fashion on just about everything since that time, each man had a different version of everything from how they met to whose fault it was that the Spirit didn't wear socks.

When Eisner's office was at 37 Wall Street, an inexperienced artist named Jules Feiffer walked in, looking for a job. "His work wasn't that good," Eisner said, laughing, "so I hired him to be a gopher. But after a while he began writing dialogue for *Spirit* balloons that was absolutely stunning. And he did coloring. Then he betrayed me by telling everyone the Spirit had no socks!"

The real story, Feiffer said, "involved much more chutzpah than that."

Feiffer was just out of high school when he went looking for Eisner, work samples in hand. "I remember, to my astonishment, that he was easy to find. When I got to his place, I opened the door and there he was. He was sitting in the outer office, where the secretary should sit—no window, just the light of the room—and he was working on John Spranger's pencils."

Feiffer loved the pre-war *Spirit* stories. And, while he believed that the art in Eisner's post-war stories was better, the stories didn't have the same power as they did pre-war. The stories seemed choppier, more off-the-cuff. "He had great ideas. But the storytelling wasn't up to his par," Feiffer said.

And only because he was a cocky teenager who didn't understand the severity of what he was saying, Feiffer told Eisner so.

"The *Spirit* stories aren't as good as they used to be," he said. "Why don't you write good stories anymore?"

Feiffer thought Eisner should just go back to the way things were. Eisner's response was not surprising.

"If you think you can do better, you write one," he said.

So that's exactly what the teenaged smartass did. Feeling complete faith in his own arrogance, he went home and wrote a *Spirit* story. Despite the faith he lacked in his drawing at that point in time, he was more than sure of his ability to write in this form.

Feiffer wrote a story as the old Eisner would, meshing it stylistically with radio suspense shows. To his delight—and astonishment—Eisner said, "That's pretty good, kid. Let's do it."

That first act of encouraging Feiffer to write rather than let his own feelings be hurt was typical Eisner. "I was snotty, he was a master," Feiffer said. "But he thought I could contribute something and he was right. It was an amazing act on his part. I remember coming home on the subway to the Bronx. He didn't offer me any money but if I wanted to hang around and erase pages, learn something, that was okay. I thought on the way home a brick would fall off a building and kill me. I *couldn't* be this lucky!"

Eisner really was impressed.

"I thought, *Jesus Christ, this guy writes!*" Eisner recalled. "He had an ear for dialect that was just brilliant."

Three months later, the honeymoon period was over and the notion that the comics business was real work set in. With his usual pluck, Feiffer demanded that Eisner pay him a salary of $20 a week.

"No," Eisner said.

"I quit," Feiffer replied, and he walked out.

Much to Feiffer's surprise—and relief—Eisner soon called him back to work. With cashflow tight, he couldn't keep much of his staff on salary at the time, but he needed an assistant. So he hired Feiffer for $20.

Though only thirty-one, Eisner was considered old hat by young men in the business—and some in his own studio—who thought, in 1948, that he was on his way out. "At my first interview, looking at my samples, Will let out that I had no talent," Feiffer said. "But when we started talking about his work, it was clear I had a complete dossier on him, going back to *Hawks of the Seas*. It was clear he hired me as a groupie; I was the only fan of his in the office."

Within a month or so, Feiffer began writing more and more as Eisner's faith in him grew. He even starting pencilling and laying out seven-page

Spirit stories on standard 20-pound white Bond paper. Eisner would take it in his office, read it, do his edit, and give it back to Feiffer for revisions. Then he would lay it out on full-size sheets and Eisner would take it over again and redo the layouts. "And he rewrote my dialogue," Feiffer recalled, "sometimes improving it, sometimes not."

On the other hand, whenever Eisner let Feiffer near any artwork—"something I dreamed of since I was five," Feiffer said—he froze. "I even screwed up doing blacks. The simplest stuff, I couldn't do. Oddly, and ironically, the form I most wanted to work in, comic books, was the one I had no gift for working in. And I still don't. I've said over the years that if I was more fluent as a comic artist, I could have been a hack. I had to opt for quality. But it wasn't my first choice."

Grandenetti remembered everyone being relatively quiet in the studio. There was little verbal exchange. "Jules and I both went to the Pratt Institute," he said. "Spranger kept to himself except when he went to Europe and was proud of the photographs he shot. And he bought a new Studebaker he was also so proud of. Marilyn Mercer freelanced for Bill. And Andre LeBlanc, a terrific artist, was there during my time, but his work didn't have that Eisner look."

Manny Stallman was an Eisner assistant for about a year. He was a sweet guy but not much of an artist. Everyone loved Stallman so much that they were afraid to tell him that his art wasn't any good. "If you told him that a leg he drew was too long, he'd break into tears," said Mark Evanier. "I suspect nothing he did ever made it on the page. But he was so proud of working for Will."

Front page of *The Spirit* Sunday section from the *Baltimore Sun*
(*Will Eisner Collection, The Ohio State University Cartoon Research Library*)

According to Evanier, Stallman's art was crude and unpopular, but he was graphically innovative.

"He worked at DC in the late '50s and early '60s. At that time, the staff was rigid. Everything had to be drawn within square boxes. But Manny felt it was his job to bring the Will Eisner approach to the world. He did these odd things in some of his stories that no one else was allowed to do because no one else would have started crying if you told him he couldn't. He spoke about Will as you would a saint. If I were Will and this man was drawing for me I wouldn't have the heart to tell him his work wasn't good, either."

Whenever there was any bad news in the studio, Alex Kotzky—once the kid, now the veteran—informed the guys. Eisner didn't like to do that.

When Eisner started working on *John Law* in 1948, he farmed outside freelance assignments to Grandenetti, such as a Fiction House back-up comic called "Secret Files of Drew Murdock." "They wanted Bill to do it," Grandenetti said, "but I was able to fake Bill just badly enough that I was able to hold on to it while I developed. I rarely signed myself. My first 'Murdock' story was so crude that Bill backed up my inks. By the second issue, I did my own. I did five or six stories; by then I developed a style of my own and broke away from that Eisner look."

Maybe so, but Grandenetti stayed with Eisner long enough that he was eventually entrusted with pencilling *The Spirit* and having his pages inked by the next new guy, Al Dixon.

Grandenetti ended up working for DC Comics, which is where his personal style—and income—blossomed.

"I was very grateful to get my $35 bucks a week from Bill," Grandenetti said. "It was a peaceful environment. At one time I remember trying to get a raise out of Bill. I think he gave me an extra $5 a week. He gave me such a tremendous break. I had no idea of the market, no idea what guys were getting for a page until I went to DC. Then I was thrilled to be getting $35 *a page*. And I developed some speed, so I was making money!"

Feiffer briefly left Eisner and attended Pratt Institute full-time for nine months in 1947, hoping it might launch him into advertising. He looked for work in the field, but, finding none, returned to Eisner's studio in 1948. "The only thing I apparently could do was write *The Spirit*," Feiffer said.

While cartoonists are not always smart or articulate, Eisner always was. And when he found a kid like Jules Feiffer who could talk intelligently about the form, it gave him pleasure.

"I don't remember Will as a teacher," Feiffer said. "He was never my teacher; he was my mentor. I learned by watching him work, by asking him questions. It shocks me how young people don't ask questions because it's not cool. But given the opportunity to be around one of my heroes, I never stopped being a pest. I asked him all *kinds* of things.

"He took me to the engravers," Feiffer continued. "He understood the printing process; he knew how paper was made. From that day to this, I didn't understand any of it. I'd nod my head and try. But he was terribly patient. And he liked to teach. There was nothing pedantic about him. He was a rabbi of the comic art form. I think that was one of the things that made our association enjoyable. We could talk about Al Capp and Milton Caniff ("Terry and the Pirates," "Steve Canyon")."

Feiffer was more comfortable as a writer in the early 1950s than as an artist, although when Eisner gave him space in the back of *The Spirit* section to develop "Clifford"—a strip about children's interactions that predated *Peanuts*—he gamely practiced his craft in front of a few million readers each week.

"It was terribly exciting and extremely terrifying," Feiffer said. "But primarily it was a work in progress. I was never certain of the art. I had not established a style for myself; I was trying to look like half a dozen other people. I was more certain of the writing than the drawing. It was a developmental process and Will gave me the room to do that."

Abe Kanegson, Will's staff letterer, helped Feiffer develop quality control standards. Kanegson and Feiffer both came from the Bronx and both went to James Monroe High School. Feiffer would show Kanegson a "Clifford" cartoon and Kanegson would say, "You can do better." Feiffer, whose ego may have been more fully formed than his art skills at that point, would grouse at Kanegson, but that's how he learned to make demands of himself.

"Abe was a lefty, as so many of us were," recalled Feiffer, whose liberal politics marked much of his work, "but he was hard left, doctrinaire. And quite a stutterer. It would be painful to hear him get a sentence out. But he was well read, quite smart. As a response to his stutter, he took up and became quite good at singing Gilbert and Sullivan songs."

When Grandenetti left the studio, Kanegson took over as background artist for *The Spirit* stories.

"After Spranger, it was Grandenetti, Kanegson, and me," Feiffer said. "I was the least necessary to the operation. But what I did provide in the office ... I was the Chris Hitchens of the place. I provided a running critique of comics. I was the first to talk to Will about comics as an art form. By then he was doing *American Angler* magazine; he wanted to get out of comics and become a publisher."

Feiffer remembered the bullpen years fondly. He said it wouldn't be unusual for some of the next generation's best art talent—Harvey Kurtzman, Wally Wood, or Dave Berg (pre-*MAD* magazine) to be found wandering in and out in Eisner's studio.

════════

One of the playful issues between Eisner and Feiffer over the years was Denny Colt's alleged religious heritage.

"Feiffer wrote an article that said everyone knew the Spirit was Jewish even though he had a turned-up Irish nose!" Eisner complained.

Feiffer still insists he was right about that.

"Jewish—I knew it all the time!" he said. "If Arthur Miller wrote *Death of a Salesman* in the 1960s, Willy Lohman would be Jewish. If Herb Gardner wrote *A Thousand Clowns* in the 1970s and '80s, Murray Burns would be clearly Jewish. That public Jewishness was simply not a staple of the culture of their time. If you were an assimilated wannabe, you stayed away from your Jewishness. Take all those writers on the Sid Caesar TV show. They were all Jewish. But look for Jewish references—there are none. They're all German. It simply wasn't part of the culture if you wanted to be in the mainstream. All of the characters were gentile.

They had names like 'Wesley,' 'Clark,' and 'Denny.' The Spirit looked like Dennis O'Keefe. What Will was doing was what everyone was doing. Jews were for laughs. He was the *schlepper*."

Like Eisner, Feiffer was Jewish, although his Jewishness never interested him as a kid and he was never religious. But he could certainly recognize Jewish symbolism, *naches* (Yiddish for good things in life), and lifestyles when he saw them. And he saw a lot of them in Eisner's work.

"Clearly, Will's Central City and my New York were more in line than Milton Caniff's China or Far East. Caniff came from Columbus, Ohio. I loved his world but I didn't feel like a citizen of it. Will came out of the Bronx and so did I. Central City was a place I could have grown up in—the filthy streets, the water dripping everywhere. I didn't think of Jewishness as a kid reading *The Spirit* but I did think of the urban experience. This guy had my history and I had his."

Feiffer rarely referenced Eisner without mentioning his former mentor's alleged cheapness. In the introduction to *The Art of Will Eisner*, Feiffer even referred to the book's subject as a "stingy-boss."

"Will himself spoke about how he used to hold onto a dime," Feiffer said. "From my own experience, that was the office joke. When I had been writing *The Spirit* for at least a year, I asked him for a raise and he said it wasn't worth it to him. But he would give me the back page. He got rid of 'Jonesy' and I started doing 'Clifford.' I got my first national distribution under my own name, but I wasn't getting paid for it."

And then there is the issue of the socks. Why *didn't* the Spirit have socks?

"Because Jules failed to color them," Eisner said. "Nobody knew what to do about the socks."

"He speaks with forked tongue," answered Feiffer. "Look at those *Spirits* from 1940. See if he's wearing socks."

―――――――――――

Eisner benefited the industry in inventive ways. The techniques and story requirements he perfected included telling a complete story in seven pages. He demonstrated every week that even a short comic book story could have a beginning, middle, and end, and that it could be both funny *and* dramatic. He told stories with consistent back stories that didn't waiver. And anybody could pick up an issue and know what was going on. He made casual and ravenous readers alike feel welcome.

Week after week, Eisner turned out classics. And for twelve years, *The Spirit* never missed a deadline. "He obviously depended on his contributors—but who cares? Who else did it?" asked Maggie Thompson, editor of the *Comics Buyer's Guide.*

Wally Wood (best known for his work on EC Comics' *Weird Science* and *Weird Fantasy* as well as his own 1960s underground magazine, *Witzend*) joined Eisner's bullpen after a fight with EC Comics. According to Eisner, EC allegedly promised to publish a magazine Wood dreamed up, but then changed his mind.

"You have business experience," Wood said to Eisner. "Can I sue him for that?"

"Not if all you have is his word—and no contract," Eisner said.

As Wood seethed, Eisner—who once more needed an artist to take over *The Spirit,* this time because he was preparing to begin work on a new Army magazine—took advantage of the situation.

"By the way, Wally, are you looking for work?" he asked.

Eisner couldn't find anybody who could emulate his style sufficiently, but he felt confident that Wood would be close enough for comfort.

———————

By 1952, Eisner lost interest in *The Spirit* sections and hardly ever drew it, except for those times that Wood faltered on deadline and Eisner bailed him out. Wally Wood came onboard as artist with Feiffer as writer to take the character into space for one of his more unusual—and less creatively satisfying—adventures. Feiffer wrote those stories while he was in basic training—much as Eisner himself wrote *Spirit* scripts when he was drafted a decade earlier.

"I did it very reluctantly," Feiffer said. "I've never been a fan of science fiction and fantasy. I had little interest in outer space when we actually had outer space exploration. I found the subject a bore. I found writing it a bore. I tried to concentrate on story and relationships. I took a story that I might write on earth and moved it to a spacecraft. There

Front page of *The Spirit* Sunday section
from the *Baltimore Sun*
*(Will Eisner Collection, The Ohio State University
Cartoon Research Library)*

was one story I wrote where the Spirit is in outer space and discovers Hitler. Will changed it (into a Franco-style dictator) because of the politics."

The end of the line for The Spirit was in clear sight by then. Eisner lost interest, Wood was gone, and Feiffer was drafted away from the business by his country, much as Eisner was a dozen years earlier.

"He was getting second- and third-rate artists, and the quality of the work really declined," Feiffer said. "Continuing was only of interest to me if I had a free hand writing it. But Will still insisted on changing stories and doing things I didn't agree with. It became a tethered situation; the fun had gone out of it and I was only doing it for the money. I was relieved to give up the job when I went into the Army."

The final reason Eisner gave up *The Spirit* in 1952 was that it no longer attracted new subscribers. *The Spirit* topped out at about twenty newspapers, and never reached beyond that. It was carried in the Bronx in the *Parkchester Review*. Other major newspapers around the country included the *Chicago Sun,* the *Baltimore Sun,* the *Philadelphia Record, Minneapolis Star,* and the *Washington Star.*

In terms of sheer numbers, *The Spirit* Sunday supplement had far more copies in circulation than any comic book in its day, including *Superman* and *Captain Marvel,* whose circulation topped one million copies per issue. And, while comics such as *Superman* and *Batman* were published monthly, *The Spirit* was printed weekly. But unless you lived in a community where the local newspaper carried it, you never heard of *The Spirit*. It was a strange duck.

The problem with continuing the comic was that the manufacturing cost was continually going up, and, after a while, it outweighed the value inherent in the feature. One year, the newspaper distributors went on strike and demanded extra pay for inserting, or stuffing, the paper with inserts like *The Spirit*. That raised the subscription cost. The other rising cost was newsprint. When Eisner went into the Army, newsprint cost about $75 a ton. When he got out, the price had almost doubled, hitting $150 a ton. Today, newsprint is about $500 a ton.

Eisner abandoned *The Spirit* completely in 1952.

"I was sorry to see it end, yes," Eisner said. "It was caused by a combination of things. It was obvious that the future of this insert in the newspaper was going nowhere. The cost of it was getting so high, I was unable to sustain the sales of it, and I realized that if I dropped anything, *The Spirit* would be the thing to drop. It was an emotional period there. Personally, I felt that I failed because it never became the great success story financially or circulation-wise that I had hoped it would be. I was satisfied with the work I had done. I had worked hard on it, produced a lot of interesting stuff, but it wasn't until years later that I was credited with being innovative. It left me with a sense of failure about what I did."

Opaque

FIVE
The Painter's Son

Billy Eisner, like most kids maturing into teens in the mid-1930s, didn't know his family was poor until much later in life. Everybody in his corner of Brooklyn suffered equally from the ravages of the Great Depression; going without new clothes or what would later be called "disposable" income wasn't an issue for him.

Eisner's mother, Fannie, on the Staten Island Ferry sometime before 1917
(Will Eisner Collection, The Ohio State University Cartoon Research Library)

Growing up in the Depression was hard on ambition and opportunity. The lack of opportunity put a perpetual economic squeeze on all but the hardiest of dreamers. For Fannie Ingber Eisner—Billy's mother—however, going without was never good enough. Born at sea as her parents emigrated from Romania, Fannie grew into a statuesque woman with high cheekbones, a swarthy complexion, and a tough exterior. She kept friends at arm's length and family only slightly closer, never growing comfortable with physical affection, not even with her children.

Her Austrian husband, Samuel, was the family's sole source of income, but only thanks to Fannie's perseverance. Through their entire married life, Fannie regularly pushed Sam away from dreaming and doing what he loved—painting—and toward the practical aspects of supporting a family.

Will Eisner, age one
(Will Eisner Collection, The Ohio State University
Cartoon Research Library)

Part of her problem might have been a result of the suspicion with which she treated everyone she encountered. Another explanation that her eldest son discovered in his thirties: Fannie was illiterate. Her husband always read the newspaper to her, a custom that seemed quaint until her children were old enough to realize she couldn't read it herself.

Fannie dreamed of owning a bakery, although she was a lousy cook. But a bakery, she believed, was a clean business and would convey status upon her. Fannie was preoccupied with her financial and social status in the community. It was a trait her husband, who was a good man and father in so many other ways, never developed, despite fathering three children.

Fannie often blistered her husband about his better-off siblings; he was too ready to accept their handouts, she said, and not willing enough to stand on his own two feet. One time, her husband's sisters delighted in pointing out that Fannie wore the same dress to two different weddings, which embarrassed and irritated her.

Eight-year-old Billy was like other kids in many ways, from collecting the baseball cards that came with his father's Murad cigarettes and playing immies (marbles) to watching cowboy serials at the movies and pretending to be Cowboys and Indians afterward.

Eisner on horse, age three
(Will Eisner Collection, The Ohio State University
Cartoon Research Library)

He also got into fights, sometimes for no reason other than because he was Jewish and that made him a target, sometimes because he couldn't control his own anger.

"I was trading baseball cards with a kid named Jummy and we got into a fight," Eisner recalled. "He cheated, and I ran after him down the street to get my cards back, and he ran into his house. This house had French doors as you went into

Cowboys and football player from Eisner's
high school sketch collection
(Will Eisner Collection, The Ohio State University
Cartoon Research Library)

the little lobby, and he put his foot behind the door so I couldn't push it open. Well, he made a fatal mistake. He stuck his face in one of the windowpanes of the French door and stuck his tongue out. In a blind rage, I slammed my fist against his face, breaking the glass, and as I pulled it out, I cut my wrist and blood gushed out like a fountain. I ran home. My kid brother, Pete, had measles, so he had to stay in a dark room and my mother was sitting with him. The first thing my mother—the classic Jewish mother—said was, 'How could you do this to me?' My father ran around all day, it was Sunday, trying to find a doctor. It took six stitches. The stitches are still visible on my wrist."

When he lived in the Bronx, before high school, Billy became a Yankees fan, attending games as often as he could. He even caught a fly ball in the outfield bleachers once and got several players—including Lou Gehrig—to sign it after the game. He lived with his parents after high school, while he was partnered with Jerry Iger, and later while in business with Busy Arnold, and they kept his room intact while he was in the Army.

Almost intact.

Coming home on leave from the Army once, his mother surprised Eisner by cleaning his room.

"You are so messy!" Fannie complained. "I cleaned up your room the other day, and you had a lot of old junk I threw out."

Panic stricken, Eisner said, *"What did you throw out?"*

"Well," she said, "you had a baseball, the stitches were all coming out, and at your age, you are not going to play baseball any more, so I threw it out."

"Oh, Mom!"

Fannie, Sam, and Will Eisner, age three
*(Will Eisner Collection, The Ohio State University
Cartoon Research Library)*

As his artistic talent bloomed on the sidewalks of Brooklyn in sprawling, extraordinarily detailed chalk drawings of Charles Lindbergh's revered airplane, *Spirit of St. Louis,* Fannie just couldn't help herself. Secretly admiring and yet fearing Billy's talent, she didn't believe it would bring him anything but a lifetime of heartache.

Fannie was frightened by the mere prospect of Billy becoming an artist. Her husband had a brother who was renowned in the family as a brilliant artist, but he was always broke.

Fannie felt that that would happen to Billy if he became an artist. "Why don't you get a nice job, be a teacher?" she'd say. "That's a steady job."

Billy lay in bed listening to his mother and father talking in the kitchen. "You shouldn't encourage him to do this!" Fannie said, over and over. "You never made a living at it, and he won't make a living at it, either!"

For the times it was good advice. But Billy's father, Sam, never confined himself to that kind of advice. As many artists do, Sam secretly admired the economic savvy of business people, but he encouraged his oldest son to follow his talent wherever it led.

Art was a talent Billy inherited from Sam, who trained in Vienna and later painted theatrical scenery for the Yiddish stage in New York. A heavy smoker most of his life, he was a gregarious man who spoke

German, Yiddish, and English, and made friends easily. As an artist, he was ambidextrous, as comfortable painting with his left hand as his right. He knew all the great Yiddish actors, including Edward G. Robinson—who was then Emanuel Goldenberg—and Paul Muni— who was really Meshilem Meier Weisenfreund. He was friendly with them all before knuckling under to Fannie's demands that he find a "real job." Sam had no real training; his talent, his son said later, "was a gift from God." To his final days, he could never draw people; he would always draw the skies and the trees, the things that a set painter—or a background artist in a Will Eisner studio—did.

Sam's painting evolved into a business when he became a furniture grainer, then a house painter and a furrier. He would often regale his children with stories of his days as a young painter in Vienna, tales that Eisner retold in his 1991 graphic novel, *To the Heart of the Storm*. Naturally, Billy always wanted to go to Vienna, because his father painted it as such a romantic place, where one sat in street cafes and drank coffee and talked to the literati.

What Fannie didn't understand until much later was that Billy's artistic talent served him well all through his adolescence and teen years. It was a skill that was respected by his peers and one that helped him make friends; it was something that got noticed by the other kids.

A lousy athlete, Billy was always the last kid chosen for stickball, stoopball, football—whatever the sport, the experience was always the same. Wherever there are boys who can run and there are balls to hit, kick, or throw, the kids will always choose up sides, and if you are not a good athlete, you—like Billy—will be the last guy picked. The streets and alleys of Brooklyn were no different than the cornfields of Iowa in this regard.

Billy was wary of other kids because he wasn't as athletically gifted as they were. Economic fears didn't occur to him until he was a little older. He looked for ways of showing off, of commanding respect in the neighborhood for something other than brawn and pigheadedness. *You can play football, or stickball,* he thought, *but I can draw.*

Billy was extremely fond of his father, in whom he saw a kindred artistic spirit. He was, at times, angry with his mother because he thought Fannie treated Sam so badly, yelling at him all the time.

At his mother's urging—and to help the family financially—Billy sold newspapers on Wall Street, including the *Brooklyn Eagle, New York Telegram, New York Sun, New York Daily Mirror, New York Daily News,* and *New York Times.* For a long time, he was angry with his mother for that. "I felt somehow shortchanged by my parents," he said, "but the family needed every penny."

It was a painful experience, until he began paying attention to the great cartoonists—George Herriman, Alex Raymond, Milton Caniff, and E. C. Segar—in the papers he sold. That's when Billy became interested in comics.

Sam noticed his eldest son's random drawings around the house when Billy was in the sixth grade and said, "I am going to teach you how to draw."

He encouraged Billy further and took him to his first art school. That didn't go especially well, but it wasn't because of anything Billy did or didn't do. Frankly, the class was just plain weird. The instructor tied Billy's right hand to one side of a gadget and his own hand to the other side. Each held a pencil. Billy's hand drew circles in tandem with the professor's movements. Sam was horrified. Of course, the only reason he took Billy to that particular school was that it was cheap.

One day, to Billy's eternal delight, Sam said to his son, "It's a beautiful day. Let's go to the park and draw."

On that occasion and the others when they stood side-by-side, two artists practicing their craft, Sam and Billy talked while they drew, usually about Sam's childhood in Austria. Billy could listen to his father's stories for hours at a time, his thick Yiddish accent punctuating each account.

Sam attended night school when he came to the U.S. and picked up English as quickly as he could, but no matter how he tried to shake it, he always spoke with a thick accent. One day, Sam gave Billy a book about Julius Caesar. "This book was given to me by my teacher at night school," he told his son, "because I learned English faster than all the other immigrants. You can illustrate this."

For a $1.50 fee, Sam occasionally put up canvas at the Metropolitan Museum of Art's galleries and copied famous paintings. He exposed his son to a lot of the good things in life, from classical artists to classical music. "It is hard to explain my father," Eisner said. "He was a man who was poor even when he had money. He was a simple man who loved classical music but probably wasn't as literate as he seemed to other people in the family—but everybody else in my family was almost illiterate, including my mother."

———————

The Eisners—Sam, Fannie, Billy, Julian, and Rhoda—lived in Brooklyn when Billy was twelve. He applied to Cooper Union, an art school in Manhattan, around this time. The experience was short-lived, however. "I remember riding the BMT train there with a friend, Ed, one hand tightly clasping the brown bag lunch my mother insisted I take," Eisner recalls. "Ed and I had both decided we wanted to be artists. Despite my talent level, I was turned down because they said I was too young; they said, 'We don't take anybody your age.'"

(When Eisner turned eighty, The Cooper Union for the Advancement of Science and Art in Manhattan—the only private, full-scholarship college in the United States dedicated exclusively to preparing students for the professions of art, architecture, and engineering—threw a birthday party for him. In his thank-you speech, he told them the story of being turned down so many years ago. "The guy said 'Come back when you are older.' So here I am!" he joked.)

———————

One of the most touching stories that Eisner told in his 1991 autobiographical graphic novel *To the Heart of the Storm* was about the confrontation he and his younger brother Julian had with neighborhood bullies. They thought it hysterical that a Jewish boy was named Julian—or "Jew-leen," as they pronounced it.

After getting beaten up in defense of his brother, Billy made a strategic decision.

"We are changing your name!" he announced. "From now on, your name is Pete … That's a better name for around here!"

The name stuck, and Will began a lifelong defense of his younger brother that eventually grew into a professional relationship. They were together every day for most of their adult lives and best friends, too.

"We lived in a tough Italian neighborhood. If they didn't like your name, you were bad news," Pete said. "Bill figured the best way to keep things cool was to change my name. And he was right."

Legally, "Pete" was always Julian. Well, sort of. His original birth certificate actually read "Julius." Then his parents changed it to "Julian Kenneth Eisner," eventually writing "Pete" on top of it. "My mother and father and certain relatives called me Julian. 'Kenneth' was actually supposed to be my first name."

(Will's original birth certificate wasn't as complicated. It read simply "Male Eisner.")

Despite the dim picture Eisner later offered of his parents in his autobiographical works, he and his brother, Pete, and their younger sister, Rhoda, were always close. "We always did things for one another," Pete said. "Although my father did not do well financially, my brother was very supportive of the whole family."

It wasn't necessarily because Eisner wanted it that way.

"At one point, my mother said, 'Your father can't make a living. You're the man of the house.' It's a good way to destroy a kid," Eisner said.

When his Air Force tour of duty ended in 1946, Pete went to college on the GI Bill. But, like Will, he found himself drawn into the constant battle to support his family. He quit school and took a job. Both the Eisner boys vowed that Rhoda would have more opportunity than they had and, indeed, they saw her attend and graduate college, the first person in the family to do so.

Even after her sons served their country in the Armed Forces and returned home to provide for her and her husband, Fannie continued exerting a strong influence on Will and Pete. She decreed that the oldest child must marry first, which put pressure on Will but was—ironically—a relief to Pete.

"She didn't like that I was so happy being single," he said, laughing at the memory.

(Years later, with Will married, Fannie turned her attention to Pete. A friend of hers brought a girl over to meet Pete. He didn't like her but did like her friend Lila and eventually married her. But first things were first. Pete and Lila's courtship was put on hold when Fannie decided that Rhoda had to get married next.)

Not many brothers were as close as Will and Pete. But, despite their friendship, they weren't in complete agreement about the way Will depicted Fannie in his books.

"No two children are the same," Pete said. "I was my mother's favorite. I did things for her; I listened to her. My brother and my sister Rhoda were more independent thinkers, and they wanted to do things their way. My mother was a dominating person; she wanted things done *her* way. She liked her immediate family. With the rest of the family, she always had problems. She was not a warm person. She may have liked you, but she was critical."

Pete, however, always got along with everybody. And while Will was renown as a friendly, easygoing guy, he never had as much patience with people and situations as Pete. All their lives, Pete was the brother with the time to sit back and jawbone, the one for whom time stood still. Will always heard the clock ticking. He always had to be doing something, keeping to his schedule. Will was never comfortable just standing around waiting.

———————

Billy made friends easily. But, until he reached high school, he didn't really know anybody else who was an artist. DeWitt Clinton High School in the Bronx opened his eyes to another world. Not only was he exposed to other young men with similar ambitions, he also discovered a competitive instinct that would drive him for the rest of his life. And from that point forward he became "Will Eisner"—not Billy.

He was intrigued by the students at school who could write. They dealt in ideas, and he wanted to emulate their talents, too. That always set him apart.

DeWitt Clinton was an all-boys public school until 1983. Its alumni roster is remarkable for the depth and breadth of its cultural impact on American society. Distinguished graduates include Jack Rudin, Lewis Rudin, James Baldwin, Edward Bernays, Avery Fisher, Ralph Lauren, Burt Lancaster, Adolph Shayes, Richard Rodgers, Neil Simon, A. M.

Rosenthal, Basil Paterson, Paddy Chayefsky, Daniel Schorr, Ed Lewis, Fats Waller, Jan Murray, Avery Corman, Nate Archibald, Judd Hirsch, Theodore Kupferman, Stubby Kaye, Lee Leonard, Gil Noble, Walter Hoving, Don Adams, Martin Balsam, Stanley Simon, Theodore Kheel, Maurice Nadjari, Arthur Gelb, Garry Marshall, Bernard Kalb, George Cukor, Larry Hart, Jan Peerce, Burton Roberts, Bruce J. Friedman, Steve Sheppard, and Stan Lee.

Eisner drawing for his high school yearbook, *The Clintonian*
(*Will Eisner Collection, The Ohio State University Cartoon Research Library*)

Back then, Eisner was a BMOC—Big Man on Campus—at DeWitt Clinton. "I was the best artist in a school that obviously produced a lot of great talent," he said. "Several of the school's writers of my era asked me to illustrate their work, but I didn't want to do it. I resisted. I felt at the time that being known just as an illustrator was demeaning. I read what they wrote, and I said to myself that I could write as well as that. I didn't need them."

In spite of his lofty ambitions, Eisner lacked good grades. He was, by his own admission, a lousy scholar. His sole interest was in the art department.

He became the staff cartoonist on the school newspaper, *The Clintonian,* and published his first comic strip there under the byline "William Eisner." "To me, creating art and being a syndicated cartoonist represented a way out of the ghetto," Eisner said. "We were all looking for a way out; that was my motivation."

While taking a journalism class together, Eisner and Ken Giniger started a campus literary journal, *The Hound and the Horn*. (Giniger later became the president of a division of Prentice-Hall and eventually started his own publishing company.)

The Hound and the Horn published articles by Giniger, of course, and by Sigmund Koch, who became a well-known professor of humanities. Another contributor, Arnold B. Horwit, went on to contribute to the Broadway musical *Make Mine Manhattan*. The magazine provided a solid, practical education for what Eisner wanted to do, because in that magazine, he was able to write and illustrate. The young publishers couldn't afford to make engraved metal plates because they had no money, so Eisner bought wood blocks so he could hand-carve engravings for publication.

One day, Eisner received his first recognition for writing when a history teacher read one of his papers. He said to Eisner, "You write very well."

At the time, Eisner was actually thinking of being a stage designer, partly because of his father's influence but largely because he worked for the school's class-night show. The fellow who wrote the show was Adolph Green. *The* Adolph Green who, with his partner Betty Comden later wrote *Singin' in the Rain,* among other cinematic and Broadway hits.

———————

Eisner was a lousy student ... in fact, he was denied a high school diploma from DeWitt Clinton because he flunked geometry. It's a fact he never revealed publicly or privately until now.

One of his art teachers talked to his geometry teacher and said, "You shouldn't deny him this because he is an artist, and that is what he is going to be; he is the best artist we have in the school." But the geometry teacher said, "Well, he flunked, and that's that."

But, until now, Eisner always said that he graduated because, in his mind, he did; he completed the same four years as all of his classmates.

"I graduated as far as I was concerned, but I couldn't attend the graduation ceremony, so I never got a diploma," Eisner said. "My parents knew, but I told them I'd make it up in summer school. Never did."

Some years ago, somebody who knew the truth asked him why he didn't go back to get his diploma. In fact, the DeWitt Clinton High School alumni group in South Florida gave Eisner a Successful Alumni Award one year. He took it, but didn't feel right about it. ("I guess when they read this, they'll demand I give it back," he said.)

The situation scarred Eisner, as evidenced by the fact that he hid the truth for more than seventy years. His wife Ann said that as a result of not receiving his diploma, Eisner is "unduly impressed by a Ph.D."

"In my field," Eisner said, "nobody asks for diplomas. Had somebody asked for it, I probably would have made a real effort, but it wasn't really necessary. As far as writing is concerned, I kept reading, so I established my own literary background. I am self-educated, if you will."

———————

While Eisner was in high school, he made his mother extremely upset by classes he took at the Art Students League of New York. One of the most prominent art schools in the United States, founded in 1875, the League's famous students have included James Montgomery Flagg, Georgia O'Keeffe, Jackson Pollock, Roy Lichtenstein, and James Rosenquist. But all Fannie knew about the Art Students League was that this was the place where her son drew nude female models. "Here was a sixteen-year-old boy and they let me do that," he recalled. "Quite a scandal for all of us!"

He studied under anatomist George Bridgman and with painter Robert Brachman.

"Brachman's class may well have been the first time I ever saw a nude woman; it surprised the hell out of me that I didn't get an erection. I expected I would have to wear a large trench coat!" Eisner said. "I still have the painting I did of one female model. It is right next to a portrait I did of my father at about the same time. One day, not long ago, we had guests at the house. My wife was showing them around and said that I did the painting of my father when I was in art school. Right next to it is the nude painting of the art school model. 'Well,' one of the guests asked my wife quite innocently, 'is that his mother?'"

The truth was, the first time Eisner saw a female model step up on the little platform and drop her robe was the first time he felt professional. It took him a moment to collect himself, as it did most of the guys. About a third of the class was girls, so when he looked around and didn't see anybody making any fuss over it, he went along. Until then, everything he knew about the female body was because he studied anatomy books, but this was totally different.

"I thought, *Boy, I'm a pro now,*" Eisner said. "It was like a ballplayer walking onto the field at Yankee Stadium for the first time."

Bridgman was a tough teacher, a little man who wanted everyone in class to draw exactly like he did. Bridgman once said, "Don't worry about where the bones are. If it looks good, it's all right."

One day Eisner tangled with Bridgman in the League's lunchroom. A skeleton hung from the ceiling of the lunchroom, and Eisner brought a pad in and started copying the skeleton in order to refine his understanding of anatomy.

Bridgman came over and said, "Get out of here! You shouldn't be doing that! In my class, you will learn anatomy the way *I* teach it!"

The way Bridgman taught anatomy was by having students draw from casts, statuettes, and large statues. He dealt in planes and taught anatomy as a mechanical machine. "The arms were on hinges," Eisner said. "It was beautifully taught." Bridgman's technique remained with Eisner. He later recommended Bridgman's book, *Constructive Anatomy,* to his own students at the New York City School of Visual Arts.

Bridgman was clever. He would look at a student's work and, if it was no good, he would say, "This is very interesting." The only time he became personal with Eisner was when he threatened to kick him out of class for trying to draw that skeleton. He said, "If you are going to learn on your own, you don't need *my* class!"

Eisner didn't care to know much about Bridgman beyond his lessons, although he appreciated that both Bridgman and Brachman taught him about the financial realities of being an artist. "I discovered over the years that a lot of painters and artists I knew weren't as intellectual as I thought they would be," Eisner said. "Writers were. I don't know why. Most of the artists were practitioners. They were tradesmen and had a tradesman's attitude."

Meanwhile, as Eisner's mother focused on the horrifying idea that her sixteen-year-old son was painting female nudes, in truth it was the corrupting influence of his fellow students that should have made her worried. Eisner fell for a tall, good-looking girl. The first time he saw her, she was on the other side of the classroom. He walked over and looked at her work.

"Gee," Eisner said, "you're pretty good."

She said, "I like your stuff, too."

That was his first "professional" liaison. It lasted just a short time—

but long enough. She had an apartment down in Greenwich Village, and invited Eisner in for a visit. It was his first romance, and his first sexual experience.

Brachman, who was a successful painter at the time, spoke with Eisner once about how he made a living in art. Eisner was still idealistic about a gallery painter being steeped in the whole business of fine art, but Brachman disabused him of that. He told Eisner that he did "portraits of fat, bejeweled ladies," and when he said "bejeweled," he said the word with utter contempt.

"But it's a good buck," Brachman added quickly. "They pay well."

Suddenly the glamour of it all disappeared. *Art is a business,* Eisner realized. He hadn't really thought about it that way until that moment.

"I was going through a period of wanting to be *something,*" Eisner said. "I thought I would like to be a gallery painter, then I realized this was not for me because the work went too slowly. It takes too long to make a painting. And I wasn't all that good." And even a painter with Brachman's skills had to teach, or begrudgingly accept portrait commissions.

Eisner never went to college. After high school, he briefly attended a commercial art school that was at the top of the historic, triangular Flatiron Building at 175 Fifth Avenue at Broadway and 23rd Street in New York. (The Flatiron Building doubled for "The Daily Bugle" head-quarters in the 2002 *Spider-Man* movie. It also served as the model for one of Eisner's graphic novels, *The Building.*) His teacher, Mr. Green, focused on the mechanics of commercial art. But it wasn't all dry lessons; the class drew with live models, too. Ironically, whenever the nude model rested, the guys in the class would all go to "lunch." Lunch, in this class, meant running to the other end of the building to leer at girls sunbathing on the roof of the next building over.

SIX
"Nice Girls Are for My Mother"

Ann Weingarten's oldest sister, Susan, was widowed in 1949, leaving her alone with two sons, Alan, five, and Carl, two. That summer, she got away with the boys to a family camp in Maine. Labor Day was approaching and Ann, who was twenty-six years old and had just started a new job as an administrative assistant in the advertising department with Paramount Studios in New York, wanted to spend a long weekend with Susan.

But how to get there? In 1949, no one she knew flew from Manhattan to Maine.

Luckily, her younger sister, Jane, was dating a man named Arthur Strassburger. Strassburger and his friend, Will Eisner, were driving to Camp Mingo at Kezer Falls, Maine, that very weekend.

"We'll give you a lift," Strassburger said.

Eisner wasn't interested in sharing the car, but Strassburger already committed them to it, so that was that. Eisner, however, tried to get out of it by calling another friend, Jerry Gropper, who was also driving to Maine that weekend, hoping he'd take Strassburger's girlfriend's younger sister off their hands. Jerry begged off saying he bought a new car and could only break it in properly by driving it thirty-five miles per hour and how tedious would driving at that speed and entertaining somebody's sister be? No dice.

And that's why a shiny, new, black Cadillac pulled up to the Eisner

The Eisner family gathered for Will and Ann's wedding in 1950. From left: Fannie, Sam, Will, Rhoda and Pete
(Courtesy Will and Ann Eisner)

home on 90th and Riverside Drive, and a beautiful young woman and her father stepped out of it. Peeking out of a kitchen window inside the apartment was a scandalized Fannie Eisner.

"What kind of girl would go with you two boys for a weekend and spend overnight on the way up?" She wanted Will to settle down, get married, and have children, but a girl whose father delivered her to a young man and his buddy in this way couldn't be the right one for her oldest son.

Eisner, for his part, just wanted to get their bachelors' trip on the road.

"What does it matter, Ma?" he said nonchalantly. "We're just dropping her off on the way. I don't care what kind of girl she is; I'm just the taxi driver. We'll drop her off with her sister and I'll never see her again."

After looking the young woman over from the window, Fannie wasn't convinced. She already had grave doubts about her thirty-two-year-old son's morality, remembering that girl he spent a weekend with in Greenwich Village before the war. She didn't speak to him for days after that incident because she thought he was "a bum."

Leaving an unhappy Fannie behind, Eisner, Strassburger, and Ann headed north with Eisner at the wheel. On the way to Dartmouth, where they'd spend the night at the Roger Smith Hotel in Holyoke, Ann did something sneaky; she laughed at Eisner's jokes.

"When I saw him for the first time, I liked what I saw," Ann said. "But I thought he was much too sophisticated for me. And I wasn't looking for a date. I was looking for a ride."

Checking into the hotel—Strassburger insisted that their rooms be on different floors for the sake of propriety—Ann went to her room while

Eisner and Strassburger headed for the bar. A short time later, she joined them for a drink. Actually, they drank while she ate. The boys ate before leaving New York and refused to stop for food en route. Ann was starving!

When Ann entered the pub, Eisner took in all of her for the first time. He hated to admit it, but he suddenly saw what so worried his mother.

The next morning, Eisner dropped Ann at her sister's cottage. Susan and her boys, Allan and Carl, liked Eisner and Strassburger, so they stayed overnight and welcomed Gropper when he arrived the next day.

When the weekend was over, Gropper drove Ann home. The weekend was a success for him, too; he eventually married Susan.

Will couldn't get Ann out of his mind for days. And when he finally returned to New York the following week, Ann called Strassburger to ask for Eisner's number, on the pretense of saying thanks for the ride.

"I already summed up that Will was absent-minded," Ann recalled. "It was possible that he wouldn't call *me* and that was no good."

She need not have worried. Eisner immediately asked her out on a date. That went well, but before they scheduled a second date, Ann heard Eisner's name mentioned at her office. And it wasn't in a good way, either.

═══════════

One of the perks of Ann's job in the New York press office of Paramount Pictures was that every time the studio released a new film, there was a gala screening for critics and employees that she was able to attend. When the highly anticipated Cecil B. DeMille epic *Samson and Delilah* came to New York, Ann took Will to see it as her date.

The movie was memorable, but not in a good way. Described as "absurd biblical hokum" by *Halliwell's Film Guide* a half-century later, Will Eisner poked fun at it in print six weeks later (March 5, 1950) in a *Spirit* parody titled "Sammy and Delilah." It featured a director named Cecil B. Schlamiel and would inspire an entire genre of satire in *MAD* magazine just a few years later. That was on Sunday. Monday, the *Spirit* hit the fan.

Paramount was not amused.

Ann was sitting at her desk when she heard screaming.

"We're gonna sue this bastard!"

"Who the hell is Will Eisner?"

Fortunately, nobody knew that Ann knew Will. Ann excused herself and ran to a desk where she could use the phone in private. Without hesitation—and somewhat petrified—she called the funny young artist whom she had dated just once, and, at the risk of losing her own job, warned, "You're going to be sued."

But she didn't know Will that well yet. He was glad that *The Spirit* made somebody mad enough to sue! And the Paramount execs were mad, but it turned out Will was incidental to their anger. They were mad because *Samson and Delilah* sucked and it made them look bad.

Pete Eisner straightens his older brother's
tie on Will's wedding day
(Courtesy Will and Ann Eisner)

"What?" Eisner was dumbstruck.

"I hate to tell you this," Ann said. "God, this is going to be terrible; they are really serious."

Sounding alarmed, barely able to contain himself, Eisner thanked his new girlfriend for the tip, hung up the phone, and immediately dialed the syndicate that distributed *The Spirit*.

"I have great news!" he said, barely able to contain his glee, "we're gonna be sued by Paramount Pictures!"

"That is great," an editor said. "Call Associated Press and tell them!"

That tip led immediately to another date, then another. Pretty soon Ann and Will were going steady. By year's end, Eisner proposed—with Fannie's blessing. Fannie actually couldn't believe her son's luck, once she became better acquainted with Ann. Ann was a private-school graduate whose Jewish family lived on Park Avenue. Her father was an esteemed stockbroker. To Fannie, Ann's father represented everything she would want in a man, unlike her own husband, the dreamer. Ironically, while Ann's family took to Eisner like a son, they never saw

Just married!
(Courtesy Will and Ann Eisner)

Fannie and Sam as more than poor, misfit relations (as Will later illustrated in his graphic novel, *The Name of the Game*).

Ann was a grown woman when she met Will. "I was not concerned about my parents' approval," she said. "I was always the maverick in the family. I never did what was expected of me. My father once said that anyone who wanted to marry one of his daughters had to ask him. The weekend we got engaged, my parents were in Atlantic City, so we drove down to tell them. I didn't have a choice of having a gift of money or a big wedding from them. *They* decided I was having a big wedding. My father was a big stockbroker and that way he could have a lot of his customers there."

Neither of Ann's parents was instantly thrilled with their prospective son-in-law. Oh, sure, he was a pleasant fellow and he loved Ann. But that wasn't enough in their world.

"My mother was pretty much a snob," Ann said. "*I* was third generation American. *His* background was not up to her standards. They wouldn't be interested unless Will was famous enough for them to brag about.

"My father interrogated Will; his theory was, 'Let's us men talk. The ladies can sit outside and wait.' Fortunately, Will grows on everybody. My father adored him. He wanted him to come with him and become a broker. Will wanted my parents to approve of him. But I was always defiant. So it didn't make any difference to me."

Ann's father made inquiries about Eisner's reputation and professional prospects. What he heard eventually won him over and earned Eisner his respect.

The couple was married on June 15, 1950.

Comic book writer Alan Moore (*Watchmen, Swamp Thing, From Hell, The League of Extraordinary Gentlemen, Tom Strong*) and Will Eisner had met just a few times, but it was always a magical pairing.

"I always enjoyed it, but I am such a cranky recluse," Moore said. "It was all right for Will. He was a sort of sprightly gadabout who zipped around the world effortlessly, but I am fairly my age, to tell the truth. I don't know how he did it."

Their most memorable time together was during a cramped car ride in London. "Because I've got abnormally long legs, they decided that I should go in the front seat next to the driver," Moore recalled, "which meant that into the back seat there was crammed three or four people. Two of them were Will and Ann Eisner. I remember that Ann had to sit on Will's lap. As we were driving through London, they were laughing in the back as if they were a couple of kids. I remember Will just saying, 'Boy, if I were thirty years younger and you weren't my wife ... ' How can you not love a guy like that?"

―――――――――――

Everyone wants an Eisner original, even his wife, Ann
(Courtesy Will and Ann Eisner)

They called each other "Love"; he called her, affectionately, "Shorty."

But what would a legendary artist get his wife, who has everything, for Valentine's Day, birthdays, and anniversaries? Homemade cards, which she loved and posted on the refrigerator.

The sexual chemistry remained strong between the Eisners for the more than fifty years they were married, and they would often tease each other affectionately, hold hands, and touch each other like teenagers, even finishing each other's stories. Of Ann's handwriting, Will liked to say, "Spider-Man was bitten by a radioactive spider. Ann was bitten by a doctor. Horrible penmanship." Meanwhile, Ann policed her husband's manners at the dinner table, shushing him if he insisted on talking with food in his mouth.

They spent all of their free time together. Weekdays were his; nights and weekends were hers. When he traveled for business, they were a package deal.

That's not to say Will was the perfect romantic. In fact, he could be downright clumsy at it. A perfect example: the wedding band he ordered for his wife on their first anniversary. When Ann first saw the engraving on the inside, she burst out laughing.

The Eisners in a festive mood
(Courtesy Will and Ann Eisner)

"We'd been married a whole year and he couldn't spell my name!" she recalled. The engraving referred to the young Mrs. Eisner as "Anne," but her name is actually spelled "Ann."

His answer was, "You know I'm a terrible speller!"

SEVEN
The Unknown Man

Will and Ann Eisner became parents in 1951 when their son John was born, and again a year and a half later when Alice arrived.

The family moved to 8 Burling Avenue in the Gedney Farms neighborhood of White Plains in 1952. Living in the suburbs was something of an adjustment for the Eisners, both of whom grew up and lived much of their adult lives in the concrete canyons of New York City.

Until then, the family journeyed only twice a year to the suburbs. Will liked to get his biannual fresh air fix, but if you

Ann, Will, John, and Alice Eisner
(Will Eisner Collection, The Ohio State University Cartoon Research Library)

told Ann she could never go to Manhattan again, she'd say, "Fine." She would miss the people, but not the environment.

The Eisner family was extremely close, with Will providing his children the emotional—and financial—support largely missing from his own childhood. He knew what they were doing in school, who their friends were, and what they liked to do for fun.

Will taught John to play chess. He surprised the kids once by bringing home an old rowboat from the pier at Long Island Sound and filling it with sand for them and their friends to play with in the backyard. And the kids always loved watching dad work at his drawing board.

"I felt that I was giving John something more than I had because I was a reasonable success," Eisner said. "Never talked to him about what he should do. One summer, we sent John and a friend to a summer school in Switzerland. He was about fifteen. Ann said to me, 'You know there are girls out there. Have you talked to him about sex?' So I went to John's room and said, 'I'd like to talk to you about sex.' He said, 'What do you want to know?' Left me speechless."

Ann, John, and Alice were able to endure Will's long absences on civilian Army business in the 1950s and 1960s by reading the wonderful illustrated letters he sent home. One letter detailed his first day at the Akasaka Prince Hotel, near the Imperial Palace in Tokyo. Among the images included in the letter was one depicting Will in the bathroom, still in his travel suit, trying to figure out which knobs would turn on the shower. Settling on one, he pulled it. Water came out from everywhere. He was drenched. "Apparently," he wrote, "the whole room was a shower."

In another letter, to Ann, he wrote: "Many Americans here who have married Japanese girls (AND I DON'T BLAME THEM—WOW!!)."

Stopping in Hawaii on the way back from Seoul, Eisner sent separate notes to each of the children.

> *Dear John,*
>
> *I got your letter and I'm glad to know that the hurricane did no damage. I'm proud of the way you are taking care of the girls.*
>
> *Your buddy pal*

> *Dear Alice,*
>
> *You wrote a very, very fine letter. I'm glad you helped John put up those tracks. I'm sure the willow tree will grow back as it did once before when you were very little. I miss you and mommy and Johnny.*
>
> *Your daddy-o*

The family went to Europe in 1966. John was fourteen and becoming a teen in words and deeds. During the trip, something Ann did or said rubbed John the wrong way. He turned to his father and said, "How can you stand her?"

Alice was very much her father's daughter. She had his temperament and compassion. Whenever she heard on TV that someone was starving, Ann had to send something.

"I had to save the world for her," Ann said.

Then there was the other side of Alice, the one recognizable by any father who has ever been twisted around his daughter's finger. Ann was the tough parent, but Will couldn't refuse Alice anything. She would con him into things. When Ann told Alice she didn't need a new pair of boots, Alice did what any determined teenage girl would do: she asked her father to take her shopping.

Sketches from a picture letter Eisner sent home from his world travels. This letter was sent from Turkey, circa 1965
(Will Eisner Collection, The Ohio State University Cartoon Research Library)

One day, John, Alice, and Will watched a Saturday morning cartoon together.

"Daddy," John said, "why aren't you famous like (so-and-so)?"

Before he could answer, Alice spoke up.

"Well," she said, "he's famous enough."

The children were as different as night and day. John was popular, athletic, and brilliant—"full of beans," his father said. For example, he had braces on his teeth for a year and he played trumpet anyway, even though it caused his lips to bleed.

Alice was none of those things, but for her parents, in her own way, she was much, much more.

A cartoonist working in Eisner's shop during *The Spirit* days had a sixteen-year-old daughter who died of cancer. The grieving father came in the office the day after she died and sat at his drawing board, crying.

"Look at him," Eisner said to his brother Pete. "If that ever happened to me, I couldn't do it."

━━━━━━━━━━

One day in 1969, Alice wasn't feeling well. Ann took her to the doctor for a blood test and none of the Eisners were ever the same again.

The diagnosis was leukemia.

Ann gave up work and everything else to care for Alice over the next eighteen months. Will, on the other hand, buried himself in his work for the Army.

"I only had her sixteen years," Ann said. "I lived with her at Mt. Sinai Hospital. I insisted on a cot there. I would go home when friends came in to relieve me briefly, change my clothes, and go back."

Alice never knew what was wrong with her. Will made the decision that she was not to know; he insisted that the doctor only tell her that she was anemic. The rest of the family abided by his decision.

"I didn't want the doctor to tell her that she was dying," he explained. "She was sixteen! When you are sixteen, you are at the bloom of your youth, and you don't think that anything can really happen to you. You think, 'Mom and Dad will take care of this.'

"One evening she came in our room and said, 'Can I get into bed with you and Mom? My bones hurt.' She had myeloid cancer, which is cancer in the bones. Today, they probably would have been able to do something by exchanging the marrow. In those days, they didn't know what to do for her. It was hard. It was very, very hard. The whole family structure wasn't great. I was trying to keep my sanity down at the office. John did not know how to handle it and we weren't sure how to help him, either," Eisner said.

Just before Alice died, she said to her father, "Daddy, buy Mom a present for her birthday. *Don't forget*! You always forget things! Buy Mom a present."

The day Alice died, sickeningly enough, was Ann's birthday.

"It was a tough day. A devastating day," Eisner said. "It was very, very hard."

When Alice died, something strange took place that Eisner never publicly mentioned until now. "The boys on the *PS Magazine* staff came up to attend the funeral," he said. "That weekend, they hit me with a bill for overtime as a result. It stuck in my throat like a stone. As a parent, the whole world has fallen all around you, and it's like a house that has crashed. You are just standing there, and you don't know what to do next, and your normal reaction isn't normal any more. You either become immobilized, which is what you do to defend yourself, or you do stupid things. And I was doing dumb things at the time."

———————

Will wanted to move away from White Plains after Alice died, but Ann couldn't bring herself to take her daughter's room apart until 1975, five years after her death.

Six months after Alice died, Ann became director of volunteers for New York Hospital-Cornell Medical Center, Westchester Division (since renamed The New York Presbyterian Hospital) located in White Plains, New York. She enjoyed the work and stayed there until they moved to Florida permanently in 1983. In a lot of ways, the work was her salvation, a place to go each day and find people that needed her skills, humanity, and good humor.

The family eventually moved into another house in the Soundview section of White Plains, leaving many painful memories behind. The new place was a modern design, with five bedrooms, a studio building in the back for Will, and lots of land.

The first time Eisner saw the property at 51 Winslow Road, he fell in love. "That house just says, 'Buy me,'" he told Ann.

———————

The relationship between Harvey Kurtzman (longtime EC Comics war artist and creator of *MAD* magazine, *Trump* magazine with Hugh Hefner, and co-creator with Bill Elder of the *Playboy* magazine comic strip "Little Annie Fanny") and Eisner was much deeper than most of their peers ever knew. Beyond their professional friendship and respect, they socialized at home with each other's families in New York and whenever they were together at comic book conventions.

"He and Harvey would have these talks and go to lunch," Adele Kurtzman, Harvey's widow, recalled. "Harvey would always ask Will for advice, and Harvey never took it. Will always said, 'Don't sign a contract without knowing what you're signing.' But Harvey, being Harvey, he never listened. Things might have been different if he had."

Eisner repeatedly told Kurtzman to read contracts carefully. "If somebody says, 'Are you interested in doing this?' don't say yes. Tell them to send it in writing," Eisner said. But Harvey made unwritten "Gentlemen's Agreements."

"If they weren't gentlemen, you didn't have an agreement," Harvey told Adele.

One of the little known ties between the two men, who were separated by twelve years (Eisner was older), were the parallel tragedies they suffered with their children.

"We have an autistic son," Adele said. "I think Harvey and Will had that bond—children—in common. When Will first came to our house and my daughter Nellie was little, I introduced them. And Will said, 'I had a little girl once, too.' It was devastating the way he said it. Harvey took solace in being able to talk to Will. Who else would understand what it's like? There's guilt, embarrassment, all kinds of feelings.

"When cancer hits a child, it's beyond reason," Adele said. "When you look back on your life, you wonder, 'How did I survive it?' Our son went into incredible rages. He stayed home for twenty-eight years and then went into a group home. He's doing well now."

———

Ann knew a great deal about the comics industry and the people in it. But she was never interested in the deals and the deal making. On the Eisners' annual trips to Comic-Con International in San Diego, she'd always pass on the "boy talk." She'd accompany her husband to meals and parties, but as soon as they were finished eating and the discussion turned to deals, trends, or idol worship (of Will), she excused herself and moved on.

"Oh, Ann, stay!" her husband would plead, mockingly, knowing it wouldn't change her mind.

"No, no, you boys discuss business; I am off," she'd say.

She literally wasn't interested, and she had a great sense of when to be sociable and when to leave.

Will and Ann read each other's thoughts. Or she rolled her eyes because she had heard it a hundred times, and she'd try to keep him honest. If he said something she disagreed with, she would absolutely get in his face and say, "Now, Will, you know that's not true," or "Will, I completely disagree with you." And he'd respond with mock indignation. "You know, I can find another girl." Friends would call it "The Will and Ann Show." To some extent it was spontaneous, and to some extent they'd been doing it for years, and knew it amused their friends.

Ann was by no means unnecessarily demure, and didn't let her husband dominate a discussion. If there was any opportunity where she could contribute her own two cents, she would. She would be careful not to say anything really negative about Will, but Ann was always Ann.

Gray

EIGHT
PS Magazine

Norman Colton, civilian editor of *Army Motors,* stayed on with the Ordnance Department when World War II ended and the magazine suspended operations.

In 1949, with the Korean War on the horizon, Colton came to see Will Eisner in New York. Colton said that the Army wanted to start a new magazine similar to *Army Motors;* would Eisner's studio—still licking its wounds after a disastrous attempt at independent comic book publishing—be interested in bidding on the production work? Eisner said sure.

"Colton was eager to have me because I had a history of success with *Army Motors* and was identified with the publication," Eisner said. "But it had to go through the process of bidding. Al Harvey, of Harvey Publications, found out about it and competed for it, but I won the bid and I helped write the contract. It was totally different than most contracts that the Army had at the time. At that time, the Army paid for services on the basis of time. My contract was based on a flat sum with a profit measurement that allowed the government to restructure the contract downward only."

Colton was one of those guys we all meet sometime in life who thinks he has it all figured out. An "operator," Eisner called him. At his own cost, Eisner designed a dummy—a sample edition of what the magazine would look and feel like. The effort paid off; the actual dummy of

PS No. 1
(Courtesy PS Magazine)

the book helped Eisner win the contract to produce what became *PS: The Preventive Maintenance Monthly*. "PS" implied "Postscript" to other, more traditional Army equipment and maintenance publications.

Once all the t's were crossed and the i's dotted, Colton dropped his own bomb on Eisner. "I would like to have a piece of this," he said.

"I can't give you a piece of this," Eisner said, surprised by his boldness. "You're an Army employee!"

"Not if you give me stock," Colton said. "I can exercise options on it later."

"That's illegal!"

"I got you into this contract!" Colton said. "I recommended you! You owe me!"

"Technically, that's true," Eisner said. "But in fact, you didn't. The quality of our work won this contract. I saw what the competition offered ... lousy!"

"*I* approved it."

"That doesn't mean anything to me," Eisner said. "Besides, I can't give you ownership in the magazine; it's against the law."

Colton, who became the magazine's first editor and continued in the position until 1953, wouldn't take no for an answer. On the pretense of production business, he came up to New York every other week, always with a new scheme for getting away with what Eisner knew to be wrong. Eisner's lawyer advised him not to discuss Colton's schemes. But the more Eisner said no, the angrier Colton became. He thought Eisner was trying to cheat him out of what he was convinced was his.

Colton was a colorful guy, small in stature, but always nattily dressed. He didn't just smoke cigarettes like the other guys; he used a long cigarette holder. "He was a strange kind of guy, a quiet guy, but an incredible promoter," Eisner said. "He would do things that really shook you up in the military. He would get things done in the military in a very, very quiet but devious manner. He was quite devious in his ways. His talent was his ability to put these things together. He was, I guess, what the Germans called a *luftmensch,* an air person."

One day, there was a new twist. As usual, Colton was expected in New York to visit Eisner. That morning, however, Eisner received a preemptive visit by two FBI agents. "Dark suits, tall, good-looking guys," he recalled. One carried a little envelope with him, the other a note pad.

"We would like to talk with you," one of the agents said.

"I don't know what this is about," Eisner said, "but I would like to have my attorney here."

"No, that won't be necessary," the agent said sternly. "We're not after you. We just want to have a conversation. Off the record."

They said that the man harassing Eisner was suspected of cheating on his Army travel expenses. Not that it surprised Eisner. But, he thought, *Oh boy,* I'm *going to jail.* At the same moment that Eisner was talking to the FBI in his studio, the phone rang. It was Colton.

"I'm at Grand Central Station," he said.

The agent signaled Eisner to have him come up. Eisner said, "Fine, I'm here; come on over."

When Colton arrived, the FBI agents questioned and detained him. Caught in the midst of a shakeup and power struggle in the Army Ordnance Office, Colton made the mistake of playing Army politics. His side lost. "He was a devious guy," Eisner said, "and when they wanted to get rid of him, he was fingered for travel expense improprieties."

Colton, whatever his real or imagined faults, may have simply backed the wrong horse at the Pentagon.

———

Jim Kidd was hired as interim editor of *PS* in mid-1953. He was a West Virginia University journalism professor who saw it as a summer job. Must have been a long summer—Kidd stayed until 1982.

When Kidd's job became permanent at *PS,* he reached out to a former student of his at WVU, Paul Fitzgerald, who was then managing editor of the *Cecil Whig* weekly newspaper in Elkton, Maryland. Fitzgerald became the first managing editor of PS, joining the magazine in October 1953 and continuing with it through October 1963.

"There had been a lot of trouble at *PS* before I got there," Fitzgerald recalled. "My job was to get rid of the cliques and get a system in place to get the railroad back on the tracks. I never met Norman Colton, but I shoveled enough debris following him that I feel like I could identify his problems. He, as I understood it, was not a journalist or a production person or an administrator. He was a promoter, a salesman. It was supposed to be a monthly publication, but the first two or three years, I think their average was not quite a magazine every three months.

"From what I saw," he continued, "the staff tried producing a magazine issue as an entity. If they hit a snag on a couple pieces of it, the whole thing bogged down."

Fitzgerald said that one of the biggest problems Colton created was constantly pointing out flaws in ordnance equipment, intending to embarrass a contender for chief of ordnance who was competing with Colton's own sponsor in the Pentagon. It was an excessive game of "gotcha" that enveloped the entire staff of *PS*.

When Colton went out the door, chains were put on *PS*. "Manuscripts were to be approved by the same guys we had been stabbing in the back!" Fitzgerald said. He refashioned the entire review process so that the military brass began reviewing manuscripts in progress, not whole issues before they went to press. Manuscripts were now approved and deposited in a bank of usable content. In this way, he had multiple issues in the pipeline at all times and could always fall back on other material if a manuscript hit a bureaucratic or technical snag.

Under Fitzgerald, *PS* was rigidly controlled in terms of technical compliance, and there was a rigid string of approvals required before an issue saw print.

In fact, there were as many as sixteen different intermediate production deadlines or mileposts put in place by Fitzgerald. They included technical clearances with command posts around the country and a policy review of a pre-print dummy in Washington that took two days every month and was usually overseen by Kidd. There were also separate reviews of pencil roughs and intermediate black-and-white art, and then the final art. The color separations were reviewed on overlays.

"I don't think there were any true writers on the staff except Jim Kidd when I came on board," Fitzgerald said. "There were technical writers; their loyalties lay with the Aberdeen Proving Grounds technical hierarchy. Jim and I changed the culture. The qualifications we set were for communicators, not technical experts. No subject matter expertise required. The military had thousands of technical experts. But it was a function of *PS* as communicators that the expertise of the experts was presented in a way to be comprehensible to GI Joe."

Fitzgerald described Kidd's sense of humor as deadpan.

"If you knew him, he wasn't a giggler, that's for sure," Fitzgerald said. "Jim Kidd was the son of a railroad signalman out of Monroe County, West Virginia. He won the Silver Star in WWII as an infantry officer. He was reared in the Depression and he was not careless with a buck—his or the public's."

"Jim Kidd encouraged and protected us," said Seymour "Sy" Reitman, a *PS* staff writer from 1956 to 1970. "Jim was straight; he wouldn't create anything funny. But he wouldn't object to something funny. Being creative was what made GIs read the magazine. They didn't read the manuals much; they wanted a magazine in a style they could enjoy, and it saved a lot of dollars on maintenance."

"Looking back at it from where I'm sitting now," Fitzgerald said, "some of what we did has a touch of sophomoric humor. Jim Kidd had a sense of propriety that established parameters that were never published or necessarily uttered. The line that was followed was a reflection of Kidd's integrity and probity."

Technically, Eisner was a contractor for the magazine, although his influence on its gestation and development is widely acknowledged. He conceived of the art and continuity section in each issue—

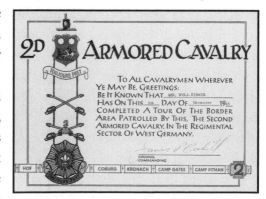

Recognition for Eisner from the front lines
(Will Eisner Collection, The Ohio State University Cartoon Research Library)

an eight-page, four-color panel strip in the center of the magazine—based on technically correct manuscripts that the *PS* staff provided him. He produced finished pages that, once they passed through the rigorous screening and approval process, went to a printer.

"Among my responsibilities," Fitzgerald said, "was the final inspections and acceptance or rejections. I also reviewed the blue lines or silver prints at the printer. Later, the dividing line was shifted so Eisner took care of the color separations and the final preparation of the film positives so there was no way in hell the printer could screw it up."

Eisner and Fitzgerald bonded over a common background: both learned the publishing trade the old-fashioned way, by hanging around print shops. Fitzgerald was the first editor at *PS* that knew the brick-by-brick process of what could reasonably be done and what couldn't.

Fitzgerald was also an ally of Eisner's during editorial reviews, when the Army brass occasionally misplaced their sense of humor.

"In all these policy and concept reviews, a lot of people in positions of authority never had a sense of humor or lost whatever they had," Fitzgerald said. "Will, Jim Kidd, and I found ourselves in a position of having to explain a joke, or what's funny. Will's frequent refrain was, 'If you have to explain a joke, it's not funny.' His point of view was that there were two generally basic and conflicting views of what constitutes humor. For him, it was the juxtaposition of the incongruous. Will said that the conflicting thesis to that was the basis of all humor was man's inhumanity to man. Will said that was the view that Al Capp held. It was a debate between him and Capp frequently when they got in contact."

Many of the solutions that *PS* presented to its readers were responses to operational difficulties or maintenance issues that arose from equipment designed at a drawing board by an engineer, sitting in a climate-controlled office in a clean shirt, that was intended for use by men in the worst possible environments. The resulting "official" maintenance requirements were therefore physically impossible at times. For example, there was a light tank in the early 1950s—the M-41—that was designed such that GIs were supposed to change its spark plugs every "X" number of hours. But they couldn't change spark plugs without pulling the engine. A GI mechanic in Korea concocted a field work-around and devised a kinky wrench that let him pull the plugs without pulling the engine. That, however, wasn't funny to the people in Washington who were responsible, nor to the engineers in Detroit.

"One idea we came up with for a cover of *PS* was these two GIs at the edge of a military reservation, in mud up to their eyeballs—or posteriors —and endeavoring to change a tire on a cargo vehicle," Fitzgerald explained. "The cover was divided diagonally from upper left to lower right. A chain-link fence represented the diagonal line. On a sidewalk is a beautiful female in a clingy dress. A breeze was blowing and there was a robin singing. The GIs were just looking. It was the juxtaposition of the incongruous. But at the review stage, someone in Washington said, 'They don't have mud like that at Army stations!' So we didn't use that ... then. It was used eventually when that particular individual moved on."

Fitzgerald and Eisner walked a tightrope with one another, always respecting, but often exasperating one another. But, through it all, the friendship remained.

Despite its inauspicious origins, *PS Magazine* and Eisner spent the next twenty-two years in each other's company. It was a profitable contract and paid for many things, including a photostat machine for the office, a luxury in those days. The magazine was a worthwhile thing to do, emotionally and financially. "It was certainly better than making the same kind of money doing comic books," Eisner said. It gave him a chance to work his way into the industrial and trade publishing field on his own terms.

Among the artists who worked in Eisner's studio producing *PS* were

PS No. 9, September/October 1952
(Will Eisner Collection, The Ohio State University Cartoon Research Library)

Dan Zolnerowich (*Sheena*), Klaus Nordling (*Lady Luck, The Thin Man*), Murphy Anderson (*Strange Adventures, Mystery in Space, Adam Strange, The Flash, Green Lantern*), Mike Ploog (*Creepy, Planet of the Apes, Werewolf by Night, Man-Thing*), Chuck Kramer (*The Spirit*), Alfredo Alcala (*Conan, Man-Thing, Star Wars, Swamp Thing*), Andre LeBlanc ("The Phantom," "Flash Gordon," "Rex Gordon, MD"), Don Perlin (*Werewolf by Night, Ghost Riders, The Defenders*), and Dan Spiegle ("Hopalong Cassidy," *Space Family Robinson, Magnus, Robot Fighter, Korak*).

Today's sixty-four-page—up from forty-eight pages—digest-size *PS* format continues largely unchanged after more than fifty years as an Army technical bulletin. Approximately eighty-five thousand copies are distributed to Army field units every month. It still features a color comic-book-style cover, and eight full pages of four-color comic book "continuity" (story) in the middle. The rest of the book features text with technical, safety, and policy information, and is printed in two colors to save money. The continuities always have the same basic cautionary tale: a soldier who ignores preventive maintenance learns about its importance in the end. For fifty years, it's always been that same lesson.

Eisner had greater freedom in the continuity section than his successors did. He used the comics as eye candy to draw the reader in. The continuity was rarely used to present technical information.

Staff writers are responsible for getting the technical details right and guiding the artists. "That's always the source of creative tension," Stuart Henderson said. "The artists tolerate the writers and think they hung the moon; the writers tolerate the artists who think *they* hung the moon."

Eisner and his studio could not have produced the continuities without the staff writers who took the photos, conducted research and interviews, and coordinated with the specialty subject experts.

Don Hubbard joined *PS* at the Aberdeen Proving Grounds in July 1954 as a writer and rose through the ranks, from production manager to managing editor, then editor. When he retired in November 1991 with thirty-seven years on staff, he held the record for most years at the magazine.

It was as production manager in 1955, when the magazine moved from Aberdeen to the Raritan Arsenal in Central New Jersey, that Hubbard began working with Eisner. Twice a month, Hubbard went to Eisner's studio in Manhattan and reviewed the work in progress. Once a month, Eisner visited *PS* at Raritan.

During Eisner's tenure, dummy week, when the magazine was finished, read, and approved for printing, was an almost sacred time. When dummy week came, no one was given leave—no exceptions. Dummy weeks were scheduled a full year ahead.

"It was always a confrontational situation," Hubbard said. "When Will did his best work, we didn't always *think* it was his best work. We would give him technical guidance and then we would review the dummy. Sometimes he went off. Will's contribution was the continuity and the covers. Sometimes he went down a road that didn't quite catch it. Or he would propose a storyline that we couldn't go along with. There was always give and take. We had to hold his nose to the grindstone to get him to do things the way we wanted. You could imagine someone of his talent and a bunch of illiterates telling him what to do! Will Eisner had a proprietary viewpoint. He said, 'I created this whole concept. Don't tell me.' He was always a gentleman but it was sometimes thorny, and he would pout if we told him to change a storyline."

Eisner's production manager always accompanied him to review meetings, taking notes on the technical matters. And the production manager would put up an argument, too.

"Will, to be honest, ground his teeth quite a few times," Hubbard said.

In one issue, the Army higher-ups forced the substitution of one continuity for another due to a policy change. But there was never an instance where Eisner and his staff were asked to redo an entire continuity because of something they did. Generally, Eisner protested change requests not over story but costs; changes meant money. So he resisted on principle.

Hubbard's favorite Eisner contribution to *PS* was a Korean War-era illustration that showed Joe Dope and another GI stop on top of a hill and study the terrain. "You really have to keep in shape to cover that kind of territory," one says to the other as they study a pair of snow-covered mountains stacked remarkably like actress Jane Russell's bust.

"Pictures From Life" and Eisner's picture letters home
(Will Eisner Collection, The Ohio State University Cartoon Research Library)

As part of his contract for *PS,* the magazine sent Eisner on location for weeks at a time to places such as Japan, Korea, and Vietnam. The Army felt it important that he periodically be with soldiers, seeing what they saw and understanding the real situations they and their equipment might find themselves in.

In 1960, Eisner and Fitzgerald embarked upon a six-week research trip together for *PS.* They flew from New York to San Francisco, then on to Guam, Japan, and Korea. It was a tense time in the international arena, coming not long after the Soviet Union shot down Francis Gary Powers' high-altitude U-2 reconnaissance plane on May 1. An embarrassed President Dwight D. Eisenhower at first reported that a weather plane had gone off course—until Powers admitted he was spying. Soviet Premier Nikita Khrushchev canceled a planned summit with Eisenhower and instead came to the United Nations that fall, and, on October 11, infamously protested Eisenhower's lie by standing before the assembly, taking off his shoe, and pounding it on the podium.

As they began the first leg of their trip on a DC9 climbing over Manhattan, Eisner pointed down at the city.

"There is a common denominator down there that is the reason why every brick or stone or yard of concrete is in its place," he told Fitzgerald. "And that's desire. Because somebody wanted or thought they needed something they didn't have—a woman, security, food, or shelter."

It was an innocuous, yet profound thought that Fitzgerald remembered for the rest of his life, and years later he saw it take form as a recurring theme in many of Eisner's graphic novels.

The trip was perhaps the most formative of Eisner's life. He wasn't allowed to leave the United States when he was a soldier himself, and now he was given the entire tableau of global war and peace in a compact package. In his numerous letters home—shared here publicly for the first time—Eisner recorded the entire experience for his wife and young children in words and sketches.

In Tokyo, their Air Force hosts were indifferent to Fitzgerald and Eisner's presence, throwing them out to the Japanese population without an interpreter, guide, or instructions. "They took us to the train station and dumped us off," Fitzgerald said. "Will and I couldn't read or speak Japanese. We just told the ticket agent, 'Tokyo.' He would hold up fingers and we kept giving him coins until we got our tickets. We were going to the Akasaka Prince Hotel. We found ourselves in a car jammed with leftist students going into Tokyo for a scheduled riot. We had to show our tickets to strangers and they would hold up fingers as to how many stops were left. We were physically obvious as strangers, helpless foreigners, because we didn't know the language."

Luckily—or perhaps unluckily—the travelers encountered some students who spoke English. But they weren't interested in polite how-do-you-dos. They berated Fitzgerald and Eisner about U.S. sins in foreign policy.

"What do you think of the conduct of Mr. Khrushchev at the U.N.?" a young man badgered them. "Do you approve or not?"

"You must remember that in my country," Fitzgerald said, "a guest in the house of my father is my guest also."

To which Eisner quickly smiled and added, "It is the custom."

The students, surprised that the Americans might have some manners, gave the customary half-bow and said, "*Ah-so.*"

On Okinawa, their assigned escort, Sgt. Kennedy, was, according to Fitzgerald, "a real soldier who knew the ins and outs of everything." For example, he ordered a helicopter for them when needed. But the real eye-opener was a private, after-hours event Kennedy arranged at the legendary Tea House of the August Moon. Here's the way Eisner described it in a letter to Ann written that evening:

> *This evening, Sgt. Kennedy took us home to his wife and six kids and after a couple of beers she and he drove us to a place where we could have dinner. The place was the TEA HOUSE OF THE AUGUST MOON. Yes, the same famous teahouse from which the movie and play was made. It is (I'm told because I never saw either) unchanged and exactly as it was when the GIs landed.*
>
> *We had dinner ... sukiyaki ... and what a dinner it was, complete with singalong geisha girls playing their stringed instruments singing cowboy songs the GIs taught them. Before long there were about eight girls sitting with us and Mrs. Kennedy had to tell her husband to inform the MAMASAN (madam) that we were not interested in you-know-what. It was an evening of great gales of laughter and tremendous fun. The women are very tiny and they all have big teeth with lots of gold dental work so when they smile they made us laugh. They giggle at everything you say, but they keep their mind on money and after each drink they say "Two dollah, prease." Made me feel like an oriental potentate.*

A geisha singer amplified the words of her Korean songs in pantomime. One of her numbers, an interpreter explained, was a traditional Japanese folk song called "The Coalminer's Song," for which she mimed a pick and shovel.

"When she finished, Will pointed to me and told this geisha—through the interpreter—that I had been a coalminer, which was true," Fitzgerald said. "I said that there were many American folk songs about coalminers. A particularly poignant one was the 'Dream of a Miner's Child.' It's an old hillbilly thing. There was then a demand that I reciprocate and sing the American song, which I did. And as I did this, Will did sketches on a napkin to illustrate and translate what I was singing. A good time was had by all."

From there, the *PS Magazine* representatives went on to Korea.

Eight years after the cessation of hostilities, there was still a high level of belligerence at the border between North Korea and South Korea, with constant provocations across the demilitarized zone (DMZ). Fitzgerald and Eisner were sent to a base that was north of the Imjim River in a remote pocket of South Korea. The only way of reaching it was over the narrow, one-lane Freedom Bridge built in 1953. The original bridge was blown up during the Korean conflict and was not reconstructed until 1998. If a conflict erupted, support for the U.S. base would never make it across the existing pontoon bridge.

"Will and I were there briefly," Fitzgerald said. "We were basically observers, getting atmosphere for effective graphic communications in the magazine. We were standing outside the headquarters one morning and a humongous water tanker-truck pulled up in front of the sick bay. A physician came out, climbed on top of the tank. He took a water sample and took it into his lab to test it. He came out, gave an okay to the driver and the truck drove off. The commanding colonel made a big to-do about it. We asked, 'Where is he going?' and the colonel said, 'He's going up on the hill to transfer water to the tank.' Later on, Will and I were by ourselves, walking across the square in front of headquarters. Will looked at me and smiled. He said, 'Are we missing something here? Like maybe an Army representative who goes with the driver to make sure he doesn't slip something in the water?' But we never said anything; that wasn't why we were there. We weren't wearing green suits. We were civilians."

Later that same day, Fitzgerald, Eisner, and the colonel were in the Officer's Club, discussing technical issues for their research.

"Colonel," Fitzgerald said, "I don't feel like I should continue this line of discussion in the bar."

He saw that Fitzgerald was looking at the Korean bartender.

"Don't worry about Kim," the colonel said. "He doesn't understand any English except 'extra dry martini.'"

Eisner agreed. "That's probably because he was given birth by a mother who was impregnated by a syphilitic camel."

The bartender never blinked.

The most rewarding meeting Eisner had in Korea came on a visit to a maintenance unit. A sergeant there, in a brown T-shirt and a dead cigar, looked at him and said, "Man, do you make this magazine?"

"Yeah," Eisner said, not knowing if he would be hugged or flattened.

"You the guy who does those pictures?"

"*Yeah ...* "

"Man, you saved my ass, you know that?"

An illustration Eisner did that explained some specific, basic-maintenance issue, such as changing a gasket, had caused the sergeant's gratitude. He said that he couldn't follow the standard technical manuals, they just were too hard to read, but he loved *PS*.

On the way back to the States, Fitzgerald and Eisner stopped over in Honolulu. As civilian travelers with the Department of the Army, they were given access to Fort de Russy on Waikiki, Oahu. But while Waikiki is a public beach, its large hotels controlled access to the shore. The few public access ways were unmarked, making them inaccessible.

"Will and I went to Fort de Russy to swim and use the beach," Fitzgerald said. "After we had done enough of that, we decided to walk up Waikiki to the commercial area. When we got there, it was too crowded and we were tired. We didn't want to walk all the way back on the sand. It was easier on the sidewalk. We were in the area of the Royal Hawaiian Hotel. The beach was almost entirely blockaded by these Hawaiian beach boys and their huge, gleaming, outrigger canoes. These guys were muscular and big, like sumo wrestlers that used weights. We couldn't find a public outlet to get off the beach! They wouldn't let you walk through the hotels if you weren't a guest. We were physically obvious as outsiders, culturally different, ethnically inferior, walking up to these full-blooded Hawaiian kings of the beach to ask for directions to a public egress. The question also branded us as economically inferior. They condescended and ridiculed us. We went away with our tails between our legs, two whipped dogs. As we were walking away from there, Will turned to me and said, 'And now, my white, Anglo-Saxon, Protestant friend, you know how it feels.'"

—————

On a separate trip to Tokyo, again accompanied by Fitzgerald, the travelers once more went by train from the airport to the hotel, which was near Shimbashi Station. Will felt like he was traveling on a child's Lionel Train, however, as he towered over his fellow riders.

"Will," Fitzgerald said, "the stations are flying by, but I don't know where we should get off."

Will leaned over and said loudly and slowly to a man, "DO — YOU — KNOW — WHERE — SHIMBASHI — STATION — IS?"

To Will, the man looked like an American's vision of a stereotypical, Japanese cartoon character from World War II. So he addressed him as a stereotypical, cartoon American, the kind who assumed that if he asked his question loud enough, the other man would understand him.

And it worked.

The Japanese gentleman leaned back and respectfully said, in perfect English, "It is indeed fortunate that you asked me ..." The man, it turned out, was a graduate of Washington State University.

—————

Eisner would just as soon have forgotten one of his later trips for *PS*.

"I lied to my wife, because I told her I was going to Japan," he said. "Well, we *landed* in Japan. But I didn't tell where I was going to after that. We landed in Japan and from there we flew over to Saigon."

Jim Kidd accompanied Eisner as far as Saigon, but then Eisner went on alone to Bearcat, a combat zone military camp.

His escort was a young major.

"He was very nervous during that whole trip because this was his last day in Vietnam, and his wife and his kids were waiting for him in Hawaii," Eisner said. "Everybody is superstitious about that, that things happen on your last day, so he was scared stiff."

They boarded a helicopter gunship and flew down to the Mekong Delta. But it was a short visit.

"We had to leave suddenly because there was incoming fire," Eisner recalled. "Shells were landing all around. It was in the center of some woods on a little island in the center of the Delta. It was like a swamp, where there were barren stretches, and I really had to get out of there. Meanwhile, this young major who was with me was quivering. And I was thinking, 'What the hell's a nice boy like me doing here? Am I going to have to die for a goddamn military contract?' I had a moment when I was scared. I ran out on the field and dove onto a helicopter that was the last one out. I jumped on unauthorized."

Incidentally, Eisner was never armed on these trips. All he had to keep him out of trouble was a noncombatant's identification card.

Eisner separated his personal beliefs from his business dealings with the Army. "Before I got there, I thought we shouldn't have any trouble, we should be able to win this," he said. "But when I came back from Vietnam, my attitude had changed completely. Militarily, I didn't think we would make it.

"I had always regarded the military contract (for *PS*) as an important point in my career," he continued. "I was proud of it. I had no military connection as far as I was concerned. It was an opportunity to demonstrate that comics were able to deal with subject matter that was not necessarily just entertainment. There was a big difference between what I was doing and what the military was doing with the comics at another level. They were using comic books as an attitude conditioner, as a propaganda tool. My use of comics was truly as an instructional tool, a means of instruction. I was very proud of what I was doing. I thought this was great."

Murphy Anderson first met Will Eisner at a party sponsored by Wham-O, manufacturers of the Hula-Hoop. The company was interested in producing a comic book and invited several creative types to meet them in a social setting. Alex Kotzky, Lou Fine, and Wally Wood all eventually did work for Wham-O as a result of that event; Anderson did not.

Several years later, in the late 1960s, as the *Batman* TV show craze petered out, Anderson heard that Eisner was looking for new artists at *PS*. He interviewed at American Visuals and was hired as head illustrator, although he continued freelancing for DC Comics on the side. Anderson would arrive at Eisner's at 5 A.M. and work until noon, then went on to DC to draw superheroes, where his drawing of *Hawkman* and *Superman* comics defined an era for the publisher.

"It wasn't too difficult for me to ape Will's style at *PS*, because I had always loved his work, and he was a big influence on my thinking back in the late '30s when the comic book started appearing," Anderson said. "I quickly formed the opinion that the best comic books were Busy Arnold's Quality books and, of course, Will was doing a lot of stuff for them. But I was a big fan of *The Spirit*, too, when that came out, and I collected all the *Spirit* comic supplements in the *Philadelphia Record*. I saved them and had them bound, as a matter of fact."

Anderson was one of the original fans who turned comic book professional. His first job in the industry, as a seventeen-year-old, was with one of Eisner's regular clients, Fiction House.

PS No. 12
(Courtesy PS Magazine)

At *PS Magazine,* Eisner laid out and created pencil roughs of covers and the center continuity sections, then handed them off to Anderson for finished pencils and inking. Eisner often took Anderson's pencil pages home at night so he could change or ink what he felt needed his personal touch. "He couldn't do much work in the office," Anderson recalled. "He spent most of his day there running the business."

For the record, Anderson is one of Eisner's few former employees who didn't suggest the man was cheap. He recalled handling assignments beyond *PS* for Eisner that qualified for overtime.

"I would stay evenings or come in early in the morning and work on them," Anderson said. "He was very generous; it was time-and-a-half for anything like that. Even though I have heard people grumble about him, I never heard anyone that could substantiate that he wasn't fair. One of the guys at DC, Chuck Cuidera, when he heard I was going to work for Will, grabbed me by the arm and insisted I go around and have coffee with him. He started telling me all about Will, what a bad move it was to go to work for Will. There was bad blood on Chuck's part, although I don't think Will ever took it too seriously."

———————

One of the constructive developments from Eisner's overseas trips was convincing the Turkish military that it needed a Turkish language *PS Magazine*. The United States was in the process of giving surplus World War II trucks to Turkey "and they were ruining them," Eisner said. "They knew nothing about maintenance."

He grimaced at the memory of watching Turkish army officers in Ankara grind—and strip—gears as they demonstrated their alleged proficiency. The officer he dealt with was at first dubious of the need for a training and preventive maintenance guide. "We have a good training system," the officer said. "What I need from America is more money!"

> *January 29, 1964*
> *Ann Dear,*
> *So far everyone who has listened to my sales pitch has concurred with enthusiasm—and this includes the Turkish top (or middle command I should say) brass.*
> *For the last three days and nights I've been working until 1 or 2 A.M. in the hotel room drawing the cartoon characters and developing the actual product!*
> *Love to KIDS & Dawg n' Nibb,*
> *Will*

Called *Askars*—Turkish for "GI Joe"—the short-lived magazine had its own version of Pvt. Joe Dope. "Nasrettin Hoca" rode a donkey backwards because he wanted to see where he had been, but "where he was going was in the hands of Allah," Eisner said.

———

Many stories in this book come from artists who developed their craft as fans of Will Eisner. Ironically, the artist whose work is most often cited as being remarkably similar to Eisner's hadn't heard of the man until he was working for him on *PS Magazine* in 1970.

"I had seen *PS* while I was in the military, but I did not know who Will was," Mike Ploog said. "When I got out of the military, I went to work at Filmation Studios, and then I went on over to Hanna Barbera. There was an ad in the National Cartoonists Society newsletter looking for an artist with military experience and that could draw like the sample in the ad. This guy sitting next to me at Hanna Barbera said, 'Hey, this sounds like you!'"

Ploog had spent ten years in the Marine Corps, the first few on the Marine Corps Rodeo Team ("It's a real well-kept secret," he said) and as a swimming instructor. When it was discovered that he could draw, he spent his last years in the service as an illustrator at *Leatherneck* magazine, creating training aids and pamphlets.

Because *PS* was extremely popular, "I had been copying Will's work and I didn't even know it," Ploog said. "At that particular time in my career, I had to copy something. I don't think I had any original ideas. And if I did, I think it would have died of lonesomeness, wandering around up there."

Ploog, who was in California, answered the ad and Eisner asked him to send out some sample artwork. A few days later, Eisner called back. "I am going to be in L.A. tomorrow for a meeting, can you meet me at my hotel?" Satisfied that Ploog was genuine and talented, Eisner didn't waste any more time. "Can you be to work on Monday?"

This was on a Wednesday. "What the hell," Ploog said. "Yeah, I'll be there." He was single, unencumbered, hated animation work, and had already dropped out of art school after just a week ("nobody took it seriously") so it wasn't a complicated choice.

"I worked on *Motor Mouse & Auto Cat,* the *Scooby-Doo* pilot, and *Wacky Races.* God, that drove me nuts! I drew so many wacky cars that if Will offered me a job in Bangkok, I would have gone," Ploog said.

(Ploog later worked on more than forty films, including three with animator Ralph Bakshi: *Wizards, Lord of the Rings,* and *Hey, Good Lookin';* three with Jim Henson: *Dark Crystal, Labyrinth,* and *Return to Oz;* he was a production designer for Michael Jackson's *Moonwalker;* and a designer on the remake of *Little Shop of Horrors.* He also contributed to *The Unbearable Lightness of Being.*)

After being regimented for ten years, Ploog—ironically, just like Eisner in this regard, too—couldn't stand people just standing around. None of the people in art school or animation were serious enough for his expectations. "It was just a bunch of guys goofing off and wandering around the halls drinking coffee." So when Eisner offered the job at American Visuals, money wasn't the issue. "I kind of doubt, knowing Will, that he offered more money," Ploog joked. "He is notoriously tight, I tell ya. I think it was just that I loved the idea of going to New York and working in New York. I was familiar with *PS Magazine,* so I thought, *Damn, this would be good fun.*"

Ploog flew from L.A. to New York, via a connection in Washington, DC. Except that when he met an old military buddy in the nation's capitol, he missed his flight out.

"I ended up catching a flight the next day, and I never even thought about it," Ploog said. "But because I wasn't there Monday morning, Will was really worried. He had the police out looking for me. And because I had a secret clearance in the military and because Will mentioned *PS Magazine,* the FBI got involved in it for days. Even after I had shown up in New York, they were going to my dad's neighbors. My dad had been dead for like two years, and they were going to his neighbors and asking if they knew anything about me. So Will had the FBI out looking for me!

"But that's Will. Will is somebody who, if you said you were going to be there on Monday, you better have been hit by a car if you're not there."

This was only the second time Ploog had ever been to New York. The first time, visiting with a friend, he loved it. The second time, when he worked for Eisner, he hated it. Not working for Eisner, that is, but living in the city.

Eisner arranged for Ploog to bunk at the Washington Hotel when he arrived and until he could find more permanently lodgings. "That was a nightmarish scenario," he said. "My first week there was the goofiest week I ever experienced, between thunderstorms and people screaming at you from the street. I moved out of there and to New Jersey.

"We often worked late into the evening there, and the first or second night that I worked for Will, as I walked across the street on my way back to the hotel, this old woman crossed the street toward me. When we met in the middle of the street, she screamed at the top of her lungs, 'RAPE!!' and I didn't know what the hell to do. I didn't know whether she was ill or what, and then all of a sudden I realized lights are coming on and there are people looking out the windows. I thought, *I am getting the hell out of here,* so I ran. There were sirens and everything. I don't know whether the sirens were for me, but it didn't matter. It just scared the hell out of me. It was like a city full of loonies."

Ploog kept moving farther and farther away from that old woman until his daily commute to work began and ended two states away, in Bucks County, Pennsylvania.

But the job itself agreed with him. His coworkers in the studio included Ted Cabarga, Bob Sprinsky, Frank Chiaramonte, and Chuck Kramer. The office was situated nine floors above one of Manhattan's most unique landmarks, a Chock Full o' Nuts coffee shop, at 34th Street and Park Avenue. The staff ate lunch at a deli across the street that it ruefully referred to as "Greasy Spoon Chock Full o' Nuts." "It was a terrible place," Ploog said, but they kept going back anyway.

The studio was in an interesting building. Employees had to make sure that they gave the elevator man a Christmas present each year. Otherwise, he would cut off their elevator service. On several occasions, the elevator didn't quite reach the ninth floor.

Eisner occupied the front office with his longtime receptionist and head of accounting, Mary Swiatek. "She was an old gal that looked after Will," Ploog said. "She was like a mother hen."

There were four rooms beyond Eisner's office, although after Kramer left, Ploog was the last artist working there. The other remaining employees were dedicated to paste-up and production work for *PS*.

One storeroom was the repository of the original lead plates from which *The Spirit* stories were printed. Eisner kept them until water or some other element ruined a great many of them; later, he gave the rest to Denis Kitchen, his publisher and friend, for safekeeping.

In another room, Eisner stored crates of toys and *tchotchkes* connected with his "World Explorer" elementary school program.

"I never got involved with it because that was something he was doing on the side," Ploog said. "But he used to get in things like silkworms, and on one occasion the rats ate all the worms and all Will was left with were a bunch of silkworm cocoons. Another time, he ended up with beads that were poisonous and could kill people if they wore them. Everything was always being held up at customs because nobody could believe that some idiot was buying two cases of silkworms. Kids would send in their little coupon and a buck, and Will shipped these things out. It was a goofy damned business, but he did pretty well at it. He made money at it."

Ploog worked almost exclusively on *PS*. Each issue, he and Eisner went over the list of items that needed illustration, as well as coming up with a theme for the eight-page continuity. Ploog would go off and draw, then show Eisner his rough work, accept suggestions from the boss, and finish it.

"Will was a real taskmaster," Ploog said. "He got a full day's work out of you. He was demanding—not in the sense that everything had to be absolutely perfect—but it had to relate to the soldiers, and that was one of the things that he really put an awful lot of work into. He wanted these guys to really relate to this book, and he wanted you to be continuously illustrating soldiers that looked like soldiers. You would think that soldiers look like everybody because they come from every different walk of life. But Will had this middle-American idea in his head of what soldiers had to look like. It used to drive me nuts. He would look at my work and say, 'I don't know this guy.' And I thought, *Well, do they all have to look like your guy?* He really wanted to humanize these people. He said, 'I want to know what this guy had for breakfast. I want to know if he has a girlfriend back in Des Moines, Iowa.' I'd sit there looking at him and thinking, 'How in the hell am I going to illustrate somebody that is going to tell you what he had for breakfast?' But then all of a sudden I got the clue: he just wanted them human. He wanted you to know as much as you could possibly know about this guy through his attitude and his expression, even his body language. That was a very interesting learning curve."

Ploog may have been the best in a long line of artists hired for their ability to emulate the Eisner style. The longer they were together, the easier it got. According to Ploog, Eisner's style caricaturized things.

"He didn't sweat reality," Ploog said. "It didn't have to look like a car but it had to feel like a car. And he did the same thing with his figures. It didn't have to be the perfectly drawn figure, but it had to look like the guy and express his expression. Through his body language and through his expression, he had to be somebody that you related to. Will was a hell of a caricaturist, but he was not a caricaturist in the sense that he drew people … (He) didn't draw a character, he drew real people. If they were bums on the street, boy, you know they were bums. If she was a hooker, boy, you know she was a hooker. He had a great insight to people, and it came through in his art."

Ploog respected Eisner for his accomplishments with *PS*, but he didn't know about Eisner's significance in the greater comics world until long after he wasn't working for him any longer.

"I was never a comic book fan," Ploog said. "The only comic books I ever read as a kid were *Roy Rogers* and *Donald Duck*. I had idols, but most of them were illustrators from the 1950s and the '60s. It wasn't until years later that I realized what an icon Will was in the industry."

In Ploog's opinion, Eisner wanted to be perceived as a businessman first and an artist second, because he felt he was most respected and appreciated as a businessman. In the latter years at *PS*, Eisner didn't even have a drawing board in his office. He worked on his desk, or he occasionally worked at an empty drawing board next to Ploog.

America's Combat Weapons,
by Will Eisner, 1960

"Pictures From Life" and Eisner's picture letters home
(Will Eisner Collection, The Ohio State University Cartoon Research Library)

"When I got to know him, I really felt that there was a certain embarrassment about being a 'cartoonist,' that there would be more respect for him if he was a businessman. Obviously," Ploog said, "he is a very good businessman."

Ploog, like Feiffer and others before him, described Eisner as close with a buck.

"He was tight," Ploog said, "right down to where everybody had pencil extenders. You know how a pencil gets too small to hold it in your hand any more? An extender is this thing that you slide the pencil into that it sits on top of and extends the length of the pencil so that you can use the last two inches of it or so."

Cheap? Maybe. But Ploog was hooked. He uses pencil extenders to this day on his own dime.

Living through the Great Depression in the 1930s, Eisner developed an underlying and never-distant fear of economic deprivation that led him to the practices that some employees saw as miserly, such as the pencil extenders. At the end of each day, when everyone else went home, Eisner rescued partially used drawing paper, cut it into squares, and used it as scratch paper. He also collected the used non-repro blue pencils (they could be used to write instructions on pages for the press workers because they didn't reproduce in print) his artists discarded. One day, as a gag, Chuck Kramer took all the little stubs that Eisner collected and made a belt of them—much as a cowboy might wear bullets— and presented it to the boss.

———

Eisner sustained a sole-source contract with the Army for twenty years. When it came time to review, he never competed at bid with any-one else for the job. But in 1971, the Army told the magazine it must solicit bids for future production contracts. By that time, Eisner had guided *PS* through 227 issues. He was ready to do other things and let the magazine go.

When Eisner gave up the *PS* contract in 1971, he said goodbye to most of his staff.

"We had a going-away dinner," Ploog recalled. "We went to the Illustrators' Club in New York. We had dinner, and everybody made toasts. Then Will got a telephone call. He got up and answered the call. He came back and said, 'Guys, I am going to have to leave you here. Good luck to everybody. I have to take off now.' And he left. And the waiter came around with individual bills for everybody. We all just sat there and looked at one another and thought, wait a minute. That son of a gun, he got a telephone call, left, and left us with the bill!"

———

That's not the end of the story, however.

Although Eisner didn't bid on the *PS* contract, his influence on the artists producing it was far from over.

"Chuck Kramer won the contract," Hubbard said. "But Chuck didn't have the grasp or subtlety. His characters became sexed up—slutty and grotesque. During the Vietnam War, we expanded the book. In some of the posters and things we did, I fought as managing editor. The art that would be otherwise a graceful, acceptable, wholesome female would be slutty, sexually overt in Chuck's hands. I was never fond of Kramer's females."

Kramer, Dan Zolnerowich, and Mike Ploog formed Graphic Spectrum Systems in November 1971 and set up shop close by to Eisner's office. They occasionally turned to their former boss for advice.

And an incident at the new production office was reminiscent of the infamous towel story at the Eisner & Iger Studio.

Trash disposal cost Kramer and Ploog almost $150 a month.

"Geez, Will, $150 a month for garbage!" Ploog said.

"Mike, you gotta get used to this kind of stuff. You are in New York City," Eisner said. "I tell you what. You bring your garbage across the street and put it in with my garbage. How's that? That will save you some money."

Kramer and Ploog were scrimping everywhere they could; the *PS* contract was not as lucrative as they expected. As a money saver, Ploog started bringing his trash across the street every night, just as Eisner suggested.

One day Ploog was in his office and three goons came in, one in a camel-hair coat with the sleeves ripped off, the coat itself about a foot too long.

"I want to talk to whoever is in charge," said the man in the coat, putting his hands in his pockets.

"That's me," Ploog said.

"How come you're not taking out the garbage?" the man asked.

"Pardon?" Ploog literally didn't know what was happening.

"The garbage, you know? The sacks out in the hall. You are supposed to put your garbage in the sacks."

"I don't know why you're so interested in our trash, but we really don't accumulate that much garbage, and so I just take it across the street to our other office."

"Oh, no you don't! You put your garbage in that sack!"

And then they left, leaving Ploog bewildered. His heart was beating harder than it ever had before. Not sure what to do, he called across the street to Eisner.

"Will," Ploog said, "these three goons just came in threatening me! They say I have to put my garbage in their sacks!"

"I was afraid that was going to happen," Eisner said quietly. "Your side of the street is with (such-and-such) brothers, and my side of the street is another garbage collector. Your side of the street is Mafia; mine's not."

Suddenly, Ploog got it. Not just that his trash disposal was handled by organized crime, but that Eisner already knew it. Eisner felt that there were some things Ploog needed to learn on his own.

When the new studio's contract expired after twenty-three issues (Nos. 228-251), Kramer, Zolnerowich, and Ploog gladly handed *PS* off to Murphy Anderson's Visual Concepts in November 1973. Anderson held the contract from issue 252 through 308 (July 1978), lost it briefly to publisher Zeke Zekley's Sponsored Comics (Zekley used Dan Spiegle as the continuity artist and Alfredo Alcala for covers) and returned for issue 315 (February 1979) through issue 368 (July 1983).

"There are certain people that are naturals at things like that. I am not one of them," Ploog said. "I don't like taking care of petty details. I still have a hard time paying my telephone bill because of the fact that I think, 'Oh, damn it, here it is again.' No, I am not inclined in a business manner."

Still, if he had it all to do over again, he would.

"I really enjoyed doing it, because it was interesting, and it stretched your imagination," Ploog said. "I enjoyed working with Will because I learned an awful lot from him. It was the big turning point in my entire art career, because prior to that, being an artist was just a job. It was like I was a mechanic. I just happened to draw as opposed to tightening nuts and bolts. And it wasn't until I met Will that I realized that there was a lot more to it. There is a lot underneath. It was his insight into how he wanted me to handle drawing and handle people that got me going, and it popped me out of my shell."

Partly as a result of Kramer's rough edges, several of Eisner's classic military characters—some going back to *Army Motors*—were either dropped (Joe Dope and Private Fosgnoff) from *PS* continuity or forced to evolve (Connie Rodd, Sgt. Half-mast).

"The Army thought they did not do justice to its image at that time," Don Hubbard said. "We didn't fight it. These characters were Will Eisner's characters and *Army Motors*'. Things changed in the Army and the audience. Will wasn't all that concerned. We were his client. He didn't have the proprietary interest that he had in *Army Motors*."

In his official history of *PS*, Dan Andree explained why the magazine's cartoon characters changed with time:

During PS' *early years, Connie was a pinup-styled siren who was often featured in provocative poses, scanty costumes, and spoke lines of thinly veiled double-entendres. Like Betty Boop and aircraft nose art, this was an acceptable portrayal of a female to an all-male readership often serving in far-off places who needed to be enticed to pick up the magazine and read it. That kind of enticement stopped in the early 1970s as more females became part of the equipment maintenance army and the idea of the pinup became arcane and sexist.*

In her early incarnation, two Beetle Bailey-type soldiers, Private Fosgnoff and Private Joe Dope, assisted Connie. As their names imply, they were screw-ups. After a few years, it was decided that showing soldiers as incompetents was not the best way to motivate. So, Fosgnoff left the Army and PS *in 1955 and Joe Dope in 1957.*

As African-Americans came to play a larger role in the Army, an African-American woman, Bonnie, was added to the PS *character staff in 1970. Since then, Bonnie and Connie have grown into their roles as professional civilian advisors to the Army's maintenance workforce.*

A few other characters have come and gone, including Sergeants Bull Dozer, Windy Windsock, and Macon Sparks. PS *welcomed Sergeant Windsock's replacement, Sergeant "Rotor" Blade, also an African-American, in September of 2002.*

Hubbard was thrilled when Murphy Anderson took over the *PS* contract. "Murphy, of course, drawing *Wonder Woman*, could draw a female better."

During the Eisner era, *PS* received just eighteen letters of a critical nature according to Hubbard, whose job responsibilities including writing thoughtful, kind responses to them. But in subsequent years,

U.S. Democratic Representative Bella Abzug from New York, on the forefront of women's liberation, and Democratic Senator William Proxmire from Wisconsin, in search of turkeys in the federal budget, brought a searing national spotlight to the magazine.

"When *Army Motors* started," Eisner said, "Its audience was a different GI. He was drafted and complained bitterly. So the humor, if it was raunchy and scandalous, was perfect. They were looking for double entendres. But in the 1960s, the military was changing. The Army became more professional. The loose humor was no longer appropriate."

The pressure to evolve mores and attitudes in *PS* increased Anderson's stewardship of the art and production.

"We were under pressure from the brass in the Army, because the people at the Pentagon were getting criticism from senators and representatives," Anderson said. "They were looking at how the government's money was being spent, and female soldiers were just starting to make an impact on the Army. It became very much an issue when I was in my ten years on the contract, and we couldn't do the risqué stuff any more. The ladies sometimes complained that they felt there were a lot of male chauvinists in the military. Of course, it had been strictly a male organization. And then, of course, color became an issue, too. We had to make sure that the black troops were portrayed correctly. The staff introduced a new character called Bonnie, but they didn't think she was pretty enough. They kept after me giving me photos of beautiful black ladies, trying to get me to incorporate that stuff. At the time, during the Vietnam War, her trademark was an Afro and I kept drawing this. They said, 'Oh, no, no! That's not it, that's not it!' Finally it dawned on me, I just started drawing Connie's face with an Afro and giving her brown eyes. You know, that stopped it. That's basically what I did."

How important were comics to *PS*, really?

"I've thought a lot about that," said current *PS* production manager and staff historian Stuart Henderson. "Somebody understood something innately, that soldiers would read something that looked like *MAD* magazine, that had humor and funny treatment of women and double entendres. And the Army knew that was the way it wanted to go. They tried it a little in *Army Motors*. They had Connie as a brunette until Will turned her into a blonde. The Army knew soldiers would read it and learn while studying the fun stuff. Who better could they find than Will Eisner? He was a corporal; he identified with the GIs.

"It's been a challenge to keep *PS* interesting and relevant with a lot of those tools taken out of our toolbox," Henderson said. "The graphics sell the book. We want the soldier to pick it up and read it. That's been frustrating for us and Joe Kubert. We come up with many interesting ideas that we can't use. Will had *PS* in a much more freewheeling time for humor and cheesecake."

Another change that Henderson lamented was Connie's strictly hands-off attitude.

"Back in Will's day, Connie interacted with soldiers," he said. "On one cover, she lifts her hair and hands suntan lotion to GIs and says, 'Can you help me out?' But Connie is no longer touching or being touched by soldiers. That's sad. Connie and Bonnie are demurely dressed, civilian instructors. They don't bend over in sexy poses. That's all gone. But they're still useful in giving information to soldiers. The Army isn't in the business of making comic books. It's in the business of using comic books to get across preventive maintenance."

NINE
Official Member,
National Cartoonists Society

Milton Caniff, creator of the classic *Terry and the Pirates* and *Steve Canyon* comic strips, brought Will Eisner into the organization he cofounded, the National Cartoonists Society. Eisner was present at the group's first meeting as the token comic book artist. He liked to say that

Walt Kelly and Milton Caniff congratulate Eisner on his award
from the National Cartoonists Society
(Courtesy Will and Ann Eisner)

the comic strip artists viewed comic book artists as the bottom rung of the creative ladder, just below pornographers.

For Eisner, who was inspired to pursue cartooning by the daily strips he read as a teen, attending NCS events was like being in a hall of mountain kings.

The meetings were usually held at what is now the Society of Illustrators Museum at 128 East 63rd Street. Eisner was still in uniform at the group's first meeting, and found himself sitting next to *Li'l Abner* creator Al Capp.

In a big, booming voice, the somewhat intimidating Capp turned to Eisner and said, "Who are you?"

Eisner, the sleeves on his uniform a little too long, his usually confident, masculine voice squeaky with teenage awkwardness, could only sputter, "I'm, *ahh*, Will Eisner."

"What do you?" Capp asked.

"I do *The Spirit*."

Capp thought for a minute, and said, "Oh, yeah, I caught that down in Philadelphia once."

Eisner took that as praise and smiled. Capp brought him quickly back to reality.

"You are never going to make it," said America's most famous cartoonist. "You are too fucking normal."

Taking his leave of Capp as quickly possible, Eisner made the acquaintance of *New York Sun* editorial cartoonist Rube Goldberg. Goldberg is best known for creating the character of Professor Lucifer Gorgonzola Butts, who designed machines that completed simple tasks in complicated ways. He was sitting in a chair, off by himself, one hand tightly gripping his cane. After the same "Who are you?" interrogation, Goldberg said, "*The Spirit*, what kind of thing is that?"

"Well, it's different than the daily strips," Eisner said. "I believe the medium is an art form and that there is tremendous opportunity for literary potential in the field."

Goldberg looked at Eisner, banged his cane down, and shook his head in disgust.

"Bullshit, boy!" he said. "You are a vaudevillian like the rest of us. It's just vaudeville, just plain vaudeville; don't ever forget that!"

"Will took me to my first NCS meeting," Jules Feiffer recalled, "and I heard my first argument about whether to admit women. Rube Goldberg didn't want women admitted because you couldn't say 'fuck' in front of them. Alex Raymond was the only one who stood up for admitting Hilda Terry ("Teena"). I don't remember Will saying a word."

Eisner at the International Comics Convention in Angoulême, France, 1983
(Courtesy Will and Ann Eisner)

Burne Hogarth, perhaps best known as the artist of the "Tarzan" comic strip and as a master of active anatomy, was an invited guest at the International Comics Convention in Angoulême, France, in 1975, the year Eisner became the first American comic artist honored with the festival's highest award. (Underground comix artist Robert Crumb was the second.) They arrived separately, but happily found themselves on the same flight back to New York.

Hogarth was running for president of the National Cartoonists Society that year, and he spent much of the flight home convincing Eisner that he should run for treasurer. Eisner was willing, but when he got home he learned that the current treasurer wouldn't give up the position without a fight.

Another topic that they discussed—and about which Eisner was far more interested—was the idea of bringing cartoonists together more often for literary and social discussions.

"The artists in France get together and sit in salons," Eisner told Hogarth. "In our country, none of us get together. The National Cartoonists Society gets together once a month; it's not the same.

"I'm going to start a salon!"

A little more than a year later he did just that, inviting artists Jules Feiffer, Art Spiegelman (*RAW, Maus*), Harvey Kurtzman, Gil Kane (best known for his stylish interpretations of "Green Lantern," "The Atom," and "The Hulk") and, of course, Hogarth to come spend time with him and Ann at the Winslow Road house.

Earlier that great day, Ann had had gum surgery. In great pain, she still made dinner for Eisner and his guests.

Hogarth, who started the School of Visual Arts in New York City with Silas Rhodes, was there. Despite his enormous history in the comics medium, Hogarth didn't want to be thought of as a cartoonist; he wanted to be regarded as a great illustrator. Eisner knew this, but apparently not well enough.

"There are two branches of the world of art," Eisner said to open his first salon. "Communications and decoration. We're in communications."

Hogarth went nuclear. He started yelling at Eisner, unleashing a blistering tirade against his host.

Ann heard the timbre and tone—rather than the content—from the next room. When they were gone she told Eisner, "Whoever that was, I don't ever want that man in my house again."

The relationship between the two men was badly strained from that day forward. They were later on a panel together and the topic was humor. "Burne had no sense of humor," Eisner said, "and I made a fool of him. Afterwards Hogarth said, 'You're like a character with a mask. You come from behind a rock and you attack.'"

Not long after that, *The Comics Journal* asked Hogarth about Eisner.

"What do *you* think about a man who has to have an award named after him so he can win it?" Hogarth replied, referring to the comics industry awards, which were named for Eisner (not *by* him).

———————

Former NCS president Mort Walker (creator of "Beetle Bailey," cocreator with Dik Browne of "Hi & Lois," and founder of the International Museum of Cartoon Art), a longtime friend of Eisner's, rebuffed Eisner's heartfelt contention that members of the National Cartoonists Society long-viewed comic book artists as being below pornographers in the industry's social strata, calling his viewpoint "a self-imposed belief." Yet he doesn't deny that his counterparts in the 1940s and 1950s were extremely selective about the company they kept.

"At one point they only wanted strip cartoonists with over eight hundred papers," he said.

As a result, some meetings only had fifteen people in attendance. "It *was* very elite," Walker said. "When I became president in the 1960s, I wanted to expand the NCS. Many fought against that, but I tripled the membership. The old members resented it. They wouldn't even let Charles Schulz ("Peanuts") in! You had to know a member. I said, 'He lives in Minneapolis, how could he meet someone?' I brought Schulz to New York and took him around. He met Al Capp and other cartoonists. Next thing you know, he won a Reuben." (A Reuben Award is the comic strip artists' equivalent of an Emmy or Oscar.)

Comic book artists weren't the only ones who felt ostracized by the strip cartoonists; editorial cartoonists also were treated like second-rate citizens in the NCS. "A guy came up to me at one of our dinners," Walker recalled, "and he said, 'Who am I?' I said, 'I'm sorry; I don't know.' And he said, 'See!'"

Strip cartoonists enjoy national and even international renown. By comparison, editorial cartoonists are big fish in their hometowns, but unless their work is syndicated, they're virtually anonymous outside their newspaper's city limits. That's why they broke away and formed their own professional group, the Association of American Editorial Cartoonists.

Mort and Cathy Walker with Eisner
(Courtesy Will and Ann Eisner)

Mort Walker shared a story that few people have ever heard.

"When I was leaving my wife—we weren't divorced yet—and I was beginning to squire my future wife, Cathy, we snuck over to the Rye Brook Hilton Hotel in the middle of the day," Walker recalled. "And who was coming out? Will and Ann Eisner! We talked in the parking lot. They were coming out from lunch and we were going in. I'm sure they weren't going in for a room like I was. I said, 'This is Cathy ...' I don't know *what* he thought."

TEN
Moving Cars, Filling Jobs ...
and Singing Dogs?

Will Eisner, a newlywed and legend in the comic book business at the ripe old age of thirty-four, recognized in 1951 that his long run in the industry was winding down. New sales of the *Spirit* Sunday section topped out several years earlier. In many major American cities, competition for circulation diminished because conglomerates often owned both the morning and evening newspapers. Meanwhile, newsprint prices were rising and publishers resisted increased rates for the product. Top talent was more interested in magazine illustration and graphic design than four-color costumed characters. And the kids were rapidly trading in the genre for another emerging medium—television.

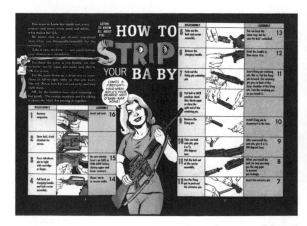

A supplement to *PS* on the M16 rifle by American Visuals
(Will Eisner Collection, The Ohio State University Cartoon Research Library)

"Grammarfun," produced by Eisner's American Visuals
(Will Eisner Collection, The Ohio State University
Cartoon Research Library)

PS Magazine was on the verge of first publication when Eisner decided that it could be the project to lead him in a new career direction. It would fulfill his belief that the medium had teaching potential, as he demonstrated in the Army from 1942 to 1945.

In the late 1940s, Eisner founded a commercial art company called American Visuals Corporation and began a twenty-year detour away from comic books in favor of working with corporate America. The shop produced *PS*, as well as educational cartoons and illustrations and giveaway comics, primarily for East Coast clients such as the Baltimore chapter of the American Medical Association. His other clients were a diverse bunch that included RCA Records, Fram Oil Filter, the Baltimore Colts, and New York Telephone. In the early years he wrote and illustrated the booklets, or at least roughed them out and drew the covers.

There were two kinds of comics produced at American Visuals. The first was "attitude conditioning," creating propaganda for everything from jobs and vacations to fire safety, political campaigns, and dental hygiene. The other was "product procedures" done in the mode of *PS*.

Job Scene, for example, was a series of comics produced for the Department of Labor. *America's Space Vehicles* was a hardbound textbook containing no comics at all. *Grammarfun* was an illustrated supplement for elementary English classes. *Deadly Ideas* was used by General Motors in its job safety program. He created the *Rip Roscoe* series for New York Telephone, touting the excitement of using a Touch-Tone phone. *Hoods Up* was a magazine "For Profit-Minded Fram Dealers." (A few observant readers noted that Connie from the Joe Dope comic did double duty as "Convertible Connie" for Fram Oil Filters.) And Eisner even drew the jacket for an RCA Victor album of music by The Singing Dogs entitled *Hot Dog Rock 'n' Roll.*

"The impression that I was an operator—I was," Eisner said. "I enjoyed business; I enjoyed the chess game."

For twenty years, Eisner explored his belief that comic books could be more than child's play, bringing the medium's potential to the attention of government leaders and business executives. He created "sequential training booklets" that instructed foreign nationals in the care and operation of military equipment, farming procedures, and social concepts. These products were purchased and distributed by the Agency for International Development, the United Nations, the U.S. Department of Labor, and the Department of Defense.

In 1957, one of Eisner's salesmen was trying to sell General Motors on an informational, labor-relations pamphlet called "Help! What Makes a Boss Tick?"

Jules Feiffer was just out of the Army, out of work, and he dropped by American Visuals to say hello to his former boss and inspiration.

"Jules," Eisner said, "would you like to do this pamphlet for us?"

Example of Will Eisner's corporate comics
(Will Eisner Collection, The Ohio State University
Cartoon Research Library)

He worked up a dummy and the salesman took it to General Motors, which rejected it, outright.

"The artwork is lousy," the automaker said.

And the salesman wasn't too impressed, either.

"Will," he said, "you are running a soup kitchen here for all your old comic artists and friends. Why don't you get some real professional artists in here?"

About a month later, Feiffer sold the *Village Voice* on a regular comic strip and suddenly he was a name in circles beyond comic books. Not long after, the salesman was back in Eisner's office.

"Hey Will," he said, "can you get that guy Feiffer back? I think we can sell his stuff now."

———

Three years later—without Feiffer's involvement—General Motors Corporation finally signed on with Eisner and American Visuals for an educational comic book. The company's initial response to the manuscript demonstrated how much tougher working with corporations versus newspaper syndicates could be:

> *June 2, 1960*
> *Dear Mr. Eisner:*
>   *Attached is the manuscript you submitted on "How Your Company Buys." This doesn't seem at all interesting and I doubt that it would do much for GM or its employees …*
>
> > *Cordially yours,*
> > *William H. Lane*
> > *Editor, Special Publications*
> > *Personnel Staff*

Six days later, Lane passed along his editorial board's comments on another sequential art training idea, "How to Get Across the Street and Survive." It must have made Eisner wish for a "Yarko" revival. "It left me cold," one corporate critic wrote.

And a week after that, Lane returned the dummy of a third concept, "Stop and Go on Ice and Snow," for good.

> *August 1, 1960*
> *Dear Mr. Eisner:*
> *The people who reviewed "How to Get Across the Street and Survive" said that they were not too impressed with it. They felt the presentation was rather scrambled. Also, they still feel there is a general indictment against motorists. Possibly the title is partly responsible for this feeling ...*
>
> *Cordially yours,*
> *William H. Lane*
> *Editor, Special Publications*
> *Personnel Staff*

Give and take flew back and forth in page after page of itemized notes from General Motors to Eisner. If Eisner thought that Busy Arnold was a nitpicker in the 1940s, he didn't know how good he had it until the 1960s dawned. The General Motors contract eventually produced several successful booklets, but the work was never easy.

At one point in the mid-1960s, American Visuals entered Chapter 11 bankruptcy protection. It was producing visual instruction guides for gas station employees, but closing the contract took a long time—too long.

"We were hiring engineers to help write materials," Eisner said. "By the time the contract got signed, we had already paid so much money out that it dragged the company down."

American Visuals spent a year in bankruptcy before reaching settlements with its creditors.

In 1966, Eisner merged American Visuals with its chief competitor in the educational comics field, the Koster-Dana Corporation. Koster-Dana was known for its Good Reading Rack Service, which put free informational and educational booklets about health care, benefits, and safety in spinning racks for employees. Its clients included General Motors.

"Koster-Dana became aware of us," Eisner said. "We recovered well from Chapter 11 and had cash on hand. They had clients but needed someone who could help the company develop its products. They called and we talked about a merger."

Eisner became president of all Koster-Dana's publishing and communications divisions—including the Good Reading Rack Service, American Visuals, Will Eisner Productions, North American Newspaper Alliance (NANA), NANA radio, and the Bell-McClure Syndicate —and owner of seventeen percent of the combined company's stock. Bell-McClure, incidentally, distributed the daily "Batman" (credited to Eisner's boyhood friend Bob Kane) and "Superman" newspaper strips.

When R. C. "Bob" Harvey—now renowned as a comics historian and author of biographies on Milton Caniff and Murphy Anderson—left the Navy in 1963, his career goal was to become a cartoonist. He hoped an original creation, "Fiddlefoot"—a hero who advertises that he rescues damsels in distress—would be his ticket. The twist was that poor Fiddlefoot is shy around girls. In one strip, his buddy blindfolds him so he won't be embarrassed coming to a beautiful woman's aid. In another, Fiddlefoot bursts through a door to save an endangered female.

"When I was drawing that one," Harvey said, "I remembered a strip in which the Spirit did that, so I copied it."

"Fiddlefoot," a comic strip created by Bob "R. C." Harvey but never published.
An editor noted similarities with Eisner's "Spirit."

(Courtesy R. C. Harvey)

As part of a presentation book he compiled for marketing "Fiddlefoot," Harvey put together some introductory pages that introduced his major characters. "I looked at *The Spirit* pages again and borrowed some more," he said.

When summer rolled around, Harvey felt ready to show his creation to some of the leading newspaper syndicates in New York. He'd leave it with a syndicate editor for a week, then return to pick it up and receive their critique. The last place he went was the Bell-McClure Newspaper Syndicate.

A week passed without word, so Harvey returned to the office to pick up his samples. There was good news, and there was bad news.

"We liked it," an elderly editor said, "but we're not buying."

That was the bad news.

"Are you familiar with Will Eisner's *Spirit*?"

"No," Harvey answered defensively. "What are you talking about?"

"Will Eisner created a character called The Spirit many years ago. And your work reminded several of us of his style," the editor said. "Will Eisner, by coincidence, is now the president of Bell-McClure Syndicate."

Okay, maybe it was all bad news.

———————

When he was fifteen—this was in 1966—Mark Evanier and several friends formed a comic book fan club. For fun, they voted on who the best artists were. Will Eisner was one of the clear favorites, so Evanier, as club president, sent a handwritten letter to Eisner informing him of the results. Eisner, as was typical of him, sent back an appreciative typewritten letter to Evanier with an original drawing.

"I showed it to the club and we had this enormous fight about whether it was my property or it belonged to the club," Evanier said. "They said I should not get free Will Eisner art out of being president of this organization. *I* took the position that Will Eisner wrote a letter to *me*."

(In 2002, Evanier—who went on to become a major name in comics and animation himself, working with Sergio Aragonés on *Groo the Wanderer,* cocreating *DNAgents,* doing a stint on the Eisner-created

Blackhawks, and writing cartoon scripts for "Plastic Man" and "Scooby Doo" among many others—was once more surprised by a letter from Eisner. Eisner found Evanier's original letter and returned it.)

"Job Scene," produced by Eisner's American Visuals
(Will Eisner Collection, The Ohio State University Cartoon Research Library)

For Eisner, a man used to doing things his own way, the glare of operating a public company was unsettling.

"I was a lousy man to work in a public company and for a board of directors," Eisner said. "The straw that broke the camel's back was that they were doing things that I didn't like, for reasons I didn't approve of, such as acquiring a company because it had a $1 million employee trust fund. At the same time, I was trying to acquire the memoirs of the late General Douglas MacArthur for the syndicate. The board wouldn't allocate money for it. They were more interested in ways of pumping up the stock. I wanted out."

Eisner said that when he took over the merged company, its stock was at $2 a share; when he ran into problems with its board, the price had already doubled.

An exit strategy wasn't difficult. The Army contract for producing *PS Magazine* was Eisner's, not American Visuals. "They couldn't keep the *PS* contract without me," he said. Koster-Dana spun off American Visuals—along with the *PS* contract—and Eisner once more started anew in the late '60s.

———

Eisner relocated American Visuals to Park Avenue, where he produced *Job Scene* for the U.S. Department of Labor. It was a series of career guidance comics intended for use in schools and government employment agencies. The Behavioral Science Center of Boston's Sterling Institute developed and tested the material; longtime Eisner associates (and *Spirit* contributors) Klaus Nordling and Andre LeBlanc contributed artwork.

Job Scene's purpose was alerting disadvantaged citizens that they had training opportunities if they only knew where to look; it was first tested in areas of hardcore unemployment and blight, including Newark and Philadelphia. Researchers found that 92.5 percent of the *Job Scene* booklets were picked up, compared with just 47 percent of the literature they replaced. A year later, the federal Manpower Administration expanded the program nationally. American Visuals produced eleven booklets in all. Nine focused on occupational fields such as *Machine Shop Work, Welding, Carpentry, Health Work, Retail Sales, The Food Field, Electronics Work, Clerical Work,* and *Auto Mechanics*. The two remaining titles, *You're Hired* and *Power is Green,* recommended basic rules of on-the-job behavior and touted the value of skill training.

Eisner also ran two more companies, IPD Publishing Co. (foreign language instruction manuals) and Educational Supplements Corporation (social studies enrichment materials, as well as "Grammar Fun" flash cards and posters). IPD Publishing was a trade name, a division of American Visuals. It was marketed with Eisner's friend David Boehm's Sterling Publishing around an idea of Eisner's. "We collected free pamphlets issued by societies and special interest organizations and sold them as a monthly bundled subscription to public libraries," Eisner said. "Sterling had a strong history in selling books to public libraries.

The business did not last long because the source of pamphlets began to dry up. Then we continued using the IPD name on other commercial publishing ventures such as educational books (*How to Build Model Ships, How to Build Model Cars, What Your Mayor Does, What Your Senator Does, What Your Congressman Does, Helicopters in Action, Combat Tanks*)."

In 1971, Eisner, then fifty-four years old, bought A. C. Croft, a Connecticut company that produced teacher study materials. He commuted frequently between New York and Branford for less than a year before selling the company off.

While at Croft one day, he received a call that began changing the tide of his career once more. It was comic book convention impresario and aficionado Phil Seuling on the other end of the line, inviting Eisner to his annual July 4th comic book convention at the Commodore Hotel in midtown Manhattan.

Around that time, Jules Feiffer—by then an established writer and artist of growing repute himself—spoke with Ann Eisner.

"What a shame Will wasted all those years doing business stuff," Feiffer said. "He could have been doing creative stuff."

"But Jules," she said, "he enjoyed that!"

The reality was that even if Eisner went back to his drawing board after the Koster-Dana experience, he still wasn't ready to produce the quality of work that would come later in his life. His experiences as strictly a businessman charged a part of his mind that writing and drawing did not. And, because he got such an early start creating comic book pages in his teens, he lacked the drive and ambition to do more of that work.

ELEVEN
The Kitchen Sink Experience,
Part I

Denis Kitchen discovered *The Spirit* in the early 1960s via Jim Warren and Harvey Kurtzman's *Help!* magazine. Harvey wrote a feature on Eisner and reprinted one of the "Sand Saref" episodes of *The Spirit,* which became an eye-opener for Kitchen. A decade had passed since the last original *Spirit* adventure; it was largely unknown to teenagers in the age of *Gilligan's Island* and Elvis Presley. A few years later, in 1966, Kitchen picked up the short-lived Harvey Comics reprints. They whetted his appetite further. He became a fan, although it wasn't easy.

The original newspaper sections from the 1940s and early 1950s were impossible to find. There were no comic shops yet and few mail order operators. Collecting was the luck of the draw. Sometimes Kitchen found a reprint in a used bookstore or flea market, but it was far and few between. These were the prehistoric days of collecting comics.

In 1969, Kitchen wrote, drew, and self-published an underground comic book in Milwaukee, Wisconsin, called *Mom's Homemade Comics* (subtitled "Straight From the Kitchen to You"). In the fall of 1970 he cofounded an alternative weekly newspaper called *The Bugle* (whose name was inspired by the newspaper in *Spider-Man*). He drew a weekly comic strip (which was self-syndicated) and drew many *Bugle* covers.

About the same time, Kitchen started Krupp Comic Works and Kitchen Sink Enterprises to publish and distribute underground comics. Initially, it was fun and daring, but profit-challenged. In the *Bugle*'s 1970 Christmas issue, Kitchen and his comix cohort Jim Mitchell placed a quarter-page ad with examples of their art for sale, and wrote, "Save a starving artist from sure death ... and give a unique X-mas gift at the same time." They didn't get any response locally, but, remarkably, a couple weeks later they received a Coney Island salami in the mail with a tag on it that said, "Never let it be said that Phil Seuling let a cartoonist starve."

Seuling, Kitchen later learned, was a Brooklyn schoolteacher and comic book buff who almost single-handedly imagined and produced the comic book convention system, and later invented the direct market comic book distribution method that essentially saved the industry from extinction.

Seuling liked Kitchen's sardonic, humorous style, both artistically and personally. He hired Kitchen to create the cartoonish ads that became a trademark of his conventions, and invited him to be a guest at Seuling's 1971 4th of July show at the New York Commodore Hotel on 42nd Street (next to Grand Central Station). It was the first convention that Kitchen attended (and, coincidentally, it was future DC Comics publisher and president Paul Levitz' first as well), and while it was Eisner's second, there was no comparison in scope. They were both in awe. It was amazing for them, coming from completely different corners of the industry, to see thousands of people in a single place with a single thing in mind: comic books. When Eisner started in comics, no one ever dreamed the industry would spawn ravenous fans, collectibles, or conventions.

In the dealers' area, Kitchen was browsing through display tables looking for old copies of *Humbug, Li'l Abner,* and *Tip Top Comics* when the man next to him read his nametag. He did a double take and said, with a heavy French accent, "Oh, Denis Kitchen!"

"Yes?" Kitchen said, startled. "Do I know you?"

It turned out to be French comics historian Maurice Horn, coauthor of *A History of the Comic Strip,* one of the earliest serious books on the subject. Later he edited *The World Encyclopedia of Comics.* He said, "Mr. Will Eisner wants to meet you."

"You gotta be kidding!" Kitchen said. "If anything, it's me who wants to meet Mr. Eisner!"

An appointment was hastily arranged, and Horn introduced them in a private room away from the crowd.

"I am so pleased to meet you—but baffled, Mr. Eisner," Kitchen said. "Why were you looking for me?"

Eisner had heard about Kitchen from their mutual acquaintance, Seuling, and was curious to meet him. Eisner looked at Kitchen, who was wearing purple tie-dyed pants and scruffy boots, and chuckled at his scraggly mustache and the hair draped well past the young publisher's shoulders.

"We were so different, right down to what we smoked in our pipes," Kitchen said.

And yet Eisner was fascinated with what this young man was doing professionally. He asked a dozen rapid questions about underground *comix*, about how they were produced and distributed.

"I understand you have established your own distribution system," Eisner said. "And I understand you and your fellow creators have absolute artistic freedom."

"Yes to both," Kitchen said.

"Well, these subjects interest me very much."

They talked at length about the alternative comix scene, how Kitchen sold comics into it, how the books were discounted, what the terms were, and who bought the product. Eisner was intrigued that Kitchen's sales were non-returnable, since high returns helped kill his short-lived comic publishing company in 1948. He was also impressed that underground cartoonists received royalties like real authors and that their art was returned to them, a rare happenstance in mainstream comics.

"I was fascinated, jealous, in fact, that Denis enjoyed absolute freedom to publish his heart's desire," Eisner said.

Kitchen, meanwhile—like Seuling before him—wanted to know all about the old days, and *The Spirit*.

After they talked for a while, Eisner said, "Show me some of these underground comics of yours." Eisner had only heard about the new breed of comix until then, never having reason to visit the head shops where they were commonly sold. At the time, Seuling himself was the largest retailer of undergrounds. He had at least three long tables in the dealers' room piled high with every possible underground. When Kitchen led Eisner to them, a young artist named Art Spiegelman happened to be loitering nearby. Spiegelman—a future Pulitzer Prize-winning author—was just beginning a career as a contributor to underground comix such as *Real Pulp, Young Lust, Bijou Funnies,* and *Bizarre Sex.*

"The whole genre is right in front of you, Will," Kitchen said.

But before Kitchen could pick up something appropriate to recommend to his hero, Eisner impulsively reached down and picked up a comic by S. Clay Wilson. It was as outrageous an underground comic as could be found at the time. Eisner opened it and quite visibly blanched at the sight of the content—*Captain Pissgums and his Pervert Pirates.* While underground cartoonists took pride in breaking all the rules, Wilson went further than anyone else.

Eisner was not expecting the graphic sex and violence to be quite that graphic! His eyebrows arched and he quickly put it down.

Spiegelman, who had been listening to their conversation, immediately rose to the vigorous defense of Wilson. Eisner didn't know who Spiegelman was at the time—and Kitchen had only corresponded with him by mail himself at this point, so he was also startled. The three of them began an animated conversation—the first of many in the years to come. Kitchen, who didn't want to alienate Eisner, tried to be the voice of reason. Eisner finally threw up his hands. "Look, guys, this has been interesting," he said, "but I gotta go."

("I think Art, back in the '70s, could be a pretty obnoxious guy," said John Holmstrom, the founder of *Punk Magazine* and a former Eisner student at the School of Visual Arts. "The first time I met him he threatened to punch me out. I was talking about The Ramones and The Dictators. He thought their music was serious; Art didn't realize it was all novelty songs. But that's Art.")

Eisner thought that was the last time he would see either of them. But, ever the businessman, he did hand them both his business card. When Kitchen returned home to Milwaukee, he put together an assortment of underground comics that he had published and on July 14, 1971, sent them to Eisner with a letter that read:

Dear Mr. Eisner,

Enclosed is a sampling of our line of underground comic books. I think you will find them generally more tasteful than the unfortunate titles you happened to pick up in the dealers' area of the Comic Art Convention (which were printed by a competitor, incidentally). As Maurice Horn knows, much more care goes into the editing of our books ...

Respectfully,
Denis Kitchen

Eisner read the books Kitchen sent, including *Bijou Funnies,* which featured the work of Robert Crumb (also known as "R. Crumb," he is the artist and writer most closely identified with the undergrounds for his work in *Zap* and *Head Comix,* his creation of enduring characters such as Mr. Natural and Fritz the Cat and the catchphrase "Keep on Truckin'"), Jay Lynch (*Nard n' Pat*), Skip Williamson and Justin Green, *Cloud Comix, Deep 3-D Comix* (Don Glassford), *Home Grown Funnies* (Crumb), and several issues of *Mom's Homemade Comics* (mostly Kitchen). Eisner was pleasantly surprised.

Kitchen then surprised Eisner by describing his ambitions beyond publishing underground comics. "I've only seen a relatively few old *Spirit* comics," he said, "but I think they deserve to be reprinted for a new generation. Would you be amenable to that?"

Two weeks later, Eisner wrote back and told Kitchen that he would like to talk further.

Dear Denis,

Thank you for your letter and samples of your publications.

You are quite right! They are more tasteful and much more professional than most. I'm particularly impressed with your own work and I was glad to see that your books have something more to say than fornication! There's a lot of exciting promise here.

Maurice is at work putting together a dummy of

"The Spirit" Magazine. As soon as we have something in hand, we shall be talking to you on more specific matters.

We shall certainly maintain contact.

Cordially,

Will Eisner

For Eisner, doing business with Kitchen Sink Press meant boarding a small vessel on which he might sail into the sunset. Not far ahead, at that time, loomed his sixtieth birthday. Eisner saw it as the threshold of old age—a sobering thought for someone who liked to think of himself as a promising young cartoonist.

To a buttoned-down type like Eisner, Kitchen's mere appearance— he was the prototypical longhaired hippie—should have sent him running in the other direction. However, it didn't take great genius to see that the underground scene was a reprise of the frontier days of the late 1930s. So when Kitchen asked to reprint some *Spirit* stories, Eisner readily agreed.

They quickly worked out a royalty rate and other details, and Kitchen called Eisner on the telephone and asked him to send the first batch of artwork.

"First," Eisner said, ever the businessman, "send me a draft of your standard contract."

"*Er,* well, Mr. Eisner, we don't *do* contracts," Kitchen said. "You have my word on it, I will send you a letter of agreement, but we don't do contracts."

"I will not do business with anyone if there is no contract," Eisner said firmly. "Why won't you send me a contract?"

Kitchen launched into a rationale about how contracts were foisted upon artists by unscrupulous publishers who take advantage of them. "I know all about how (*Superman* creators) Jerry Siegel and Joe Shuster were ripped off and Harvey Kurtzman was ripped off," he said, "and I'm not going to do that to *my* artists."

Eisner listened carefully and then gave his young and idealistic friend a short lecture on how he was completely wrong. He pointed out that Kitchen's prejudices *were* prejudices, that there was no reason a hippie couldn't enter into a contract. He just needed a contract that was agreeable to both parties.

"In truth, a contract is not an imposition," Eisner said. "A good contract is something that protects both parties by clarifying the issues. For example, your handshake is good for me, but what if a bus hits you tomorrow? How am I supposed to convince your partners what our deal is?"

"That is very unlikely," Kitchen said.

"Maybe so," Eisner agreed, "but, I don't want to have to deal with your partners if something does happens. Besides, what if *a bus hits me* tomorrow? How will you explain to my widow what the deal was if there is nothing in writing?"

Eisner wore down the self-righteous opposition as Kitchen clung desperately to his bias against anything that smacked of the Establishment. His last defense was, "Will, I hate to spend money on attorneys."

Eisner couldn't argue with that. "I don't blame you one bit," Eisner said. "I hate to spend money on attorneys, too, so I'll tell you what; I will write one myself and send you a contract that you can use if you want to."

Kitchen thanked Eisner and hung up. In retrospect, the irony was sweet. While Kitchen's notion was that publishers imposed contracts on artists, here, the exact opposite had occurred: an artist imposed a contract on him, the publisher. He later told Eisner that Eisner had done him a huge favor.

When Kitchen asked Eisner about reprinting *The Spirit* newspaper sections as modern comic books, it was a wild idea for them both. There was no outcry for the age-old feature. And why would Eisner want his cemetery-dwelling but clean-cut detective sold on shelves next to the work of S. Clay Wilson?

Kitchen later admitted he didn't have a clue as to whether he could really sell *The Spirit* in the head shop and off-campus college bookstore market. More than eighty percent of his customers bought underground comics alongside rolling papers and beads. It was a big gamble for

Kitchen Sink Press'
The Spirit: The Origin Years No. 2

him—and zero risk to Eisner—to think that *The Spirit* would sell there. But to their delight, it did sell.

The hippies saw *The Spirit* as a cool outsider, an improbable suit-and-tie hero devoid of superpowers whose crazy adventures and offbeat style somehow fit into the psychedelia of the era.

Not all the head shops instantly embraced *The Spirit*, of course. The shop owners who used to say things like "Never trust anyone over thirty," said to Kitchen, "What the hell are you doing? These aren't head comics. These are geezer comics!"

But Kitchen believed in the importance of diversification. On one hand he thought a revolution was right around the corner, but part of him also believed the counterculture would be over shortly. He knew underground comix were a phenomenon and that it couldn't last forever. He was correct.

═══════════

Kitchen Sink Press was never run as formally as Marvel Comics or DC Comics. The company averaged one new comic book every month. Sometimes Kitchen did two or three at once; sometimes two or three months would go by and he wouldn't have produced any new ones. (At the same time, Kitchen was running a commercial art studio and art directing *The Bugle;* he was working, just not exclusively on comic books.) With an erratic production schedule, Kitchen might talk to an artist passing through Milwaukee and say, "How about doing something for my new anthology?" And the artist would say, "Okay, I'll start working on it; I'll have it to you in three or four months." A year might pass, however, before the piece arrived, but whenever it did, Kitchen published it, assuming it met his standards.

And, unlike now, when a comic book is carefully marketed and announced months before publication to distributors and collectors, Kitchen Sink Press didn't do any pre-press marketing. When a new title was assembled in Kitchen's office, he generally took it to the printer for a standard initial run of ten thousand copies. (A Crumb title might start with fifty thousand copies.) Samples were then sent to drug paraphernalia distributors, independent retailers, and burgeoning comics distributors such as Phil Seuling and Bud Plant. "Here is our new book; how many do you want?" Based on experience, Kitchen assumed he could sell at least ten thousand of anything. All the underground publishers periodically put out product that might be substandard, but, by and large, they could still sell ten thousand copies of it. The only issue was how quickly Kitchen reprinted a title. It might take a year to unload the first ten thousand. But if it sold it out in a few months, he printed another ten thousand and when that sold out, another ten thousand. A popular underground comic book never went out of print, whereas mainstream comics like *Spider-Man* or *Superman* were printed monthly and replaced sequentially so there was a new issue every thirty days.

Unsold mainstream comics—often representing more than fifty percent of a print run—were routinely pulped by distributors, an inefficient and resource-unfriendly process that Kitchen held in disdain.

Marvel and DC were normal publishing houses putting out a normal product; monthly production was the way their business model worked. But for hippies, it was just that there were these cool comics, and why shouldn't they be on the racks indefinitely? The good ones are still in print. Kitchen's rationale was that you could go into a bookstore and always find a classic such as *Huckleberry Finn* because it withstood the test of time. He felt that if a Robert Crumb comic was good, people would keep discovering and reading it, and it would be just as good today as last year, and it would still be good five years from now. Undergrounds also enjoyed a high pass-along rate because they would end up in a lot of college dorm rooms, crash pads, and communes, places where ownership was nebulous. The original owners didn't read a comic once, stick it in a plastic bag, and put it away in a humidity-controlled, hermetically sealed vault for the rest of eternity.

Kitchen created a place in this generational marketplace for Will Eisner's *Spirit* by marketing the book as the *Underground Spirit*. And while the insides were largely reprints, Eisner created racy new covers and a few new interior pages to accommodate the audience. It was not your father's *Spirit* newspaper section. On the cover, Eisner drew a bare-chested woman. But it turned out that they were fake breasts; a drug dealer opened one of them like a safe and said something about how he kept his stash in there. It was a crazy joke, but Kitchen loved it. (There were more

Will Eisner surprised many by drawing this cover for the underground comix *Snarf* No. 3

new pages inside that were racy as well. Eisner took advantage of his newfound freedom.)

For Eisner, working in the medium again with no net and no rules was liberating.

The first issue of the *Underground Spirit* sold out and Kitchen reprinted it. But just as he sent a second issue to press, Eisner got a call from Jim Warren.

TWELVE
Jim Warren's Dream

Jim Warren first encountered Will Eisner's *Spirit* in the *Philadelphia Record* as an eleven-year-old boy in 1941. But he didn't read it.

"Other people read it, but I didn't," Warren said. "I studied it—every panel, every black shadow of India ink, every architectural rendering of a section of a house, layouts that could make the eye go exactly where Will wanted it to go. It was unbelievable to me. This man, for me and for the rest of the world, single-handedly changed so-called comics into a sequential art form. 'Sequential art form,' that's a technical term. A timeless thing of beauty was what Will produced."

Two decades later, Jim Warren was a magazine publisher. In August 1960, with Harvey Kurtzman as his editor and partner, he launched *Help!* magazine, which ran until September 1965. The magazine featured standup comedians such as Sid Caesar, Jerry Lewis, and Jonathan Winters on its covers, reprinted comics by Winsor McCay (*Little Nemo*), George Herriman (*Krazy Kat*), and Milton Caniff (*Male Call*), and introduced to America such future underground innovators as Robert Crumb (*Fritz the Cat*) and Gilbert Shelton (*Wonder Wart-Hog*). It was hip before its time, bursting with talent and creativity.

"We had an incredibly small budget," Warren said. "One day, Harvey matter-of-factly said to me, 'I have always liked Will Eisner's work.' I jumped up, and I said, '*You* like him? The man changed my life!' Will agreed to let us reprint seven pages from a classic *Spirit* story in *Help!*"

Fast-forward to 1973 and Jim Warren was essentially America's most successful alternative yet mainstream comic book publisher. If Marvel and DC were the mainstream, and Kitchen Sink Press and Rip Off Press were the underground, Warren Publishing was somewhere in the middle. It was mainstream in that its major titles—*Creepy, Eerie,* and *Vampirella*—were available on most U.S. newsstands. But it was alternative in that it published comics in a magazine format and in black and white. Warren's gore and horror fests were as likely to be found racked next to *Time* or *Good Housekeeping* as *Batman* or *X-Men.* And where Marvel and DC made household names of Stan Lee and Jack Kirby and the underground comix made Robert Crumb and Gilbert Shelton famous, Warren developed his own stable of craftsmen, including renowned fantasy and horror artists Richard Corben, Esteban Maroto, and Jeff Jones.

What Warren didn't have was a product that would draw in comic book buyers who disdained the blood and guts stuff.

Many of the men and women who worked for Warren in those days became stalwarts of the comics business behind the scenes for decades to come.

After a tour of military duty in the 1960s, W. B. DuBay's first professional art interview in New York was at a Park Avenue studio where he had been directed after answering an ad in the *New York Times.* They were looking for a layout artist for "a little military magazine."

"Will himself interviewed me," DuBay said. "I think he was impressed with my credentials. I'd just been discharged from a two-year stint as editor of the Army's biggest post newspaper and had won a few design awards in the process. Moreover, I showed him I could draw anything in any style he wanted, including his. And I was particularly good at diagrammatic cutaways of the Army's biggest diesels."

As it turned out, another military veteran, Mike Ploog, got the job. DuBay was more disappointed than at any other time in his life. After six months and a stint at Warren Magazines, he went back home to California.

Several years later, DuBay returned to New York. During his time away, he wrote and drew several horror stories for Warren's *Creepy* magazine, and Jim Warren hired him back as editor of *Creepy* and *Eerie*. Warren's office, curiously enough, was right around the corner from the place of his life's biggest rejection.

"Being in the neighborhood," DuBay said, "I knew that I'd eventually have to stop in and say hello to my hero, even if he didn't remember me.

"So, I popped in one day and introduced myself as Jim Warren's new editor. Ever the gentleman, Will did his best to remember me. We chatted and laughed and I told him again how I wouldn't be the man I was without the inherent heart of *The Spirit* and those *PS* lessons in engine maintenance. And then I asked him when he was going to republish all of those beautiful old *Spirit* stories."

"Soon as I find the right publisher," Eisner said.

He mentioned DC and Marvel as possible suitors.

"Right then and there, the deal was sealed in my mind," DuBay said. "And I knew that I'd get to edit a brand new Warren-published title."

(Carmine Infantino, a respected artist and longtime editor of DC Comics, was another person sniffing around the rights to *The Spirit*. In fact, he was interested in both the character and Eisner's instructional comics operation. "I had heard that Will was doing work for the Army," Infantino said. "I met him and we talked about it. I talked to Warners [Warner Communication, which owned DC at the time] and they weren't interested. There wasn't enough money for DC Comics to get involved in producing the educational comics. As for *The Spirit*, I discussed with Will whether he would come over and work with us, maybe create some new characters. The reason was that he was talking to Stan at Marvel about the same thing. He was a genius at storytelling and designing pages.")

Super Comics' *Spirit* was an unauthorized reprint series

DuBay went back to the Warren offices and marched into the publisher's office.

"When are we going to publish that new title?" he asked.

"As soon as I find one that meets our standard of quality," Warren replied.

DuBay's smile must have lit up the room. And it only got brighter when he told Warren that he'd just been up to see Will Eisner.

Promotional ads by Eisner for the debut issue of Harvey Comics' *The Spirit* No. 1
(Will Eisner Collection, The Ohio State University Cartoon Research Library)

Harvey Comics produced two issues of a new *Spirit* comic book in October 1966 and March 1967. Eisner (with help from Chuck Kramer) wrote and drew a new seven-page Spirit origin for the first issue and a second new story for the next issue. The rest of the pages were reprints.

But it was the two widely distributed reprints published by Denis Kitchen's Kitchen Sink Press in 1973—with all-new wraparound covers by Eisner—that put *The Spirit* back on the mainstream radar.

When Jim Warren heard from DuBay that Eisner was talking with Marvel and/or DC about the possibility of reprinting *The Spirit* sections from the 1940s and 1950s, he immediately telephoned Eisner, described his operation, and asked if he could take him to lunch.

"I took him to a snazzy place—I think it was the Friar's Club," Warren recalled. "I pulled out all the stops to impress him, which is difficult to do because you don't impress Will. Will is a guy who can see through any kind of pho-niness. I pitched him on Warren Publishing doing this project instead of any other company. I said that although we couldn't pay like the other companies, I had the passion, energy, and the love to do it right."

Nearly an hour later, when Warren finally stopped pitching, Eisner the businessman said, "What exactly are you offering me?"

Warren realized that he needed to start acting like a publisher—not a fan—and make a rational offer for *The Spirit* rights.

"But I couldn't," he said. "I just couldn't. I was unable to adapt the emotional/mental mindset to negotiate with *the* Will Eisner. Negotiation is someone who says, 'I want X,' and then you say, 'Well, we will give you X less something,' and then after six hours you meet halfway. I couldn't do that with him. I hated negotiating with creative people, but with Will Eisner, it was like negotiating with God. How do you do that? You say, 'What do you want?' And he says, 'This,' and you say, 'okay,' which is exactly what happened."

Eisner's terms were simple—to a point. He asked for $1,000 an issue, paid in advance, plus a royalty from profit sharing.

That was the simple part. The complication was Denis Kitchen.

With his company's broader and more traditional newsstand distribution system, Warren told Eisner that he could easily distribute up to 100,000 copies of a monthly *Spirit* magazine.

Those numbers were hard to ignore, much as Eisner was indebted to Kitchen for bringing the character out of retirement. Eisner called him immediately and broke the news.

Warren Publishing's *Spirit* Magazine No. 13

"I am really impressed with how well these have sold," Eisner told Kitchen, "especially in your rickety distribution system. But I just got an offer I can't turn down from Jim Warren. He thinks he can get 100,000 in circulation every month. No offense; I hope we can still do some business, but after you sell the second issue out, I am not going to renew the contract."

Kitchen was crushed and Eisner didn't blame him. But Eisner was a businessman and he had somebody who would not only sell many more copies but could sell them on a regular schedule, and in more respectable places than Weird Harold's Head Shop. Making royalties on *The Spirit* after twenty years was like receiving an inheritance from a forgotten uncle.

And it wasn't a total loss for Kitchen, either.

"To clear my conscience," Eisner said, "I demanded that Warren buy Kitchen's unsold inventory. It was probably this move that gave birth to a thirty-year relationship."

Eisner made buying out Kitchen Sink Press's remaining *Spirit* inventory a condition of his deal with Warren. "Will felt guilty because Denis is a nice guy," Warren said. "I said to myself, 'This man Eisner also has a loyalty to people—something rare in our industry.' I instantly said, 'Of course we will.' And I sent him a check immediately. Who else would do otherwise? And I didn't negotiate Denis's price one dollar; we bought it at exactly the figure Will represented to me, because I knew I was dealing with two people who weren't running a scam. One was Will Eisner, and the other was Denis Kitchen, and both of these men had reputations for integrity and honesty in an industry that is not exactly famous for those qualities."

(Years later, Warren told Eisner that he would have agreed to $5,000 or even $10,000 an issue. "I would have sold the farm, I would have mortgaged the house, I would have sold my first-born because working with you had been a dream of mine since fifth grade," he said.)

Warren insisted he never saw Kitchen's *Underground Spirit;* his interest in acquiring the rights was based on hearing that DC and Marvel were in hot pursuit. "I don't recall seeing Denis Kitchen's *Spirit* and contacting Will and saying, 'Hey, we can do better.' I don't remember it happening that way. But if Will said it did, I defer to him.

"My recollection was that I was competing very hard against Stan Lee because Stan had come out with a shabby imitation of our *Famous Monsters* magazine (Marvel's was called *Monsters Unleashed*). It was humorous, Jim Warren going head to head with the mighty Stan and the mighty Marvel Comics! Stan, of course, is a creative genius, and yet he was taking my stuff and copying it blatantly, and I was ready to strangle him. I would have if he weren't six-foot-four. A lot of people have come up to me and said, 'I am your biggest fan,' and I always reply, 'No, you're not. Stan Lee is my biggest fan, he's six-foot-four.' I thought of *The Spirit* magazine venture as like, 'God, I have to keep it out of Stan's hands,' and besides, it's the great Will Eisner and I can't possibly let him get away.

"I knew I was competing with giant companies who could offer Will more money," Warren continued, "but I believed that I had a big advantage. Warren Publishing would create *The Spirit* magazine with such tender loving care. Also, I didn't really care if we made a profit or not, I just wanted to have it out there. I wanted the world and a whole new generation to see what I had seen when I was eleven. One of the reasons I went into this business was because of Will Eisner. Will showed me that comics could be something a hell of a lot different than just *Popeye*. Not that *Popeye* was bad, but Will's creative and technical talent was incredible. He took it out of the realm of comics for me and into another dimension. Back then, to me, anyone who referred to *The Spirit* 'as comics' would be like calling baseball a game for little kids. It was something totally different—it was two planets, two galaxies away."

The deal was that Eisner could come into Warren's office, use it as his own if he chose, and supervise every aspect of the production process. "There was no doubt that Will's word was law," Warren said. "It wasn't that he had creative control, he had control, period. If Will would have said, 'Jump out of the window seven stories,' I would have jumped. And so would the entire Warren Publishing art and production team."

One day Eisner challenged the status quo. He drew a cover for the magazine that someone else colored—"in circus colors," he said. When the art was delivered for his approval, Eisner flew into a rage. He flew over to Warren's office and prepared to raise hell.

"Jim was in a meeting with someone," he recalled. "His secretary wouldn't let me in, but I pushed my way in, slammed the art on his desk, and said, 'Over my dead body, Jim!' And I walked out."

Warren, true to his word, changed the colors.

===

The first issue of *The Spirit* magazine was celebrated in unusual style for a comic book, with Warren throwing Eisner a party in a private room at New York's famous Plaza Hotel. The twenty invitees included the editorial staff of the company and some special guests, such as artist Richard Corben. They gathered around a single, enormous, round table that some described as akin to King Arthur's.

The banquet manager, a man in his forties, asked to speak privately with Warren.

"Yes, what is it?"

"Is that really *the* Will Eisner?" he asked.

"It certainly is."

The banquet manager let out a low whistle. He was impressed. After that party, Warren's social standing at the Plaza improved considerably.

The first issue's cover art was not unlike the regular cover art style of *Creepy* and *Eerie*. The second issue was closer to the original concept of Eisner's Sunday sections. "We wanted a full-cover painting for *The Spirit*. We wanted to retain that linear Will Eisner look. But it didn't come easy. Particularly since I wanted to present our version of *The Spirit* in the best possible light," Warren said.

Warren Publishing's
Spirit Magazine No. 2

Inside, *The Spirit* was, well, peculiar. The first four pages (which included the table of contents, letters to the editor, and a text feature) and the last four pages (which advertised genre books and monster model kits) were printed on a less-expensive salmon-colored paper. The next twenty-eight pages were standard newsprint, on which original *Spirit* stories were reprinted. Then came an eight-page color section with another *Spirit* story, then twenty-eight more pages on newsprint.

W. R. "Bill" Mohalley was production manager for Warren Magazines from 1972 until the company quit publishing a decade later. His boss might have been a huge fan of Eisner's work, but Mohalley didn't think it was either the right time for a *Spirit* revival or that Warren was the right place.

"(*The Spirit*) was something different than the usual monster magazines for us," said Mohalley. "It was a different pace. I don't think it sold like gold. It was '40s stuff, nothing up to date. To me, it looked old-fashioned, not for a young audience. But it was interesting. To me, it wasn't the right time for this thing. It was like a golden-oldie magazine. But we tried."

Eisner chose the stories and art, and Mohalley and his staff put the magazine package together for Eisner's approval. The production gradually grew more complicated, from straight reprints of Will's original art to the addition of textured overlays.

"We would go through a story like a kid with colored pencils," Mohalley said. "We would do a beard or a coat, for example. We did it by hand. You don't know how much trouble we went through. We tried to go through the story and make sure it's consistent, that the coat was the same, that the beard was the same. There was so much to do that I had to take it home and do it at night. I'd often stay up till one in the morning doing that."

———

The Spirit immediately made its mark on the comic book community. The first Warren issues outsold the Kitchen Sink edition by tens of thousands of copies. A new generation of comic book fans discovered the character, and the next generation of comic book artists and writers were influenced beyond their wildest expectations.

But as the months wore on, the appeal wore off.

"The magazines didn't sell as well as they deserved to sell because they could not be marketed properly," Warren said.

This was before the days of comic book stores. In order for Warren to reach the comic book fan and sell fifty thousand copies, his magazines had to appear on newsstands in front of a million people. Today, if a company is selling a product for pregnant women, the company wouldn't advertise it in *National Enquirer, National Geographic,* or *Playboy* magazines. Instead, it would niche advertise, targeting magazines aimed at pregnant women with a readership that is full of potential customers. That approach didn't exist back then. There was simply no niche marketplace for what Warren was producing.

Comic book publishers had their own standalone spinner racks (*"Hey, Kids! Comics!"*) or their own sections of the newsstand. But Warren Publishing had to fight for every square inch because the distributors and the retailers didn't know where to put *The Spirit, Creepy, Eerie,* and *Vampirella*.

"On the first day, God created the magazine distributor," Warren said. "On the second day, He created the amoeba. Then we went up the ladder from there. Magazine distributors didn't know what the hell our product was, didn't want to know, and didn't want to learn. I had to fight day and night to get them to listen to me. Had Commissioner Dolan been real, he would have arrested them for stupidity."

THIRTEEN
What If ...
Will Eisner Ran Marvel Comics?

S tan Lee called Will Eisner twenty years after production ceased on *The Spirit* and he turned his back on the comic book industry.

The creator or cocreator of every major Marvel Comics character from Spider-Man and the Fantastic Four to the X-Men and the Hulk, Lee—born Stanley Lieber, himself a graduate of Eisner's alma mater, DeWitt Clinton High School—was editor and publisher of the Marvel line in 1972. Lee, in fact, had overseen Marvel—a company started and run for decades by his uncle and boss, Martin Goodman—since his teenage days in the 1940s. Every modern Marvel comic book began with the line "Stan Lee Presents." He was the first brand name talent in the maturing business. But after more than a decade of incredible growth and fame, Lee was ready to move on. He wanted Eisner to replace him at Marvel so he could go to Hollywood and make movies.

Lee felt that Eisner might be the only comic artist around who had the respect of cartoonists and who also had the business experience to manage an enterprise of Marvel's size and scope.

When Lee rang in the 1970s, Eisner figured it was a social call. Eisner had been out of comic books for twenty years. Comic book conventions were still a relatively new phenomenon, and the direct sale comic book market was still a few years off. Eisner, recently separated from *PS*, was not yet a "revered legend," more like an old-timer with a portfolio.

"I hear you are at liberty," Lee said.

Eisner laughed. They chatted for a minute or two. Eisner still didn't know what was coming.

"Why don't you come down to my office at Marvel," Lee said. "I would like to talk with you about something."

So Eisner went. When he arrived, Lee didn't mince any more words. "To tell you the truth," he said, "I need somebody to replace me here. I want to go to Hollywood. I love the Hollywood scene. This isn't for me any more. But they won't let me go unless I can find a suitable replacement."

Eisner was pretty stunned that that was why Lee wanted to see him, thinking originally that perhaps Lee wanted him to do a book for Marvel. Many artists from the Golden Age of Comics were turning up for a last hurrah at Marvel, DC, or Charlton, and Eisner figured that Stan opened his Rolodex and his wandering finger landed on "E." Eisner remembered Lee being surprised to learn when they met years earlier that Eisner wrote all the *Spirit* stories. Lee said he had been impressed that Eisner could write *and* draw.

"You have business experience," Lee said. "You'd be ideal for this job."

During the course of the conversation, Lee's boss from Marvel's then-corporate parent joined them. The meeting quickly became a job interview. He wanted to know what Eisner thought about comics, where he thought the industry was going, and what he would do about it.

"Well," Eisner said, "one of the first things I would do is abandon the work-for-hire system that you have here."

There was a noticeable evacuation of air in the room. Lee winced.

"Oh, we can't do that," Lee's boss said. "That's impossible to do here."

"I don't see why," Eisner said. "First of all, allow the writers and artists to keep copyrights. The book publishing business does that and does it quite profitably. Then return their original art to them. You asked me what I would do in my role here; that's what I would do right away."

Other comic book artists that Eisner knew sustained a certain amount of animosity toward Lee. Jack Kirby, for example, always maintained that he brought the idea for Spider-Man to Stan. Until the *Spider-Man* movie debuted in 2002, Lee generally took sole credit. The movie credited the character's creation to Stan Lee and artist Steve Ditko.

"Stan wasn't terribly popular among other artists, either," Eisner said later. "He was regarded by and large as an exploiter, which is the fate of all publishers. Creators will always regard publishers as exploiters. I guess it is something that psychiatrists can discuss better, but I have always regarded it as a child/parent relationship. Artists need somebody to hate. In the comic field, the publishers are close at hand."

After more idle chat between Lee and Eisner, it became clear that Marvel was unprepared for Eisner's independent-artist approach to corporate policy. It's understandable that the company was startled by Eisner's ideas; there wasn't yet a large comic book industry press, so his views were still pretty revolutionary. In any event, Eisner could see where the conversation was going. Finally he said, "Gentlemen, I don't think this is for me."

Lee walked Eisner out to the elevator. He tried one more time.

"C'mon, Will," he said, "Why not?"

"Stan," Eisner said, "this is a suicide mission."

"The pay is good," Lee said in desperation.

"I understand that," Eisner said. "But money is not what I am interested in right now. I have money."

The idea of working for Marvel was not attractive to Eisner, but not because it was Marvel. The idea of working for any large corporation again after the Koster-Dana fiasco was unattractive.

"I never had the outlook necessary for the mainstream comic book market," Eisner said. "I could never do superheroes well. My heroes always looked like they were made of styrene foam. The Spirit evinced psychological problems. Spider-Man did, too, of course. Stan once told me that he 'liked the idea that the Spirit was human and not quite superhero-ish.'"

Lee's memory of meeting with Eisner was hazy at best, but he didn't doubt Eisner's account. "Will certainly would have been a good choice for me to want to run the place if I were not there any more," he said.

When Eisner laid out his conditions, Lee knew they would never be accepted by the corporate bosses.

"At that time, that wasn't the way it was done in comics," Lee said. "I am sure that whoever was the publisher then wouldn't have been willing to go along with that. But it would have been fine with me. I just wanted

Will to be part of Marvel. I wanted in some way to have an association with him, because I certainly would have thought that he would be a great asset to us. You can quote me on that. Unfortunately, I had nothing to do with the business arrangements. I would have said to whoever the hell handled the business, 'I want to hire this guy,' or 'I would love this guy to work with us,' but then he would have had to talk to the business department and make the deal, because I was never part of that.

"I wasn't a big reader of *The Spirit*," Lee added, "because it was never in a newspaper that I read. I was in New York, and as far as I know, it wasn't in New York, but I had heard about it and I had seen bits and pieces of it here and there, and I was always incredibly impressed with the artwork, with the layouts, mainly with the first page, with the opening page. Each title was done differently on each weekly episode where the title 'The Spirit' was really part of the artwork. And that impressed the hell out of me. I thought that Will was a really fine designer.

"He is really one of the only creative people in the business who was also a businessman who was able to make money at it and was smart enough to own everything he did. And I have always admired him for that."

Writer and former Marvel Editor in Chief Marv Wolfman (*Superman, Batman, Tomb of Dracula, Green Lantern, Spider-Man, Fantastic Four, Daredevil*), who joined Marvel Comics in 1972, clearly remembered Lee's interest in hiring Eisner.

"Stan was a huge fan of Eisner's work," Wolfman said. "I remember him talking about getting in touch with Eisner to head up something."

Roy Thomas, longtime Marvel Comics writer (*Spider-Man, Conan, Avengers*) and editor in chief from 1971 to 1980, also knew that Lee reached out to Eisner. "I have a memory of it," he said. "I suspect it was between 1972 and 1974."

If Eisner took the job, it would have caused many more changes.

"It would have hastened my departure to DC by about ten years," Thomas said. "I don't think I could have worked for Will."

As for Marvel Comics publishing *The Spirit*, Thomas doesn't think that would have worked for anyone.

"The things Will Eisner did had a lot in common with Stan," Thomas said. "But if Stan were to do *The Spirit*, it would have been more like a Marvel Comic, and then it wouldn't be *The Spirit*."

When Eisner said no, Lee made a run at Harvey Kurtzman. He turned the job down, too.

Artist Batton Lash (*Supernatural Law*) remembered the week that Stan Lee offered Eisner his job at Marvel Comics. Lash was a student in Eisner's first cartooning class at New York City's School of Visual Arts. Eisner didn't make a big deal of the Marvel proposal, Lash recalled. Eisner would often tell his students to pull their chairs up close and he would talk about a variety of subjects. On this particular day, Eisner told a more memorable tale.

"Superheroes aren't selling," he said. "Even Stan Lee is losing interest. He called me the other day and asked if I wanted his job while he goes out to make movies."

Being matter-of-fact about passing on the biggest job in comics was typical Eisner.

"I don't think Will ever regretted turning Stan Lee down," Lash said. "But I get the impression Stan was flabbergasted."

Conversely, Eisner didn't tell his students that Jim Warren was about to begin reprinting the *Spirit* stories from the 1940s; they discovered it on the newsstands like everyone else.

Lee and Eisner maintained a cordial, often joke-driven relationship based on mutual respect and one-upsmanship—a trait only Lee brought out in Eisner. They would often meet at conventions. "My wife claims that we are like two vaudeville comedians fighting each other for center stage," Eisner said. "Apparently, Stan brings out a great deal of competitiveness in me."

Even before approaching Eisner about running Marvel, Stan Lee wanted to put out a magazine that would compete with *MAD, Cracked,* and *Sick.* He thought there might be room for a humor publication with Marvel Comics' wit.

Lee told Roy Thomas that he wanted Eisner to create and run the magazine. "I think he was thinking of the *National Lampoon,* which was a hit," Thomas recalled. "But Stan didn't want to go as raunchy."

Thomas went to lunch with Eisner as a follow-up to Lee's interest in a magazine with the working title *Bedlam.*

"I don't remember much, but we talked about whatever Stan wanted," Thomas said. "Eisner and I kicked around some ideas. I remember seeing some sketches that Will may have done."

Eisner even sent out a letter dated February 20, 1973, to several artists' and writers' agents soliciting their interest. It read:

> *Dear Sir,*
>
> *I have been engaged by Stan Lee and Marvel Comics Group to help them launch a new slick paper satirical magazine. Of course, since I am aware that you handle many talented professionals who I believe have something worthwhile to say, I am writing to you to find out whether any of your clients would be interested in accepting an assignment or making submissions for our landmark premier issue and hopefully beyond.*
>
> *Will Eisner*

Marv Wolfman said that he and fellow writer Len Wein (cocreator of the characters Swamp Thing and Wolverine), both then around twenty years old, received a telephone invitation from Eisner to come by and talk about working with him on a possible new humor magazine.

"I knew what *The Spirit* was, but this was before the Kitchen Sink and Warren reprints and it had not taken hold of fandom at that point," Wolfman said.

When they arrived at Eisner's Park Avenue office, the duo was greeted warmly and they listened to Eisner's pitch. He gave them some background on his work, discussing *The Spirit*, *PS*, and other publishing projects.

"He was talking about doing a humor magazine of the *National Lampoon* variety. A lot of college humor," Wolfman recalled.

The conversation lasted several hours. When it was over, both sides were disappointed.

"As much as we would desperately like to work with you, Mr. Eisner, it's not right," Wolfman said. "It won't work."

Eisner was puzzled.

"To do a college humor magazine today would mean an incredible amount of anti-government, anti-establishment material. Don't you think that would conflict with your Army contract to produce *PS?*" Wolfman asked.

Eisner honestly hadn't thought about that. And he conceded the logic—and smart business sense—in their decision to pass on the work.

"It really hurt us," Wolfman said. "We would have loved to work with him. It would have helped so much. That was a bittersweet meeting. We could have learned a lot about the industry—a lot sooner—instead of picking up bits and pieces over the next few years."

Wolfman and Wein didn't walk away empty-handed, however; Eisner did sketches of the Spirit for each writer.

"Later on, when I was doing *Crazy* for Marvel, we licensed some of Will's material from his *Gleeful Guides* series that fit in," Wolfman said. "I always loved his work; Stan loved his work."

Meanwhile, when Thomas reported back to Lee, he found his boss had cooled on Eisner for the project. And while Eisner produced several humorous, satirical books, it's not surprising that he might not be the right person to guide a college humor magazine.

"Stan felt it wasn't quite the direction he wanted to go. They weren't on the same wavelength," Thomas said. "This was during Nixon. It would have been difficult."

After Eisner passed on *Bedlam,* Lee also talked with Harvey Kurtzman about the project. Kurtzman—the master of the genre who created *MAD*—dropped into Gil Kane's office at Marvel, told his friend why he was there, and shook his head.

"Oh God," Kurtzman said, "am I back to this?"

Kurtzman passed.

Lee eventually got his magazine together and called it *Crazy.* Ironically, he offered the editor's job to Denis Kitchen (editor of Marvel's short-lived *Comix Book* magazine), who also declined. *Crazy* lasted from 1973 through 1983.

One more "What If ..." story about Eisner and Marvel:

Shortly after Jim Shooter became editor in chief of Marvel in January 1978, he and Eisner met for lunch at the Princeton Club. Shooter, who had recently agreed to begin producing an annual series of character crossover comics with DC, asked if Eisner would be interested in doing a one-shot *Spider-Man vs. The Spirit*. No character had ever crossed over into the Spirit's world before.

"I don't think it would be a very good idea," Eisner told Shooter, joking, "because the Spirit would kick the shit out of Spider-Man."

Shooter didn't laugh.

"Give it some time, think about it," he said.

"I don't have to think about it," Eisner said. "The Spirit would make a fool out of him."

Shooter recalled that Eisner was not just skeptical of the *mano-a-mano* interaction between the characters.

"At the time, I barely knew what the Spirit was—and what I did know was because of Jules Feiffer's book, *The Great Comic Book Heroes*," Shooter said. "Will could not abide by anyone else handling the Spirit in any way. I suggested *he* could draw it, but he said no. It wasn't happening. And the state of Marvel Comics in 1978 was pretty ugly. We weren't good then. I didn't blame him for being skeptical of our ability to do a good job; he was rightfully worried about the notion of us messing with his character."

Still, the old Eisner charm took the sting out of rejection for Shooter.

"Will was even nice when he was telling me to go to hell. Made me look forward to the trip!"

FOURTEEN
Cat's Tale

Cat Yronwode, born Catherine Manfredi, was a single mother and comic book fan who lived in an isolated rural cabin near the town of Cabool, in the Missouri Ozarks in the 1970s. Visually impaired and unable to drive, she tried freelancing magazine articles on crafts, gardening, antiques, and comics history as a way of earning a living. But it wasn't until she landed a weekly column for Alan Light's influential and widely read comics fanzine *The Buyer's Guide* and a job as comic strip editor for Ken Pierce Publications that her comic book hobby began to pay off.

When she was home, comics helped Yronwode pass the time. The daughter of a special collections librarian at University of California Los Angeles, her particular interest was putting credits to old comics that often carried inaccurate or incomplete creator credits.

Her first interest was in cataloging and identifying the work of Steve Ditko, the cocreator and original artist of *Spider-Man* and *Doctor Strange*. From Ditko, she moved on to an immense challenge, Will Eisner's *Spirit* sections. A fellow collector she met shared her interest in *The Spirit*. But he didn't have all the issues; Yronwode thought maybe Will Eisner himself might.

Looking for an excuse to contact Eisner directly, she called Gary Groth, publisher of the comic book industry criticism and review magazine *The Comics Journal,* and asked if she could interview Eisner on assignment for the *Journal*. Her secret goal was discovering whom the inkers were that worked on *The Spirit*. Not exactly something the world was crying out to know, frankly, but Yronwode was not your typical comics fan, either.

"If you can get to him, go ahead," Groth said.

Yronwode wrote a letter to Denis Kitchen requesting an interview with Eisner, giving Groth's name as a reference. Kitchen called Groth.

"Who is this guy 'Cat Yer-Ron-Woodie'?" he asked.

"First," Groth replied, "Cat's not a guy. Second, it's 'Iron-wood.' She's okay."

Reassured, Kitchen arranged a first meeting.

Most writers working without pay for a small publication—and who literally lived a thousand miles away from the subject—would make an appointment for a telephone interview.

Not Cat Yronwode.

She *went* to New York City in the company of her friend, Denis McFarling, and stayed at the home of another comics fan, Ken Gale.

In preparation for actually meeting Eisner, she haunted the stacks of the New York Public Library, looking for old *Spirit* sections in the newspaper morgue. Many already were knifed out by collectors.

When she finally met Eisner at the School of Visual Arts—Yronwode arrived barefoot just as he began teaching a class—he handed her a book to read and promised they'd talk when class was over. The book was hot off the press: *A Contract with God* by Will Eisner.

"I was laughing, crying," Yronwode said. "I was blown away."

When they finally talked, she got right to the point. "All the *Spirit* sections are gone from the Public Library," she said. "Can I come to your place and index yours?" It tells a lot about both these characters that she invited herself to the home of a perfect stranger—and that he said yes.

"I went to his house and met Ann," Yronwode said. "We had a lot of things in common, among them that we both had a daughter who died. We're both Tauruses. We really hit it off."

She arrived still barefoot, but packing an already encyclopedic knowledge about Eisner's body of work and career, "more than even he could remember," Ann said.

SPECIAL WILL EISNER ISSUE!

The Comics Journal

$1.25

May
No. 46

Who was that masked man? A feature-length interview with the man behind The Spirit

"A Contract With God" Dennis O'Neil reviews the groundbreaking new book by Will Eisner

News
Marvel's *Epic Illustrated*, DC's Digests, a new book from Warren, and news from the alternative press

Reviews
Wonder Woman, Li'l Abner, The Buyer's Guide, and others

"Axa"
The brilliant new strip from England

"Changes In The X-Men"

New Feature!
Checklist of May releases from DC, Marvel, and Warren

The Comics Journal No. 46 including Cat Yronwode's first interview with Will Eisner

Meanwhile, the interview—which started after that initial encounter at SVA—went on for some time. They met again at the Princeton Club. It was there that Yronwode told Eisner that she was a single mother living on $200 a month in welfare in the Ozarks.

"We're going to have to work on making a capitalist out of you," Eisner told her as they left the club and he paid for her cab fare.

The interview appeared in the May and June 1979 issues of *The Comics Journal* (Nos. 46 & 47). It dealt with three main topics: *A Contract with God,* Eisner's lost history as an artist, and the previously uncredited identities of inkers who worked on *The Spirit.* In the process of producing the interview, Yronwode—with the help of Eisner fans Jerry Bails (co-founder, with Roy Thomas, of the *Alter Ego* comic book fanzine in 1961, and author of *Who's Who of American Comic-Books*), Jerry Sinkovec (editor and publisher of *The Comic Reader*), Mark Hanerfeld (editor of *The Comic Reader*), and John Benson (editor of *Witzend*)—also began her now legendary "The Spirit Checklist." She and Benson shared an interest in the work of Wally Wood, another artist who worked on The Spirit, and Benson told her to ask Eisner about Wood's contributions to the series.

Bails, Sinkovec, and Yronwode were members of an association of comic book indexers called "APA-I" or the Amateur Press Association for Indexing. Bails and Sinkovec mailed their Spirit sections to Yronwode in Missouri. After indexing them, she mailed them back.

"Hanerfeld and Benson met me in New York, showed me their *Spirit* sections, and said, 'Ask Will this,' or 'Ask Will that,'" Yronwode said.

As their friendship blossomed, Ann Eisner called Yronwode, who was back in Missouri, working in McFarling's print shop, about her possible interest in cataloging Will's artwork. At the time, it was stored in boxes, cartons, and file cabinets in a converted bedroom at the Winslow address, having moved from studio to studio with Will from all the way back in the Eisner & Iger Studio days. Ann liked the idea of organizing the chaos. "Cat can stay with us," she said.

"Ann called and asked me to work for them," Yronwode said. The Eisners were coming off a bad experience in which Eisner's previous assistant allegedly stole original art from him and was fired. "Will needed help organizing his stuff. He said, 'It's all over the place, could you please come help?' When I was indexing, I pointed out there were errors in the Harvey reprints. Other errors had appeared in print as well. For example, a reprint of the 'Lady Luck' sections by Ken Pierce was credited entirely to one artist although there were several contributors. Pierce had gotten the silver prints from Will, who had hastily credited the work to Klaus Nordling. I wrote a note to Ken and said, 'How could you leave off Fred Schwartz's credit?' Ken then hired me to edit his second collection of 'Lady Luck'—and all his other comic strip reprint collections as well."

Yronwode didn't take much convincing. With the Eisners paying her way, she packed a suitcase and moved into the Eisner's guest room for the next six weeks. "It was one of the happiest times of my life," she said. "I got to do fan stuff, I got to gopher for Will. It was like a Grimm's fairy tale. He was Rumpelstiltskin and he put me into the art room and said, 'Spin straw into gold.'"

Eisner's workspace was next to the house in a small building that the previous owner, an architect, had built as a studio. The ex-bedroom where Yronwode spent her solitary days was on the second story of the house. It had shelving all around, plus file cabinets, and a fireproof vault. Yronwode's job was cataloging, indexing, and organizing it all, making sense of five decades of art and commerce. She started at one end of the room, setting up the shelves by year and began sorting. This was before computers; she inventoried it all on index cards.

It quickly became clear that Eisner was one of the comics industry's great pack rats. He saved everything, a personality trait that usually served him well. Yronwode found almost all the work the prolific Eisner ever produced in that room, from copies of his high school newspaper to original art for the corporate comics he created for Sears and General Motors. But keeping everything and keeping it all organized were two different traits.

"The art pages were in brown paper envelopes," Yronwode recalled. "The envelopes and the artwork were intact, aside from the fact that old paste-ups were falling off due to Eisner's use of rubber cement, an unstable mastic that loses its adhesiveness and stains white paper brown over time. One of my main tasks was to collect and carefully re-glue the hundreds of tiny art corrections that had been pasted down with rubber cement during the 1940s and had come loose in those fraying envelopes."

Sometimes her enthusiasm for the job overwhelmed Yronwode. She'd come down from filing with an obscure piece of art in hand and say, "This is so cool!"

And sometimes, Eisner's little secrets slipped out. For example, Yronwode discovered that when Eisner began licensing *Spirit* reprints to Harvey and Warren, he couldn't help but change things. There were 1940s pages with 1970s art pasted on top. She also noticed the way characters in his early comic books recurred from one Eisner project to another. "Everyone said he drew Lauren Bacall a lot. But it was actually a girl he once dated who looked a lot *like* Bacall. 'Skinny Bones' was the name he gave the Bacall character." One time when Yronwode asked Eisner about a female character's origins, Ann chastised her husband. "I don't want to hear about your love life before you met me!"

Intimately familiar with Eisner's early Centaur and Fiction House comics as well as *The Spirit* and his recent graphic novel, *A Contract with God,* Yronwode recognized something else about the women—or a woman—portrayed in several stories.

"He has this woman he loves/hates. She always gets killed. She always has another boyfriend. In a way, it's so transparent, it's sad. I don't think he realized how much he was wearing his heart on his sleeve. That was something that really made me love him. I saw something about his naiveté and his innocent immersion in his art. When I asked him who that woman was, what her real name had been, he told me right away, and then, really puzzled, he said, 'How would I know somebody would put all these stories together and figure it out?'

"My thrill about working there was I got the answers to all the questions I asked," she said.

Yronwode quickly took charge, using the library skills she learned from the years she spent at her mother's side at UCLA. It became a life any comics fan would envy; full days spent sorting through the originals, personal letters, and other miscellany of a life in graphic art, plus breakfast, lunch, and dinner (Ann was an excellent cook) with a legend.

To the Eisners, Cat was more than just an employee.

"Cat was one of the people we would have adopted as a daughter," Ann said. "She was bright, always full of anecdotes and stories."

She filled a gaping void in their lives, providing a view into what their lives might have been like if their daughter Alice had survived. One day, for example, Will and Ann were asleep in bed and Cat came barreling in—in much the way Alice once did—but instead of asking about clothes or shoes, she wanted to ask some arcane question about *The Spirit*.

"I was still suffering from recent tragedies," Eisner said. "She became a real professional after a while. To me, well, there was something very deep there. I think—in the back of my mind—that she was replacing my lost daughter, and she seemed to be the age of what Alice would have been, and I couldn't help it. Ann accused me one day of talking to Cat like she was our daughter."

A typical day in the Eisner household began early. Will and Ann got up together, ate breakfast together, and read the *New York Times* together. Yronwode became integrated in the household routine.

"To me, it was like being home at my mom's," Yronwode said. "Nice Jewish food—smoked cheeses, salmon, grapefruit. Will had a grapefruit every morning and half a bagel. We'd talk about the news. It was inspirational to see what a loving couple they were. They teased, but they were very in love and happy together."

Ann went off to work each morning as director of volunteers at New York Hospital-Cornell Medical Center, Westchester Division. Eisner either played tennis or headed off to his studio. He would call up to Yronwode at midday and they'd have lunch together, usually fruit and cheese. She treasured these one-on-one sessions. "I was between relationships. My daughter was at her dad's; I was on my own," she said. "I was struggling economically. They afforded me a window into a better life. My life turned around because of their influence."

One day there was a late-morning bomb-threat at the hospital, and the building where Ann worked was evacuated. Employees were sent home early for the day. Minutes after she arrived, in walked her husband, drenched in sweat from his morning tennis game. He was in his fifties; she was in her forties. With Yronwode in the room with them, Ann kissed her husband and said, "You're so gorgeous!" Then, turning her back to Yronwode, she took Will by the hand and led him away to the bedroom.

"They represented to me the acme of marital fun and fidelity," Yronwode said.

The two women struck up a friendship, despite the many differences in their ages, styles, fashions, and politics. They went to a psychic fair together once and had fun. Ann took Cat shopping a few times, which was entertaining for both because they deplored each other's taste. Ann was dowdy and conservative; Yronwode wore skirts down to her shoeless ankles. Each tried to bring a different joie de vivre into the existence of the other.

On another occasion, Eisner was at the dinner table, opening mail. He read that a European group had made him the recipient of its annual award.

"Ann, Ann," Eisner shouted to the kitchen to share the good news. "I just got an award from Europe!"

Coming into the room, a smile on her face, Ann said, "Now you can go tell your mother that you *could* make a living as an artist."

Eisner stood up from the dinner table, looked upward, and said, "Mother! I'm making a living as an artist!"

―――――――――

Eisner encouraged Yronwode to meet his publisher Kitchen face-to-face. Her conversations with Kitchen led to another long-term relationship. Kitchen bought the rights to serialize her "The Spirit Checklist" in *The Spirit Magazine* (Nos. 22-28) for $35 per typeset page, with

Yronwode doing her own typesetting. She soon became associate editor for Kitchen's *Spirit* reprints, writing the "Dept. of Loose Ends" column with annotations on every tale. She conceived of and helped coordinate *The Spirit Jam*, in which Eisner wrote and drew the beginning and end of a *Spirit* story and the pages in-between were contributed by an all-star assemblage of the modern era's top comics writers and artists, including Terry Austin, Brent Anderson, Brian Bolland, John Byrne, Milton Caniff, Chris Claremont, Richard Corben, Howard Cruse, Archie Goodwin, Kitchen, Harvey Kurtzman, Frank Miller, Denny O'Neil, Peter Poplaski, Marshall Rogers, and Bill Sienkiewicz. (On the last page, Eisner drew Kitchen and Yronwode along with himself.)

Spirit Jam

Yronwode was the kind of hippie who refused to compromise. The world might compromise to her, but it would never be the other way around. The strength of her convictions would cause strong reactions from those around her, either envy or enmity.

When Kitchen Sink Press sent her W-9 miscellaneous income statements for tax purposes, Kitchen said, "She would return them with anti-government diatribes and declarations that she refused to pay taxes."

The turnabout in Yronwode's life continued as she took the job of reprint editor for Kitchen's (post-Warren) *Spirit* magazines. She was obviously the perfect choice; no one else on earth knew the stories and inventory as well. Yronwode immediately took charge, sending Kitchen better and more related stories. Not that Kitchen ever had a choice in the matter; previously, Eisner or his brother Pete would grab a set of stories off the shelf and send it. No master list existed and neither of them gave much thought to the overall continuity of the reprint series before Yronwode explained that contemporary fans wanted to experience the same story-flow that readers had originally enjoyed in the 1940s.

While in White Plains, Yronwode also took on the job of ghost-writing one of Eisner's Poorhouse Press books, a calorie-counter guide called *What's in What You Eat*. Bob Pizzo, then an Eisner student at SVA, did the art and Eisner laid the book out. Yronwode completed the text after her return to Missouri.

Another potential Poorhouse Press title from that era got off to a rocky start in its development phase. Under the working title, "30 Days to a Brick Shithouse Figure," Eisner used physical fitness guidelines from the U.S. Air Force as his inspiration. Will and Ann were at odds over the book; she was upset about it but couldn't initially articulate why.

"It's so awful!" Ann said.

"It's going to sell," Eisner protested.

Yronwode took Eisner aside and suggested not publishing the book.

"Why?" he said, clearly puzzled by the unusually strong resistance being mustered by the women in his home.

"No offense," Yronwode said, "but you're offending everybody here."

Eisner tried a new title on the women, "30 Days to a New Sexier You," but once more, Ann broke into tears. Eisner just didn't get it. He repeatedly tried changing the title, including "40 Days to a New Beautiful You."

"Ann is a very sexy woman," Yronwode told him, "but by publishing that book, she thinks you're telling her that in thirty days, if she becomes anorexic, you'll find her sexy."

Now he got it. "30 Days" was never published.

Once Eisner's art room was organized in 1979, it was time for Yronwode to move back to Missouri. (She returned one more time, in 1983, to organize Eisner's archival donation to the Ohio State University.)

For the next four years, Yronwode worked out of Eisner's own home as a freelancer, offering publishers her services as a writer, editor, typesetter, production and paste-up artist, and complete packager of projects from concept to press.

Among her clients were Eisner's Poorhouse Press (for whom she wrote, edited, and helped paste up *The Art of Will Eisner*) and Denis Kitchen (writing and typesetting "The Spirit Checklist," editing reprints in *The Spirit* magazine, writing articles for *Will Eisner's Quarterly,* editing graphic album reprints of *The Spirit,* and writing material for another Kitchen periodical, *Yesteryears*).

She also was an art agent for Ann Eisner and, beginning in late 1980, wrote a weekly, multi-page news and reviews column called "Fit to Print" for *The Buyer's Guide.* It was through the wide circulation of this column that many fans and professionals still remember her best today.

=========

Eisner often told Yronwode that he hoped she would marry again; Ann was delighted to try her hand at matchmaker. It was one more thing they tried to help her achieve stability in her life.

Ann felt Yronwode's social life suffered while she was living with them, so she threw a party for Yronwode, inviting all the (mostly) single, male cartoonists the Eisners knew in New York.

"They hosted a party for me with all these comic book men I was flirting with," Yronwode said. "All these men came up; they all wanted to meet Will. One of them was Dean Mullaney, the co-owner of Eclipse Comics, a small independent publishing house. He was the most flirtatious. Ann said to me, 'Who's that ugly man?' I said, 'Ugly?' Dean had acne scars, but I didn't notice; I wasn't wearing my glasses."

The gathering attracted a wide variety of talent, including Terry Austin, Jim Shooter, and Denny O'Neil. Ann hoped Yronwode would be smitten by one of the young men, and she was—Mullaney. Ann didn't care for Mullaney and tried to discourage Yronwode. But Yronwode was a woman who followed her own counsel.

"When she left us, she was madly in love," Ann said.

Mullaney and Yronwode became engaged, although Ann still bore reservations about him. They relocated to California, and when their wedding day arrived, the Eisners were there and met Cat's family for the first time.

While working for Eisner, Yronwode went in search of an answer to an enduring Eisner mystery: Where was all the original art from his twenty years of producing *PS Magazine*?

As she tamed the room full of Eisner's civilian art, Yronwode became interested in seeing more of his *PS* work. Specifically, Yronwode wondered what became of the original art pages he did for the magazine. It was the only major work of his that Eisner didn't possess; the Army kept it.

Researching the issue, Yronwode was told the art was stored under lock and key at Fort Knox in Lexington, Kentucky. She convinced Denis Kitchen to pay her way to the base to investigate further and to inquire whether the Army might consider releasing the art to Eisner.

After the staff reminisced about Eisner and his time at the magazine, Yronwode learned about the heartbreaking *PS* production and storage process.

"In each box was all the art for each *PS Magazine* and all the training manuals Will did. And it was all in order," she said.

Until she began looking through the boxes.

Eisner had discovered vellum by then. Vellum is thin and translucent, like tracing paper. Eisner, in another example of his classic frugality, pencilled *PS* pages on scratch paper and instructed his staff to put the art on vellum and ink over it. "But vellum doesn't last," Yronwode discovered. "It turns brown and decays. It oxidizes as we speak. Some of the most beautiful art he did for the military magazines was gone. That's what came out of his military experience—inexpensive ways of drawing."

The vellum habit carried over from his military work to *A Contract with God,* which Eisner created in the same fashion. The work may be a classic now, but the paper on which it was imagined and brought to life had a short shelf life. While Eisner's post-World War II *Spirit* sections were created on sturdy Strathmore pages that stood the test of time—and which he had the foresight to keep and store properly for decades—he and the Army never gave the *PS* pages the same respect. Of course, the collectors market for such art was still in its infancy when he left *PS,* so it's somewhat understandable why he did the work on the cheap and didn't think it would have a life beyond immediate publication.

"I taught him something" as a result of the disturbing *PS* discovery, Yronwode said. "If he wanted to sell art, he had to go back to Strathmore. I said, 'Don't think of me as pushing, but I represent your fans. And they want stuff on Strathmore that they can frame.'"

═══════════

Once Yronwode located Eisner's *PS* art, she discovered two problems. First, to release the material the Army would have to declare the art "surplus property." It would do that if Eisner agreed to bid on it. But before he could make that decision, they told Yronwode that all of his original art and files were shipped off to another base, Carlisle Barracks, in Pennsylvania.

Here the story takes a tragic turn, not unlike the stories that end in "My mother thought my comic books/baseball cards/fill-in-the-blank were garbage and she threw them out when I went to college."

Unfortunately, some idiot in Carlisle decided on his own that—despite the staff's careful packing and request that the work be stored—the original art was no longer of any practical use. So they destroyed it.

"We packaged the original art in 1993 when we moved from Lexington, Kentucky," said *PS Magazine*'s Stuart Henderson. "They threw it away. They said, 'You've got the printed books.' And we said, 'We didn't send you four hundred boxes of printers' boards to have you throw them away!' There was an official Army inquiry. To this day, if I find somebody selling those on eBay, I'll make sure somebody spends the rest of their life making little rocks out of big rocks at Sing Sing."

"They apologized profusely because the destruction was never authorized," Eisner said. "But you know how the Army is."

Lost in those boxes was not just Eisner's art but several years' worth of Murphy Anderson's work, too.

═══════════

There is no doubt that Yronwode's tenure with Eisner had a great influence on him. She brought a comic fan's perspective to his studio—and also to the classroom.

"I watched him teach at the School of Visual Arts," she said. "He'd rattle off these rules; I told him he had to write it all down. *Comics & Sequential Art* was something I encouraged him to do. He started with a lot of theory. I challenged him: 'Why do you do this?' I interviewed him to talk about it. I wrote it down and said, 'Here is what you told me.' I always presented myself as the curious fan: 'Here is what the curious fan wants to know.' I tried to show him how much people cared about his work."

In subsequent years, during the time that Yronwode was Eisner's exclusive art agent, he still valued her input enough to show her advance pages from his latest graphic novels and to solicit her ever-blunt appraisals. "He's a great storyteller and I didn't mess with that," she said. But she might take note of a woman's dress in a Depression-era story and criticize the fashion. "This woman needs a 1930s dress; you're just faking it," she'd tell him. "You know architecture but not women's fashion." And to back up her assertion, she would send him a page from an old Sears Roebuck catalog with the appropriate style for the era.

———

Ann Eisner had never read a *Spirit* story—with the exception of the "Samson and Delilah" parody published more than two decades earlier—until one evening in 1980 when Kitchen and Yronwode were visiting the Eisners for dinner.

One of them asked Ann what *Spirit* story was her favorite. When she said she hadn't read any, except for the one that parodied her onetime employer, Kitchen and Yronwode's jaws dropped.

Ann loved her husband for himself. Until that point, his work as an artist and his influence upon generations of artists was no different to her than if he was an aerospace engineer at NASA.

"If you could only pick one *Spirit* story for me to read," Ann later asked Yronwode, "which would it be?"

She read one, and then asked Yronwode for another. "Give me a funny

one and a tearjerker." She read them as original art. One day Eisner
came in from his studio for dinner and Ann gave him a big kiss. "I read
one of your stories today," she said. "It was so funny!"

Yronwode said that next, she encouraged Ann to attend a few conventions with her husband and get a dose of how people loved and
admired him. "She started seeing what people like me saw in him,"
Yronwode said.

During the process of cataloging and inventorying Eisner's art, Ann
asked her husband, "What are you going to do with all of that art?"

"I'm going to have it buried with me in a special coffin," he said.

"Why don't we sell some of it?" Ann asked.

After a great deal of hesitation about parting with his work, he agreed,
but he insisted on selling the stories as a package. He believed that people would keep the stories together. That wouldn't happen, but the timing was right for going to market. The new comic book fan market
hungered for original pieces, and since the reprinting of the first *Spirit*
strips by Kitchen and Warren, recognition of Eisner as the industry's
rediscovered master was growing daily.

There was one complication, however. When Walt Kelly, the artist
behind the "Pogo" comic strip, died, his wife Selby was reportedly hit
with a tremendous federal tax bill because the value of the original art
she inherited was so high. Eisner and several members of the National
Cartoonists Society even held a fundraiser for Selby so she could pay
the IRS and not sell the art.

Around the time the Eisners decided to market his art, Harvey and
Adele Kurtzman and Klaus Nordling and his wife were visiting.
Yronwode asked Kurtzman what he would do with his inventory if he
were Eisner.

"You have to die with no art," Kurtzman said. (For a man whose business sense was not the best, it was a rare moment of clarity.)

"I said, 'Will, you have all this art, who you going to leave it to?
Ohio State University?'" Ann recalled. "We give a lot of money to char-
ity. We have a small foundation. Maybe it's Alice's influence, but I said,

'Let's use that money (from the sale of the art) to make it possible to help the things we believe in.'"

Eisner then formally gave the art to Ann to sell. But there wasn't any big rush. There was so much of it that creating a glut would depress prices. And he wasn't in a huge hurry to part with his portfolio after keeping it with him for decades.

"It was a source of pleasure and pride to him that his art was valuable," Yronwode said.

Ann recommended naming Will's assistant as his official agent for selling original art. After all, who knew his work and inventory better than the woman who cataloged it?

Yronwode went through and ranked all the stories. First to go were broken up story pages. She also sold pencil sketches that Eisner had previously just been throwing out.

"Nobody will want my pencil sketches," he said.

"Oh, yes they will," said his agent.

She, of course, was correct. The first sketches sold for $20 to $40 each. Small change, perhaps, but they were more valuable in frames in collectors' homes than as landfill. And the sketches led to requests for specially commissioned pencil sketches and paintings.

═══════════

When the Eisners prepared for their move to Florida in 1978 (as seasonal residents first, they moved there full-time in September 1983), they wanted to throw away all the detritus of a storied life.

In the summer of 1983 — three years after spending that first six weeks as their guest and two years after writing *The Art of Will Eisner*, Yronwode was still working for them and for other publishers when Ann telephoned and said that, as a side effect of their moving to Florida, they were throwing out a lot of personal memorabilia. She and Will were not sure what was valuable and what was not. An entire trashcan had already been filled and put at the curb, but not yet picked up. Will, being a pack rat, was distraught and thought that Yronwode could help them. She immediately agreed, and suggested Will bring in the trashcan immediately.

The Eisners knew that Yronwode's mother had been a Special Collections librarian at UCLA, handling the papers of famous authors, and that Yronwode had contacts at a number of university libraries. They also knew that she had donated thousands of comic books and many boxes of comics industry ephemera to Michigan State University Library in East Lansing over the years. They wondered if MSU might be a place to send their unwanted personal papers.

"Much as I personally liked the folks at MSU," Yronwode said, "I told Ann that the Ohio State University would be a better recipient for their donation. Lucy Caswell had recently established a repository of comics art at OSU's journalism library, following a generous bequest of the art and papers of Milton Caniff, a former Ohio state resident whose 'Terry and the Pirates' newspaper strip had been a leading early influence on Will's approach to dramatic storytelling. I knew that Will would greatly enjoy the idea of having his works archived alongside one of his mentors and that obtaining the Eisner collection would put the nascent OSU collection on the map."

The Eisners asked Yronwode to contact Caswell privately to assess her interest. She was quite enthusiastic, to say the least. With that squared away, the Eisners paid Yronwode's plane fare to New York and she again went to work in the art room, as well as in Will's studio. She spent about three weeks there, collecting, filing, documenting, boxing, and labeling the Eisner donation. With Ann's permission, she also selected one complete Spirit story, "Hurricane," in the form of original artwork, as the centerpiece of the collection.

Among the items Cat Yronwode saved from the trash was a box of 8mm silent films that Will and Pete Eisner had taken of themselves, their family, and their friends during the late 1930s and early 1940s.

"I encouraged Will to do a story about how he became a comic book artist," Yronwode said, "how he went straight from high school to being a professional artist, how he catapulted from being this poor kid to being a guy who had a partner thirteen years older. I was also tired of seeing Will fall short as a memoirist and slip into Jewish comedy shtick."

One of Eisner's most popular graphic novels, *The Dreamer,* came out of Cat Yronwode's perpetual requests that he buckle down and put his memories on paper. "He first started telling me these stories because I was fascinated with his life," she said. "He was the same age as my father, who was the son of Sicilian immigrants. My father was a painter who, like Will, also went to the Art Students League. They both grew up in mixed neighborhoods of Irish, Italians, and Jews. Will told me wonderful stories of people I knew. I could envision them as Will would draw them. I'd say, 'Why don't you draw them?' He'd say no. And I'd insist—'Do Buck and the boat!'"

One of the filmstrips that Yronwode salvaged was of the boat that Eisner and his friend Buck built in high school.

"The film of the boat was sadder to me than the story as Will described it," Yronwode said. The films suggested to her that Eisner was even more of an outsider than his stories implied. "It was Will taking pictures of all the details of the beautiful boat—but Buck, when he held the camera, showed very little of Will and it was out of focus."

Yronwode represented Eisner as his official art agent for several years, long after she and Dean Mullaney moved to California and the Eisners relocated to Florida. She said that the relationship unraveled when he "priced himself ahead of the market. Then things didn't sell as fast and I didn't make as much. That's where we came a cropper. If the last complete story sold for $8,000, Will priced the next one for $10,000. It didn't sell and I made no commission."

With Yronwode living in California and the Eisners in Florida, communications became strained.

The arrangement had worked well for several years. Will and Ann enjoyed not only their continuing involvement in Yronwode's life, but they also enjoyed helping her financially. Meanwhile, Yronwode became the editor-in-chief of Mullaney's Eclipse Comics, one of the earliest and, for a while, most successful independent comic book publishers.

At some point, Yronwode didn't sell any more art, however, and there was a falling out between the two women. Yronwode felt hurt when Ann took the agency away from her.

"Ann cut me off," Yronwode said. "I put out a catalog and sold pretty much everything in it. I thought it went well. Ann wanted me to do another catalog right away. Then Will asked for an increase in prices over the last catalog. I guess I delayed, because Ann sent me a very angry letter. It was personally hurtful. To this day, I don't understand it."

The Eisners disputed Yronwode's story about how the relationship unraveled, supporting their view with correspondence Ann and Pete sent Yronwode. They repeatedly asked for reports on what she was doing but Yronwode didn't respond. Finally, Ann wrote and said she assumed that Yronwode's other business responsibilities interfered with her representation of Eisner's art.

In a final letter, Ann told Yronwode that she didn't want their personal relationship affected by a business decision. Ann never heard from her again.

Ann subsequently engaged Santa Rosa, California-based Mark Cohen as Will's agent. Cohen—whom the Eisners met through Yronwode—was renowned for his large collection of *MAD* magazine's original art. He commissioned a large group of cartoonists—Will included—to do self-portraits of themselves and was a co-founder, with Jeannie Schulz, of the Charles M. Schulz Museum in Santa Rosa.

Cohen represented Eisner until his death from cancer in 1999, when the agency passed on to Denis Kitchen.

"It came to a horrible end and I don't know why," Yronwode said. "I loved hanging out with them. They're wonderful people."

The last contact between Cat Yronwode and the Eisners came in 1997, when Ann sent an invitation to a surprise eightieth birthday party for Eisner at the International Museum of Cartoon Art.

"I got an answer back from her secretary," Ann said. "It read, 'Cat Yronwode will be unable to come. Please wish Will a happy birthday for her.' That was it! A note from her secretary?"

"I guess I am no longer important to her," Eisner said. "Whatever. You never know. She may not know herself."

That summer at the San Diego Comic-Con, Ann saw artist and writer Scott McCloud (*Understanding Comics, Reinventing Comics*)'s wife Ivy talking with Yronwode. (The McClouds had attended Will's surprise party.) Yronwode smiled at Ann, but Ann didn't return the gesture. "There are certain lines everybody has," Ann said. "When you hurt my husband, that's a line you can't come back from."

FIFTEEN
The Kitchen Sink Experience, Part II

The Warren newsstand *Spirit* magazine looked great and sold well initially, but its circulation tapered off and Eisner's business relationship with Jim Warren diminished.

After sixteen issues, Eisner decided not to renew his contract with Warren (though they remained friends) and called Kitchen. "There are still a lot of stories that are unpublished," Eisner said, "but I wonder if there is any life left in them. What do you think?"

"Are you kidding, Will?" he said. "I would *love* to continue it."

Whereas Kitchen opened the door a crack for *The Spirit*, Warren kicked the door in like the Incredible Hulk, establishing that the market could easily support publication of fifty thousand or more *monthly* copies of a *Spirit* comic book.

Figuring there were enough collectors who wanted to continue getting the magazine as Warren had printed it, Kitchen followed the Warren numbering system. Where Warren ended with issue number sixteen, Kitchen Sink Press began again with issue number seventeen.

That publication continued until issue forty-one, at which point Kitchen split the publication in half. For the first time, *The Spirit* sections were reprinted in comic book format, in chronological order, and as full-color reproductions. Meanwhile, Kitchen Sink Press created a new magazine called *Will Eisner's Quarterly* that featured newly created non-Spirit material as well as articles about his career.

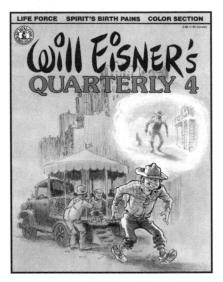

Will Eisner's Quarterly No. 4

"My sense of the marketplace," Kitchen said, "was that there were Spirit fans and fans of Will's new work that we've come to know as graphic novels. It tended to be a polarized audience. When Will ran his new stuff in the *Spirit* magazine, I'd get lots of complaints: 'We want more Spirit.' Finally we decided, let's give them both. Let's do just *The Spirit* for people who want it and the *Quarterly* for new work and historical articles about Busy Arnold, Quality Comics, and *PS*."

Eisner, who enjoyed having his own name on the magazine, also continued the popular "Shop Talk" interview series in the quarterly (later collected in a book of the same name). These were in-depth, revealing, and sometimes raucous interviews Eisner conducted with comic book and comic strip greats, including Milton Caniff (*Terry & the Pirates, Steve Canyon*), C. C. Beck (*Captain Marvel*), Jack Kirby (*Fantastic Four, Silver Surfer*), and Neal Adams (*Green Lantern/Green Arrow, Batman*). Eisner enjoyed the professional give-and-take of "Shop Talk" and spoke often of restarting the series.

Kitchen Sink eventually reprinted every episode of *The Spirit* from the post-World War II period (when Eisner returned from the Army and took back creative control) through the strip's conclusion in 1952.

By then, the Eisner projects replaced underground comix as the cornerstone of Kitchen Sink Press' business. Other living legends, such as Harvey Kurtzman, Milton Caniff, and Robert Crumb, joined Eisner on Kitchen's growing list.

———

Despite having Denis Kitchen as a common link, frequent publisher, and number-one fan, Eisner met Robert Crumb only once. They went for dinner to a restaurant in Greenwich Village with Harvey

Kurtzman. Crumb, who was a great admirer of Kurtzman, wore his familiar porkpie hat.

When Kurtzman got up to use the men's room, Eisner tried making conversation with the reluctant Crumb. It wasn't easy. Then Crumb asked Eisner a question.

"Do you know any girls with big legs?"

———————

Over the years, the relationship between Eisner and Kitchen grew from business into the personal realm. They visited each other often, and became part of the fabric of one another's lives.

The link between Will Eisner and the comic book underground was Denis Kitchen. Kitchen bridged the generation gap between the comic greats like Eisner, Caniff, and Kurtzman, and the underground comix stars like Robert

Denis Kitchen and Will Eisner
(Courtesy Denis Kitchen)

Crumb, Skip Williamson, and Jay Lynch. Unlike other underground publishers, Kitchen did not feel the need to discard mainstream cartooning in order to appreciate underground cartooning.

"I felt more at home at Kitchen Sink because I didn't feel required to turn up my nose at people like Al Capp," artist Howard Cruse said. "There was a certain appreciation for the 1930s tradition among people like the Air Pirates (Dan O'Neill, Bobby London, Ted Richards, Shary Flenniken, and Gary Halgren). But most felt that nothing happened from the '50s until they were the great revolutionaries. I felt there was a great arrogance in this. The underground broke into a new threshold of cartooning possibility and I think Eisner recognized that."

Eisner saw that Kitchen was interested in expanding cartooning. And undergrounds were a hint of the opening of the comics field to the things Eisner wanted to do.

Once Eisner was introduced to the underground comix movement, there was no turning back. Not only did he begin doing business with

Kitchen to adapt *The Spirit* for a new era, he began selling other work into the marketplace.

"Will was always talking up the underground," former Eisner student and office assistant John Holmstrom said. "He was thrilled to be working in the underground, not to have the restrictions and censorship. Harvey Kurtzman and Will were always trying to find a way to get comics accepted instead of just as kids' crap. They were frustrated that comics were grownup material in other countries but frowned on in this country."

Holmstrom offered the February 1977 issue of Al Goldstein's *Screw* magazine as an example. That issue featured four pages by Holmstrom, an Andy Warhol profile, and cartoons by Bill Griffith

("Zippy the Pinhead"), Art Spiegelman, and a four-page "Will Eisner's Gleeful Guide to the Quality of Life."

"It was pretty graphic stuff for Will," Holmstrom said, "including a couple topless women."

The irony of it, Holmstrom said, is that Eisner thought undergrounds were the future. "He and Harvey Kurtzman agreed on that. But (by then) it was the end of the underground." By the time Eisner discovered comix, the 1970s were ending and a new cultural era was beginning.

Inside front cover to the fanzine *Comic Art News and Review* No. 23 (July 1974), in which future *Cerebus* artist and writer Dave Sim interviewed Will Eisner
Courtesy and © Dave Sim

Dave Sim organized *Cerebus Jam* in 1985, a comic book featuring his aardvark character Cerebus interacting with other famous comics characters. The jam was a way of working with artists Sim admired and bringing fresh attention to his ongoing *Cerebus* comic. It ended up as a fairly aggravating experience. But he had one person with whom he dreamed of partnering—Will Eisner.

He called Eisner, who was by then a friend, and said he'd like to tell a Cerebus story with the Spirit. "Will's reaction was the same reaction as I would have had; 'This is going to turn into a lot of work, and you are going to make it sound like a little bit of work, and I am not going to be interested.'" Sim showed Eisner a pencil rough of the entire four-page story with as much of his part done as possible.

"I will rough in the Spirit and Commissioner Dolan," Sim said, "and if you are willing, you tighten it up, correct the pencils, and I will do the inking."

Sim then sent another draft with his best approximation of the Spirit and Dolan, drawn as much in the Eisner style as possible. "The closer I could get it and make it so he just had to correct the pencils, the better the chance that I would actually get him to work on it," Sim figured.

When the pages came back to Sim a few weeks later, he was startled to discover that Eisner tightened up and inked *all* the figures.

"Hope you don't mind that I inked the figures," Eisner said later, "but I was like a fire horse getting a whiff of the smoke; the moment I had it all tightened up, I just had to go in there and start inking it."

"No, Will, that's fine," Sim said, barely containing his glee. "I will let that one go. I am a little steamed, but you are Will Eisner, I will let it go."

Up until that point, Eisner had only created two new *Spirit* stories and covers for the short-lived Harvey Comics revival of the character, a political Spirit story for the *New York Herald Tribune* in 1966, and covers for the Warren and the first two Kitchen Sink underground re-prints (which also included a few new interior story pages). "And it was gorgeous," Sim said of their collaboration. "It was like he hadn't been away from it for fifteen minutes let alone the thirty years."

———————

Christopher Couch worked for Kitchen Sink Press from 1994 through 1999, and cowrote *The Will Eisner Companion*—an introduction to

Eisner's graphic novels and *The Spirit Archives*—for DC Comics. He also taught Eisner's work at the University of Massachusetts in Amherst and at the School of Visual Arts in New York. At KSP, he was Eisner's editor, as well as the brother-in-law of Eisner's hands-on independent editor, Dave Schreiner. (Kitchen told Couch, "I hired you because you have a good pedigree.")

Schreiner edited every Eisner graphic novel for twenty years, from the second one, *Life on Another Planet,* to *Fagin the Jew.* He died in August 2003, the very week that Fagin was published.

Couch called Eisner's relationship with Schreiner "very intimate."

"Dave told me that when he first started working with Will, he sent him letters and Will said, 'Dave you're being too polite.' After that he never stinted giving his opinion. And whether Will accepted the advice or not, he respected it."

Schreiner went through each book with a fine-tooth comb, line by line, and thoroughly vetted the story structure.

What distinguished Schreiner and made him so effective as an editor—

Special "Spirit" adventure for the *New York Herald Tribune,* January 9, 1966
(*Will Eisner Collection, The Ohio State University Cartoon Research Library*)

and fun to be around as a friend—was that he was one of those guys who not only knew a little about everything, he knew a lot about everything. He knew classic, modern-American literature as well as modern popular culture and sports trivia. And he really understood how fiction worked.

A Contract with God is described in shorthand as a graphic novel, but it is basically four short stories. The short story is a form in which Eisner is a modern master. But when he literally switched to producing graphic novels, full-length stories such as *Dropsie Avenue,* it was an area in which he was not yet experienced.

"He relied heavily on Dave," Couch said. "They worked really hard on *Heart of the Storm.* That's the capstone collaboration of Dave and Will. Dave was the expert in literature who helped Will master the novel form. Not that Will couldn't do it himself, but it's like the relationship between Maxwell Perkins and Ernest Hemingway. Dave was the kind of editor who got writers and artists to do what was inside of them and get it to be hugely successful."

———

By the mid-1990s, working at Kitchen Sink Press was no longer a lot of fun. Not for Denis Kitchen, and not for his employees.

"That was a pretty hellish time," Couch said.

By then, Will Eisner's role with Kitchen had grown from being a friend, business mentor, and creative contributor to being a member of the KSP board.

"Will worked really hard to help keep the doors open," Couch said. "He came to Massachusetts regularly to meet with Denis and strategize. He told him to keep his chin up (through financial hardships) and keep fighting. We used to call him 'Uncle Will.' We just loved him. Whenever he came to Northampton, we wanted to spend as much time with him as possible."

After 1994, Kitchen Sink Press was a far different operation from the company that Denis Kitchen started in a small Milwaukee apartment in the 1960s. In 1993—on April Fool's Day—Kitchen merged his operation with Massachusetts-based Tundra, owned by Kevin Eastman, cocreator of *Teenage Mutant Ninja Turtles*. And, while KSP technically swallowed Tundra, it was Kitchen who relocated to Northampton, Massachusetts.

Artistic success came easily to the new company, but financial success was more difficult. The entire comic book market went into a tailspin the year of the merger. Independent comic book stores were closing by the hundreds by the end of 1994, leaving fewer places for KSP's popular books to be sold.

In 1995, Kitchen and Eastman sold control of KSP to Los Angeles-based Ocean Capital Corp. Kitchen remained president and a board member but answered to investors and a board of directors, most of whom were not hippies but Hollywood suits who saw the company as a mill for concepts—such as *The Crow* by James O'Barr and *Cadillacs and Dinosaurs* by Mark Schultz—that could be adapted to movies and TV.

"A" list producer Robert Rehme (*Patriot Games, Beverly Hills Cop III, Lost in Space*), who kicked off the Academy Awards every year as president of the Academy of Motion Picture Arts and Sciences, was on board, as was "B" list producer Larry Kuppin (*Jimmy The Kid, Evita Peron;* he also played a derelict in *Hellraiser III*). Kuppin was also cochairman of New World Entertainment when it owned Marvel Comics.

"It was no longer truly my business," Kitchen said. "I was still technically in charge, but it was a mutation of KSP. I had two or three allies on the board, but Ocean controlled the nine-member majority. They did show respect for me and, as we set up the board, said, 'Who should balance these Hollywood guys?' Kevin Eastman was already on the board because he had been a major shareholder. I said, 'Will Eisner.' They acknowledged that on every level his inclusion made sense. They could boast that they had three generations of cartoonists on board—Will, me, and Kevin. They also liked that Will had been involved in publishing."

In addition to milking KSP for its potential crossover concepts, Ocean Capital envisioned an initial public offering (IPO) that would make everyone rich.

But Ocean reneged on its investment promises, leaving KSP in a financial lurch. The company's prospects further darkened when Ocean's chairman and IPO engineer, Joel Reader, hung himself on Christmas Day 1996. (In February 1990, while working as an investment banker for Oppenheimer & Co., Reader took *Young Frankenstein* and *The Producers* creator Mel Brooks' film production company public. "Brooksfilms initial public offering is a flop," read the *Los Angeles Business Journal* headline. A year later, Reader was with L. F. Rothschild, where *Forbes* reported that he loaded Divi Hotels NV with all the debt it could borrow, and the company crashed and burned as a result.)

"The last board meeting we had," Kitchen recalled, "Kuppin was on a conference phone call with me and Will and the others. He said, 'What the hell am I wasting my time for? My investment is lost. This is a waste of time.' And he resigned and hung up. When it was over, Will made a point that the minority of cartoonists was on the verge of taking over the company. Will said, 'One more guy dropping out and we have control!' I was distraught over this guy dropping out and Will saw it as a strategic advantage!"

Longtime DC Comics *Batman* editor and writer Denny O'Neil admired Eisner's Spirit characterization over the years because it remained consistent; more than just being about the title character, the comic became a way of telling stories. "The reason I preferred Batman," he said, "was that he was also a great vehicle for telling stories, and there were more stories you could tell with Batman than someone who was three degrees less powerful than God. Maybe that was something I picked up from reading Eisner when I was a little kid."

When Kitchen Sink Press was Eisner's publisher, O'Neil and Eisner talked about telling a story in which Eisner's Spirit would meet Batman. "It would not be us directly working together, but for me to write a story wherein Batman meets the Spirit," O'Neil said. "It intimidated me—I'm going to do Eisner's *Spirit*? Right. But he seemed okay with it."

O'Neil met with a Kitchen Sink editor and they talked about possible formats, whether it would be a miniseries or a long graphic novel. When Kitchen Sink imploded and DC acquired rights to the Eisner graphic novels and *The Spirit* reprints, the talks continued. "It was one of those projects that everybody thinks is a good idea but there was no compelling reason to do it," O'Neil said.

(In 2004, Eisner met with DC Comics Publisher Paul Levitz at Comic-Con International in San Diego to talk about a number of issues and agreed to allow The Spirit to join the DC Universe of characters and comics beginning in late 2005. Eisner made sure he had a clause in the contract giving him creative control, of course.)

When Kitchen Sink Press finally succumbed to falling sales and a cumbersome corporate structure and ceased publication in December 1998, all of the company's rights to Eisner's books reverted to him. At that point, he was free once more to do whatever he wanted. That was the good news for Eisner. But for Denis Kitchen, it was a professional low.

From left: Will Eisner, Alexa Kitchen, Denis Kitchen, and Pete Eisner
(Courtesy Will and Ann Eisner)

He was dazed over the loss of the company that he founded and that he nurtured for thirty years.

But where Kitchen saw tragedy, Eisner once more saw opportunity. He called Kitchen and said, "Would you be my literary agent?" Kitchen was stunned. But it made perfect sense to Eisner. He said, "I think that is the logical extension of our relationship. I want you to find a new home for my work."

There wasn't even a pause in his answer; Kitchen went directly from being Eisner's publisher to being his literary agent, forming the Kitchen & Hansen Agency in 1999 with Judy Hansen, a former vice president of Kitchen Sink Press and alumni at the Doubleday division of Random House and Simon & Schuster. Kitchen also assumed control of the sale of Eisner's original art through the separate Denis Kitchen Art Agency. His art agency, founded in 1991, already represented the estates of Harvey Kurtzman, Russell Keaton, Al Capp, and other artists.

Black & White

SIXTEEN
An Artist Rediscovered

The Great Comic Book Heroes
by Jules Feiffer

Jules Feiffer wanted credit where credit was due.

"Dare I say that it was *The Great Comic Book Heroes* that reinvented Will Eisner?" said the author of the 1965 book that launched the modern age of comic book fandom and made the field respectable for the next generation of creators. "He was forgotten. I thought the two most important creators in the strip world were Milton Caniff and Will Eisner. Caniff had plenty of accolades. Will's name was unknown."

Feiffer is correct, of course; just as one generation of future comic book creators was first introduced to *The Spirit* in the 1970s by Jim Warren's black-and-white reprints, an earlier generation in the 1960s discovered Eisner through Feiffer's book and an excerpt from it in *Playboy* magazine.

Feiffer wrote:

The Quality books bore his look, his layout, his way of telling a story. For Eisner did just about all of his own writing—a rarity in comic-book men. His stories carried the same weight as his line, involving a reader, setting the terms, making the most unlikely of plot twists credible.

His high point was The Spirit, a comic-book section created as a Sunday supplement for newspapers. It began in 1939 {sic} and ran, weekly, until 1942, when Eisner went into the army and had to surrender the strip to (the joke is unavoidable) a ghost.

For all the grouchiness and teasing in their latter-day relationship, Feiffer couldn't hide the pleasure it gave him to provide his former mentor a boost in recognition and respect.

"One of the most compelling, most satisfying aspects of anyone's career is collateral assists," Feiffer said. "Just as when people tell me a book of mine or cartoon of mine helped their kid, these things are terribly important to me. *GCBH* helped make comics a big thing again when they were dying out. I had not been a fan for a long time and never was a fan of the 'Marvel Age.' The book was a hope it would do something for Will. I'm thrilled it went way beyond what I hoped for. What *GCBH* did was make Will have second thoughts about his abandoned career as a cartoonist. With fanzines and the underground, he was launched back into the world."

Feiffer's cause was certainly aided by the fact that becoming a publishing entrepreneur did not work out as well as Eisner once hoped.

"Had Will become the Henry Luce of ordnance publications," Feiffer said, "we might never have seen the rebirth of Will Eisner as a cartoonist. Like so many of us, I suspect he backed into this latter day career."

═══════════

Maggie Thompson, editor of the *Comics Buyer's Guide*, had been a friend of Eisner's since the 1960s, when she and her late husband, Don, edited one of the first mimeographed comic book fanzines, *Comic Art* (1961-68). They tracked Eisner down and proudly put him on their mailing list, starting a relationship that lasted the rest of Eisner's life.

It was Don who introduced Maggie to *The Spirit* sections. "They blew me away and we collected them devotedly," she said.

In the 1973 book, *The Comic-Book Book* (coedited by Don Thompson and Dick Lupoff), Maggie Thompson contributed a chapter on Eisner and the influence of *The Spirit,* introducing thousands more people to the artist and his oeuvre. In the course of her own study, she elaborated upon a point of contention that was first raised by Jules Feiffer in *The Great Comic Book Heroes:*

> *Sartorially, the Spirit was miles apart from other masked heroes. He didn't wear tights, just a baggy blue business suit, a wide-brimmed blue hat that needed blocking, and, for a disguise, a matching blue eye mask, drawn as if it were a skin graft. For some reason, he rarely wore socks—if he did they were flesh-colored. I often wondered about that.*

Thompson, in her chapter of *The Comic-Book Book* ("Blue Suit, Blue Mask, Blue Gloves—And No Socks") couldn't help but bring it up again when describing the Spirit's brief and unexpected return to print in the *New York Herald Tribune*'s Sunday magazine January 9, 1966:

> *The Spirit wore a single-breasted suit, a narrow tie, and button-down collar. Otherwise, he was the same old Spirit—except for the socks. People have pointed out that the Spirit never wore socks; the leg that showed between cuff and shoe was almost invariably colored "flesh" in those old sections. The reason has been cloaked in as much mystery as why the Spirit always wore gloves, even to bed. But in the* Herald Tribune *that Sunday, the Spirit wore baggy socks—and even appeared briefly without his gloves. It's as though Eisner decided to break the traditions with that "final" appearance.*

Eisner responded to Thompson with a sketch of the Spirit saying, "It was a joke! I had socks!"

In the 1970s, there was an explosion of Eisner's influence, past and present, on the comic book scene. Experiences and opportunities for the writer/artist came from all corners of both the industry and the world, making them difficult to organize and categorize, because they all defined the man and his growing mythos.

For example, Eisner's work has long been recognized and revered within the comic book and graphic novel industry. But his remarkable creative output is now credited with touching all kinds of media.

Scott McCloud, author of *Understanding Comics* and *Reinventing Comics,* cited Eisner's influence in everything from novels to movies. He said that Michael Chabon (Pulitzer Prize-winning author, *The Amazing Adventures of Kavalier & Clay*), Frank Miller (writer/artist, *The Dark Knight Returns*), Art Spiegelman (Pulitzer Prize-winning author, *Maus*), Steven Spielberg (film director, *E.T., Close Encounters of the Third Kind, Jaws,* the *Indiana Jones* trilogy), Quentin Tarantino (writer/director, *Pulp Fiction*), and Matt Groening (creator, *The Simpsons*) are among those who have spoken publicly of being influenced by Eisner's work. Brad Bird, writer and director of the Academy Award-winning animated film *The Incredibles,* paid homage to Eisner in his film *The Iron Giant,* when a child shows the Iron Giant one of his *Spirit* comic books. And in *The Incredibles,* the featured characters' masks are all similar to *The Spirit*'s. Here's what Bird told *Washington Times* reporter Joseph Szadkowski in a story published in October 2004:

Scott McCloud (*Understanding Comics*) and Neil Gaiman (*Sandman*) surround Will Eisner at his eightieth birthday party
(Courtesy Will and Ann Eisner)

"I started getting into The Spirit *after reading an interview with William Friedkin and was amazed by how cinematic the character was. My first love has always been movies, and it struck me as a comic-strip version of* Citizen Kane.

"The angles were tremendous and the lighting was dramatic. It was even arranged on the page that was cinematic. Panels were not just broken up into geometric squares, they were longer, shorter and abrupt with a feeling of almost movielike timing.

"And I think this was one of the first comic strips to do that, and I love the fact that Will Eisner had all of the draftsmanship that one would look for but wasn't afraid to get broad or cartoony with some of the expressions.

"I also tipped my hat to Mr. Eisner's work in Iron Giant. *The kid pulls out stuff that the giant would enjoy seeing, and he pulls out a copy of* The Spirit. *I thought that not a lot of people know about this and it is a great thing.*

"I think Will Eisner is a genius ... "

"In comic book fandom, there was a disproportionate number of media-savvy, precocious readers who went on to do amazing things," McCloud said. "So the name 'Will Eisner' has great currency in design firms and movie production. Many prominent directors know Will's name. Like *Citizen Kane, The Spirit* helped codify storytelling language that other artists took advantage of. If his name doesn't travel far beyond our industry, his readership does. And it goes back several decades. The minds in media that create media know the name Will Eisner."

The difference between Eisner and the creators of better-known characters such as Superman and Batman, said McCloud, "is the difference between the man who built the first internal combustion engine and the man who created the tail fins on the Thunderbird. Will built the engine that everything runs on."

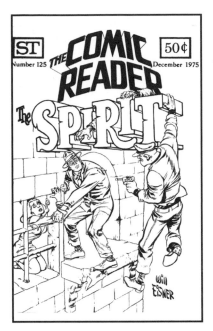

The Comic Reader No. 125,
December 1975

In researching his documentary, *Will Eisner: The Spirit of an Artistic Pioneer,* filmmaker Jon B. Cooke was surprised to learn that Eisner created the assembly-line method for producing comic books in the late 1930s. "He talked to the *Philadelphia Record* about the importance of comics in 1941. *1941!* It stuns me. The guy was so insightful. He was the only one in that era who was aware. He had no mentor. There was no one pointing the way for him. At twenty, he recognized comics as an art form. I don't think anyone else thought it was more than disposable, throwaway entertainment. This guy is an art god. And he is so cool."

When Eisner received the 2001 Sparky Lifetime Achievement Award from the Cartoon Art Museum in San Francisco (named for "Peanuts" cartoonist Charles Schulz), he was the first artist outside of the western United States to be so honored.

"Our board felt that the time was right to expand it beyond the West Coast," said Museum Curator Jenny Dietzen. "Will Eisner's name was the first one mentioned. He was honored not only for his work as a creator but also for his work as an advocate for the art form, which has been tireless. He's been around for the entire life of the comic book industry. What he's done for it is really phenomenal."

Other winners include "Peanuts" creator Charles Schulz (the first recipient and the artist for whom the award is named), "Bugs Bunny" creator Chuck Jones, *Toy Story* creator John Lasseter, *MAD* magazine artist Sergio Aragonés, "Donald Duck" artist Carl Barks, "Brenda Starr" cartoonist Dale Messick, and Marvel Comics' legend Stan Lee.

"It's quite an illustrious group of people," Dietzen said.

Eisner's renown is even stronger outside the United States, according to Professor Lucy Caswell, curator of the Cartoon Research Library at Ohio State University.

"That he is so well known internationally says there is merit in what he has done," she said. "We've had international film crews come here to do documentaries on Will. The queries we receive about Will are mostly international. It blows me away."

Being rediscovered in his fifties, after two full careers, and enjoying new fruits of his labors in acclaim and remuneration made Eisner's third act the greatest of his career.

"What was most wonderful," Ann Eisner said of her husband's career, "was that Will could make a living at what he loved doing. He never had to do anything else."

Through the years, the Eisners, like anyone else, went through some periods where they needed to economize. But it never bothered them.

Yesteryear No. 59
(Courtesy Denis Kitchen)

Eisner would tell his wife, "I can always do something to make money." And he always found a way. He was a highly principled person who frequently turned down jobs when they failed to challenge his creative side.

"I was so proud of him," Ann said. "Mostly I was proud of the way he handled the attention he got at comic book conventions. He didn't need to do what other people did, such as saying, 'I did this, I did that,' or, 'I'm wonderful!' He had enough confidence to be himself. He was just gracious about things; he was just a good human being."

Fans often approached Eisner through Ann. "Young guys would say, 'Will Mr. Eisner sign an autograph?' I was a patsy for that," Ann said.

At the same time, Eisner discontinued the practice of drawing sketches for fans meeting him at conventions. The righteousness of this decision was confirmed when he gave a university talk several years ago. A ten-year-old boy came up to him and innocently said, "Mr. Eisner you're the best, will you draw me a picture?" And, of course, Eisner did. Then he went on speaking with other people. As he left the lecture hall, he saw a crowd gathered around the boy, who was standing on a chair, auctioning off Eisner's drawing to the highest bidder.

"That's it!" Eisner snapped in disgust.

═══════════════

Another incident occurred in 1973, when Eisner attended Cosmocon, a comic book convention at York University in Toronto, although the result was different. He met a young man there named Dave Sim, who in 1977 would launch his own independent comic book universe featuring an aardvark named Cerebus.

But, thirty years ago, Sim was a typical fan, publishing a fanzine called *Now & Then* with one of his buddies. In one issue, they interviewed idiosyncratic *Creepy* and *Eerie* magazine writer T. Casey Brennan. Brennan said something in the interview about how, if you show violence in a comic book, you should show the *results* of the violence. Brennan said there shouldn't be bloodless comic books. Trying to be a little more innovative than most fanzine material, Sim took that quote and showed it to artists attending Cosmocon and solicited their response.

"I saw Will Eisner talking to somebody," Sim said, "and I thought, *Man, wouldn't it be a coup to get Will Eisner to read this and get his side of it?*"

Holding Brennan's quote on a piece of paper in hand, Sim walked over to Eisner. But Eisner, pulling his arm up into his suit jacket, said, "I left my right hand at home." He thought Sim was asking him for a free sketch. He wasn't doing sketches any more.

"No, no, no!" Sim said.

He explained about the Brennan quote and asked for Eisner's opinion. "The funniest thing was that he took the piece of paper in his left hand and was reading it and was so completely engrossed, he didn't notice that he hadn't put his right arm back down again. So he was standing there reading it with his arm hiked up into his jacket. I am sure there must have been a half dozen people who went, 'That's Will Eisner. Why is he standing there with his arm hiked up into his jacket?' Or, 'I hope Will didn't lose his right hand.'"

A year or two later, Eisner returned to Cosmocon. This time, he spotted Sim first and did something completely Eisner-esque.

"Hi, I'm Will Eisner," he said, putting out his right hand. "Do you remember me?"

Dave Stevens (*The Rocketeer*) designed this ad for a "Spirit" T-shirt. Originally published in Kitchen Sink Press' *Spirit* magazine in August 1982, it also launched Bob Chapman's Graphitti Designs company

(Courtesy Bob Chapman)

In some ways, Bob Chapman owes the success of his business, Graphitti Designs, to Will Eisner.

His screen-printing company produced its first comic book inspired T-shirts in February 1982. There were few shirts being mass produced for comics at the time, as hard as that may be to believe today. One of Chapman's T-shirts featured Dave Stevens' Rocketeer, another featured Will Eisner's Spirit. It was the best of the new and the best of the old.

"I didn't know what the hell I was doing," Chapman said. "I played the learn-as-you-go system. I got on the phone with Will and told him what I wanted to do. He was intrigued and receptive; here was a character (The Spirit) that was forty years old and he had never been on a T-shirt. I had met these other people in comics and never been impressed with their business savvy. Will was way smarter. There wasn't any haggling; Will set the tone and I followed his lead."

The initial one thousand Spirit shirts sold out at $8.95 each, thanks to an ad drawn by Stevens in Kitchen Sink's *Spirit* comics.

But ... the source artwork that Eisner provided Chapman for the shirt was not his best work.

"Will provided three or four pictures that I didn't like," Chapman said. "But I didn't have the balls to tell Will. They looked like they came from a coloring book! The lines were too thick; it didn't best represent Will's work. Dave Stevens was the troublemaker in this. I showed him the art that Will provided and Dave said, 'They're crap.' They were derivative of Will's Warren work. I don't think Will knew what I was looking for. I was in an awkward position; I had to find a way around what Will gave me. Then I found a back door: Dave and I found something in a Kitchen Sink magazine that was classic Spirit. We were able to lift that from the book, shoot it, and clean it up. I said, 'Will, we feel this design would be a better design.' I didn't tell him the truth about the others. But for Will, that was fine. He didn't want to create a new piece of artwork; he wanted to use existing material."

Chapman crossed a professional threshold when he signed a contract with Eisner.

"Here was somebody who had every right not to talk to me," Chapman said. "I don't know why Will gave me the opportunity. But he did. I was thirty years old. Will set the tone—you can do business and mutually exploit other people and enjoy it. It was a wonderful foundation. And all of a sudden I had a degree of implied legitimacy. I was dealing with Will Eisner! When I called Milton Caniff or Jack Kirby, I was legitimate all of a sudden—and that was as far from the truth as was possible!"

———

Finding reasons to reprint old *Spirit* adventures isn't difficult—the art is outstanding and stands alone, while the stories hold up well to generational changes sixty years after they first appeared.

What might seem tougher to explain is the reappearance of a minor Eisner character that most readers only know *as* the Spirit.

Eisner, who recycled nearly everything he touched, created John Law in the spitting image of the Spirit. So much so that when the first four John Law stories—created for Eisner's short-lived comic book line in 1948—went unpublished, he erased Law's badge, pasted the Spirit's mask over Law's eye patch, and no one was the wiser. ("Meet John Law" became the two-part, January 8 and 15, 1950 *Spirit* sections "Sand Saref";

"Ratt Gutt" became a Spirit adventure titled "Ratt Trapp" on January 29, 1950; "The Half-Dead Mr. Lox" was published on February 19, 1950, converting the character of Nubbin the Shoeshine Boy into Willum Waif; and the final reworking of a Law story was "The Jewel of Gizeh" on March 12, 1950.) Cat Yronwode and Dean Mullaney collected the unaltered stories as the one-shot comic *John Law, Detective* at Eclipse Comics in 1983.

In 1998, fifty years after John Law's first publication, an Australian writer/artist named Gary Chaloner was commissioned to do a story for what would have been the ninth issue of *The Spirit: The New Adventures*. But when that title was canceled after eight issues, Chaloner pulled a stunt only Will Eisner could love: he turned a Spirit story into a John Law tale.

When he first approached Eisner for permission to revive John Law, a series of overseas telephone calls ensued. The two men already enjoyed a friendship dating back to an Eisner appearance at the Sydney Opera House for a 1986 Australian comic book convention. Chaloner, who was launching his own Cyclone Comics line at the time, became Eisner's accidental chaperone. Years later, when Eisner authorized Chaloner to revive John Law, he signed off by saying, "We better watch out Gary— if we're not careful, we just might do something good here."

Why bring back a character most people didn't know was missing in the first place?

"I was attracted to the possibilities of picking up where Will left off in 1948," Chaloner said. "The basics were there for a good character. It's as simple as that. Will had produced four tales featuring Law that were eventually turned into *Spirit* stories. These stories also covered Law/Colt's origin and have become classic and much loved *Spirit* stories.

"Those stories are *Spirit* stories now, but back when they were originally produced, they were Law stories ... classic Law stories! You can't hide the fact that Will was on a roll when he wrote and produced that stuff. *The Spirit* strip received the benefit of them in the end, but it's a testament to the initial Law concept that those four stories are so fondly remembered."

For Chaloner, turning his *New Spirit Adventures* stories into John Law episodes was a bit of justice. Comic book karma came full circle.

Robert Overstreet commissioned Eisner to draw the cover of his 1976 *Overstreet Comic Book Price Guide*, over the publisher's objections. It doubled sales from the previous year

"Like Will did so many years earlier with his Law stories," Chaloner said, "I wasn't going to let a perfectly good story go to waste."

The new *John Law* was first published in a new medium, another typical move for an Eisner character. Chaloner launched his Law strip on the Internet, as a subscription-only feature on www.ModernTales.com. *John Law* didn't appear in print until after it established an online following.

"I don't think this *John Law* project would have gotten off the ground at all if it weren't for the Internet and e-mail," Chaloner said. "E-mail made communicating with Will that much easier, while the Net provided the perfect kick-start for the series. I hate to think how I would have gotten anywhere without it."

In the development stages of the series, there was a time when every idea Chaloner proffered was beaten into print by another creator or publisher. For a time, he thought *John Law* would be a modern day crime series with a supernatural twist. But at the time, "every man and his dog seemed to be releasing supernatural-cop comics," Chaloner said.

Disheartened, Chaloner e-mailed Eisner for his thoughts.

"Don't worry about what anyone else is doing," Eisner wrote back. "Have faith in your ideas and the end result will stand for itself. You can't control what other creators are doing, so don't waste time worrying about it."

Interestingly, the only guidelines Eisner insisted on for *John Law* was that the character be as different from Denny Colt and The Spirit as possible. The rest was basically up to Chaloner, because the character came with little back-story. Chaloner kept the patch over Law's left eye, but put the character in gray suits rather than the Spirit's rich blue. He also made Law taller and broader than Denny Colt. Finally, he moved Law's base from New York to the West Coast.

"Will wasn't shy in coming forward about sequences or layouts that he thought could be improved," Chaloner said. "He was always ready with suggestions and was always just an e-mail away if I needed advice. Hey, I would have been crazy *not* to pick the brain of a storytelling master like Will. Will advised me to keep the stories 'human', so I've tried hard to make the new stories about people ... about Law the man ... not a police procedural. Telling human stories is an Eisner trademark, so I'm more than happy keeping that tradition for John Law."

During the 1970s, the best-known name in comic book fan circles was Robert Overstreet, creator and publisher of the *Official Overstreet Comic Book Price Guide*. Overstreet's book is the most comprehensive, authoritative resource for comic book prices.

And Overstreet is a big Will Eisner fan. So much of a fan, in fact, that for the 1976 edition of his price guide, Overstreet hired Eisner to draw the book's prestigious cover, the second professional artist to do so (Eisner's onetime protégée, Joe Kubert, was the first).

"When I was young and learning to draw, I went to school on Eisner," Overstreet said. "I called him and asked what he'd charge. I didn't know if I could afford him. He said, 'What do you normally pay?' And that's what he charged me—$300."

The 1976 edition, Overstreet's sixth, was the first distributed in bookstores. By a coincidence, Overstreet and Eisner shared a common publisher, Crown, which published Eisner's *Gleeful Guides*.

"When they saw the cover to my new price guide, they called and told me that Will's cookbooks did not sell," Overstreet said. "They worried that with Will's cover art, this would not sell either. They told me to call him and ask if I could take his name off the cover. I called him on Christmas Eve, 1975. His name was on the cover twice. They wanted one removed. Will said, 'That's okay, go ahead.' And then I didn't do it. The book sold fine. In fact, our circulation doubled—we sold more than forty thousand copies that year. It put the price guide on the map."

Eisner did this sketch as a surprise for Diamond Comics Distributors' Steve Geppi
(Courtesy Steve Geppi)

The most powerful man in comic book publishing is in Will Eisner's corner.

But before Steve Geppi built Diamond Comics Distributors, Gemstone, Alliance Game Distributors, Diamond Galleries, and became a minority owner of the Baltimore Orioles, he spent five years (1969-75) as a mailman.

Geppi was born in 1952, the same year that Eisner stopped producing *The Spirit* sections. But in his early years in the comic book industry, he stumbled upon someone with a great collection of *Spirit* sections. He eventually bought them for his own.

Then, inexplicably, he sold the collection to Bob Overstreet. And then he bought it back—plus a second set. But the original newspaper sections were too valuable to actually read, so Geppi and his friend Kim Weston started making two sets of color photocopies of each section so they could each have a set for reading. Every week, Weston took a few originals from Geppi's home in Maryland into Washington, DC, and made copies.

"This took forever!" Geppi recalled. "I wanted my originals, but I wanted a set I could actually hold. So we bootlegged *The Spirit* for two! That's how much I loved Will."

(By the time they finally finished making copies, DC Comics had begun printing *The Spirit Archives,* rendering the whole exercise moot.)

Over the years, Geppi took retailer and convention organizer Phil Seuling's original idea of a direct sales channel for comic books—targeting distribution straight from publishers into comic book specialty stores and to mail order businesses—and grew his company, Diamond, into a virtual monopoly. No other distributor comes close to the power and reach of Geppi's operation, which has grown beyond distribution into publishing, valuation, and professional sports.

What does all this have to do with the U.S. Postal Service?

After years of success in comic book distribution, Geppi's employees—who knew of the special place in his heart for Eisner—commissioned the artist to do a special illustration of the boss. Eisner produced a full-color image of Geppi as a super mailman, bursting in to save the Spirit, who was tied up and left for dead (as usual) by the bad guys.

"Tell you what Spirit," Geppi said in the watercolor drawing, "I'll save you if you'll help me build a distribution business!!"

Geppi saw to it that every employee received a print. The original hangs in the Diamond lobby.

———

Of course, not everything Eisner touched during the period in which the public rediscovered him turned into gold.

After he illustrated a tennis story for *Esquire* in 1977, he was approached by a syndicate interested in a daily strip built around a sports-oriented family. "The Joggs" was closer to his work for the Department of Labor than *The Spirit*. It was forced, stiff, and ultimately forgettable.

———

Naming someone the "most influential" anything shouldn't be done lightly. When *Wizard Magazine* decided in May 2002 that the time was right for naming "The 10 Most Influential Artists in Comics," a six-man committee of editors and writers started by throwing out fifty names, then quickly culled the list by half.

"Then we got down to rankings," said Jim McLauchlin, who was a writer and editor with the magazine for ten years before taking the job of editor in chief of Top Cow comics in 2003. "The thing we agreed on right off the bat was that number one was either Will Eisner or Jack Kirby. After thirty more minutes, we agreed number one was Eisner. That was the easiest part of that process. Eisner. Bam! *Next!*"

Here's how the magazine justified its top pick:

When comics started, the recipe was simple: "Put words and pictures on paper." Pretty much everything after that was the invention of Will Eisner.

Bob Jones sent Eisner this photograph in 1989 showing someone painted "The Spirit" on the Berlin Wall
(Courtesy Will and Ann Eisner)

The irony of Eisner topping that list and also subsequently being dubbed "Granddaddy of the Graphic Novel" was that his later work rarely received the kind of press in *Wizard* that a new project by Alan Moore or Frank Miller might. Some people believed that the magazine didn't care about what *was*, only what is, particularly what Marvel and DC publish.

"I can't tell you how many times I've had to listen to stupid crap like that," McLauchlin said. "Read the magazine. Is there a monthly ten-page article on the grandeur of Will Eisner? No, there's not. But in the list of the ten most influential artists, there he is. In the fifty great moments, there he is again, three or four times."

McLauchlin was a little biased. He had a small stack of handwritten letters from Eisner, sent over the years in response to stories McLauchlin wrote for *Wizard*. He always flagged positive stories or comments about creators and sent them copies. Some replied; most didn't. Eisner always wrote back.

"Will was one of those people who could have been stuck in the past, but he wasn't. His ideas were always fresh. His thought processes were new. If you talked to him on the phone, you wouldn't know if he was twenty, forty, or sixty. He topped himself with every project," McLauchlin said. "In the comic book world, there were only two instances when I geeked. Those were the first time I talked to Gil Kane and the first time I spoke to Will Eisner. They were goose-bump moments. Obviously, the guy had life experience. You can put yours and mine together, multiply it, and not match his. Every time I talked to Will Eisner, I couldn't help but smile. And I hung up the phone in a warm afterglow and went, 'That was cool.'"

Will Eisner at a Brazilian celebration of his career, October 1999
(Courtesy Will and Ann Eisner)

Wizard Publisher Gareb Shamus was another Eisner fan. But what surprised him was discovering, early on in the magazine's existence, was that Eisner was a fan of *his*.

"Will was such an insightful guy," Shamus said. "His whole life was dedicated to promoting comic books, storytelling, and getting people interested in the medium. Here came *Wizard*—there wasn't another product like it. He was so appreciative of a *Wizard* coming along to get people interested in the field. Will Eisner and Stan Lee so appreciated what we did because we got people excited. Will ... loved seeing the vibrancy of our industry through our eyes. I never thought a guy like him thought about us that way. I was trying to bow down to him and he reciprocated. It was so complimentary."

In the late 1980s, DC Comics hosted an educational seminar for everyone in the comics industry. It paid Eisner for conducting a two-hour session in a *Time* magazine conference room on how to do comics. More than two hundred people were in the audience as Eisner drew sketches on an overhead projector, explaining as he drew.

Mike Gold, who helped organize the event said, "There was that magic moment when you realized that here was a guy who has forgotten more than I'll ever know."

———

Brazilian documentary filmmaker Marisa Furtado de Oliveira was introduced to *The Spirit* by a boyfriend in 1986, when it returned to print in her native Brazil in *Gibi*, a black-and-white publication with covers done by Brazilian artists. "I liked so much the stories and the shades and fluid art, so well done and unique," she said. "It was a big surprise to me when later on, I found out that it was originally published in color. I still prefer them in black and white."

Five years later, she bought a magazine with a story featuring Eisner's work about astrology. Furtado not only recognized Eisner's style but herself in the way his work described her birth sign Aries. The text said "Aries girls love to be hairdressers," and in a funny drawing he showed a girl burning a woman's hair. (At the time, Furtado was a hairdresser.)

Later that year she produced an art installation in a bar in Copacabana, a mural covering the roof, the walls, and the doors. It included a massive collage of three hundred comic book characters. A friend, Heitor Pitombo, loaned her several magazines for reference. Pitombo was working on a big comic book project himself, organizing the First International Comix Biannual, a festival that included seventeen museums in Rio de Janeiro.

"Will Eisner is coming!" Pitombo told her, full of excitement. "Moebius and Bill Sienkiewicz, too!"

"Who is taking care of the reception of the foreigners?" Furtado asked.

Third from left: Ann Eisner, Will Eisner, and Marisa Furtado de Oliveira at a comics festival in Brazil
(Courtesy Will and Ann Eisner)

"Nobody—until now," Pitombo said.

Furtado saw an opportunity and grabbed it. Fluent in French, Spanish, English, and Portuguese, she was a natural choice.

"The night before Eisner's arrival, I couldn't sleep. I was so excited!" she recalled. "Of course, as the head of the reception group, I charged myself with escorting Will and Ann during their visit. We spent four incredible days together. My friendship not only with Will but with Ann Eisner, also, started after our first shaking hands."

Eisner was well known in Brazil; his work has been faithfully published in South America since the 1940s. At the 1991 Festival in Rio, Eisner spent three hours signing books for his fans, enchanting them with his gracious and sympathetic attitude. Each person received a personalized autograph, a word of thanks, and a handshake.

"I was twenty-eight years old and got tired much before him," Furtado said.

When the festival ended, Furtado and the Eisners continued their friendship by mail, with Ann inviting Furtado to visit them in Florida. In 1992, Furtado took them up on their hospitality. She also visited Denis Kitchen at his Wisconsin farm, where Kitchen Sink Press was then based. (Kitchen was recently divorced and Furtado's visit was, in part, a sly attempt at matchmaking on Ann Eisner's part. But Ann's timing was off. Kitchen had just met Stacey Pollard, who would become his new wife.) Furtado availed herself of Kitchen's deep Eisner archive and his catalog of Eisnerania, providing a more personal tour of Eisner's work than Will himself could do.

Around the time of Eisner's eightieth birthday, in March 1997, Furtado decided to produce a pilot about comics for Brazilian TV. Her partner at the time, TV scriptwriter Paulo Serran, suggested they do an Eisner documentary. That May, by luck, Eisner alerted Furtado that he would return to Brazil for an international comic book convention in Belo Horizonte.

"We went there ten days before Will and Ann arrived and built two sets for the main interview that I conducted with Will. I also interviewed many other artists at that convention—Brazilians and Europeans—about Will's body of work, and his influence on theirs," Furtado said.

That material—which included an Art Spiegelman interview conducted while he was in Rio—was enough to produce the pilot, and, as Furtado and Serran found more money, they traveled to the United States for interviews with American artists such as Jerry Robinson, Bill Sienkiewicz, Denis Kitchen, Lucy Caswell (head of Cartoon Research Library at Ohio State University), Thomas Inge (professor in Massachusetts), Pete Eisner, and Ann Eisner. The three-part documentary—released on DVD in the United States in 2005 under the title *Will Eisner Profession: Cartoonist*—is remarkable for its interviews, Eisner-influenced sets, and the way Furtado animated scenes from a wide variety of Eisner's body of graphic work, which earned it an award from the Brazilian Cartoonist Society. It is a rare and insightful peek into the Eisner world.

Many Brazilian artists—not only in comics but also in theater, music, and movies—have publicly acknowledged Eisner's influence upon their work. Here is an excerpt from an essay by famous Brazilian children's comics author Mauricio de Sousa:

> *The first time I became aware of Will's work, I was eight years old. I was beginning to like comics, learning to read ... The narrative took my attention, the different way of storytelling that Will used in making* The Spirit. *It was a police story; no way it was for children. But I liked it very much, nevertheless.*
>
> *These stories were published in* Gibi, *a thrice-weekly publication, in stores all over the country. And on the last page of* Gibi, *The Spirit story was printed.*
>
> *I liked it so much that I cut it out very carefully. I collected them, made a little album. Using school paper, I made a cover and sewed it on. I drew a title on the cover and this was my special collection of* Spirit *comics.*

SEVENTEEN
School of Visual Arts

William Eisner took care of his family from the time he was thirteen. When he did things for people, in his own way, he never expected anything in return. The stories of his assisting young artists are legendary.

So are the tales that students tell from his seventeen years at New York's prestigious School of Visual Arts.

In the early 1970s, the School of Visual Arts (SVA) was a trade school with a reputation for training generations of art directors and technically proficient graphic designers.

"I went there because when I was a kid and read the bios of artists that I admired, they all said they went there," said artist and writer Batton Lash (*Supernatural Law*), a student of Eisner's at SVA.

In 1974, Marvel Comics' longtime secretary "Fabulous" Flo Steinberg recommended to John Holmstrom that he attend either the Rhode Island School of Design or the School of Visual Arts, which was founded by Burne Hogarth and Silas Rhodes. SVA won out when he learned that two of his heroes, Steve Ditko and Wally Wood, both went there.

But once enrolled, Holmstrom discovered the school didn't actually teach the art and business of comic books.

"There were a couple guys there, including myself, who petitioned the school to start comic art classes. They weren't doing it and a bunch of us weren't happy," Holmstrom said.

They approached Alumni Director Tom Gill, who had worked on a strip himself and was only too happy to help.

"Who do you want?" he asked.

With no names beyond their reach in the greater New York metropolitan area, Pomerance, Holmstrom, and the others presented a dream list of teaching candidates. At the top of the list were Will Eisner and Harvey Kurtzman.

"We were dumbfounded when the school said yes. And they landed the two greatest cartoonists of all time!" Holmstrom said. "We were thrilled."

Around that time, Holmstrom met Lash, a native of Brooklyn. They became fast friends.

"Batton was a charming guy. You couldn't find a nicer guy," Holmstrom said. "He was one of the first people I met when I came to New York from Cheshire, Connecticut. I didn't know a soul in New York. We became great friends because we were both nuts about comics and Steve Ditko in particular."

And they both couldn't believe their luck in being art students at a school where Eisner and Kurtzman would soon be among their teachers. "I knew the gravity of that," Lash said. "I knew about Kurtzman and *MAD;* the *Spirit* wasn't around at that time, but I knew Will's influence. When I read bios of other cartoonists, they all mentioned him."

(Eisner remembered the timeline slightly differently. He recalled Silas Rhodes inviting him to lunch and inviting him then to teach. Later the next semester, Eisner said, he nominated Harvey Kurtzman to join the faculty.)

That July, Eisner did something that further impressed Lash and Holmstrom. He sent personal letters to all his students inviting them to a meeting at his Park Avenue office.

"I remember going into his huge office where he had a huge desk and wood paneling," Holmstrom said. "He was the nicest guy you could imagine."

"We had no idea what to expect," Lash said. "What shocked me and John was that only five or six people showed up. We were expecting twenty-five to thirty, at least! It was exciting to have that audience. We sat in his outer office, waiting. Then Eisner came out. He took a chair, spun it around, and sat like a coach talking to his team. He told us he wanted to duplicate a shop where he would overlook all of us working on stories, kibitz, and show us how it's done.

"We were impressed that he reached out to this extent," Lash said. "When the class started, it was friendly hellos, but we couldn't trade on that orientation. It was, 'I'm glad you showed up, but let's get to work. There was a curtain. You never got too close to him.'"

Holmstrom sensed that some of Eisner's steeliness was caused by the reality of facing a bunch of scruffy, counterculture art types every week. "I think Harvey and Will were both nervous. Neither had done this before."

The SVA building where Eisner taught was the school's main building on East 23rd Street. His classroom was on the second floor, just atop the staircase, and a few feet away from the student lounge. Graphic design legend Milton Glazer taught in the same classroom at night.

Eisner's first class began with thirty students. After the first week it was down to nineteen. "I had no academic background," Eisner said. "Silas Rhodes said, 'We don't want teachers. You're known to run a shop and train guys.' And that's the way I ran my class. I never graded students. My operation was pass/fail. If you didn't show up three or four times, you failed. As long as you showed up, no matter how good or bad, as long as you kept doing the work, you passed."

Kurtzman's class was the complete opposite of Eisner's.

"Harvey invited some students to his home," Lash said. "Harvey was a little more open to being manipulated than Will was. I say that with all due respect. When I saw Will work a room, he knew how to weed out the wise guys and quiet the boisterous heckler. And he was like this in class. I think all students are undisciplined, loud, and irreverent. But there was this underlying respect for Will. When he spoke, you listened. Sometimes, Harvey's class was like *Animal House*. Everybody talked at once. I can imagine how Will's real shop was run. The guys were always bullshitting, but when Will came to the door, they ran back to their pages."

Guest speakers were a regular occurrence in the class. The first year they included Mike Ploog, Gil Kane, and then-DC Vice President of

Operations Sol Harrison. Later, Eisner's class hosted artist/writer Frank Miller and renowned French cartoonist Jacques Tardi.

One memorable student in class with Holmstrom and Lash "thought he was Batman," Holmstrom said. "He walked around with a utility belt. He kept his art supplies in there. He drew a bat symbol on his shirt. And every time he got an assignment, he drew Batman."

He also harassed guest Sol Harrison about the way DC handled Batman.

"Write a letter," Eisner told the student.

Most of the people in Eisner's class arrived wanting to work for Marvel and DC. But Eisner wasn't interested in that. He talked about European comics and European artists. He talked about a day in the future when comics artists would own their work. It frustrated some students whose attitude was, "Just tell us how to draw Superman!"

One day he talked about the medium as the message.

"It's not the draftsmanship that is so important," he said. "One Robert Crumb is worth a dozen Frank Frazettas to me—even though I admire Frazetta." (Frazetta, who started his career drawing romance comic books, is best known for his fantasy and sword 'n' sorcery paintings.)

Lash recalled that moment like it happened yesterday.

"The kid next to me was about to pass out," he recalled. "Will said the most blasphemous thing! He slammed the kid's idol, and the kid wasn't in class the next week."

Eisner's point—clearly lost on some—was that it was what Crumb was saying in his work that made him important. Frazetta, he said, was a brilliant painter.

"People think you're born with talent," Holmstrom said. "But this was like boot camp, and Will was the drill sergeant. Batton and I did twice as much work as we were assigned because we wanted to soak up the opportunity."

Eisner was a hard taskmaster. He was critical, especially of weak storytelling. And it could be tough getting him to say something nice about your work.

Will Eisner's Gallery of New Comics 1974
(Courtesy Batton Lash)

SVA was a bastion of underground thought and creative tension in the late 1960s and early 1970s. Over the years, the school has trained creative luminaries such as Chris Stein, cofounder of the punk band Blondie, and pop artist Keith Haring. When Holmstrom and Lash attended, there was a great commingling of punk fashion, punk rock music, and underground comix, as well as the mainstream arts. Some instructors were only a few years removed from keeping jars of pot in the art supply cabinets. "They taught street fighting for the demonstrations," Holmstrom said. "It was a weird school. The first year, when Batton and I took this English class, a teacher showed us a weird film. At the end, he mixed in a beaver shot and the Three Stooges. That's when things started to change; the teacher got fired for doing it. There were some conservative types who said, 'We came to learn, not for this.'"

What, exactly, did one do in a Will Eisner comics class?

There was a reason the class was organized like a bullpen. Each semester, the class was assigned the production of a comic book anthology. The first edition of *Will Eisner's Gallery of New Comics* featured stories and art by Lash, Ken Laager, Bob Wiacek (who became a top-flight comic book inker, eventually working with Neal Adams), and many others.

"It was awesome," Holmstrom said. "I was editor of the second issue and actually got to finish the drawing Will did for the cover. I finished the bricks and filled in the blacks. I was thrilled."

Along the way, Eisner provided his students with feedback by putting their work on an overhead projector and pointing out the flaws and possible points of correction.

"It turned everything I knew about comics inside out, upside down," Lash said. "I discovered comics were hard work. Some people in class were a little intimidated. Most thought they were going to learn to draw Spider-Man. No matter what I brought in, it was shot down. 'The anatomy's weak.' 'You're too ambitious here.' 'Embrace your strengths!' It sounds harsh, but that's the way it was. And Holmstrom and I were the savvy ones! With nineteen people in the class, by the time Will got to the tenth person, the critiquing got skimpy. We noticed that the first five people got the best critiques. We never wanted to be first, but second or third.

"It was like we did a tour of duty," Lash continued. "I don't want to give the impression he was General Patton. He ran a tight ship, but it was still informal."

Lash didn't recall Eisner ever drawing the Spirit in class, although the instructor's stick figures were always better than most. Lash even kept one as a souvenir. "Not because it was worth something," he explained, "but even then I thought, *One day I will look back on this and feel very fortunate to be in this class.*"

(When Gil Kane did a chalk talk in Kurtzman's class, he did one paper sketch for demonstration purposes. But when he was done, Kane put it in his briefcase. "You guys are not getting this one!" he said.)

———

Despite copying the mass-manufacturing design of the Eisner & Iger Studio, Will wasn't interested in training SVA students as factory workers. "I'm here to train you to tell a better story and package it better," he told them. "I'm not here to help you get a job at Marvel or DC." As far as he was concerned, the major comic book publishers were cranking out sausages, not art. He always thought comics had a higher calling and he would lecture his students about where comics were going. "Nostalgia is for chumps," he said. "You should look ahead. When I look back, all I can think is that the bathroom situation is so much better today!"

"He would talk about what we know now as the graphic novel—bigger books, more pages," Lash said.

Lash and Holmstrom were as hip and antiestablishment as anyone in the school, but they couldn't deny how cool it was being in classes taught by Eisner and Kurtzman. But that worship provoked two different reactions. Eisner saw something special in Holmstrom. And while he wasn't prone to favoring one student over another, Holmstrom certainly gained his respect.

Eisner's reaction to Lash was decidedly different.

"John and I were like Frick and Frack in Eisner's class; we were like Gallant and Doofus," Lash said. "John was doing everything right and I couldn't do *anything* right. Will was very patient with me. I could tell I was not destined for greatness."

Lash was in Eisner's class every Thursday morning. And every Thursday afternoon, he took a video production class.

At the end of each semester, Will scheduled a sit-down with each student, asking them, "What do you want to do?" and then critiquing each one. When Lash's turn came, he was ready with his answer.

"I came to be a cartoonist," he said.

"Well," Eisner said, "I know you're doing this funny video (a student musical of George Romero's cult horror film *Night of the Living Dead*). That may be your thing; cartooning may not be your forte."

Needless to say, Lash was crushed. "But I could tell during the year that my work was not resonating with Will. He saw that I was working but also saw that I had strength in other areas. He said, 'You always have ideas. But maybe filmmaking or stage work is where you belong.'"

But Lash's story had a happy ending; Eisner's constructive criticism encouraged him to settle down by the end of the year and focus his talents in different directions.

"Will's advice forced me to expand my horizons and broaden them," Lash said. "That summer, I stopped buying comics—except *The Spirit* reprints. Now that I didn't have to face Will every Thursday, I could appreciate the line work, how the story was told. Every story was a different approach. The small stories became big stories when you thought about them."

For the next six years, Lash steered clear of comic books. After graduating, he took on various art-related jobs, including doing paste-ups for an ad agency and being comic book artist Howard Chaykin's assistant. As a freelance illustrator, Lash did drawings for *Garbage* magazine, a children's workbook, the book *Rock 'n' Roll Confidential,* a reconstructive surgery firm, and other projects. He also created courtroom graphics and prepared charts for *The New York Daily News* advertising deparment for sales meetings and in-house presentations.

"Looking back, that six-year period was the best thing that ever happened to me," he said. "Part of the problem with the comic book industry is that a fan becomes an assistant editor, then an editor, or a freelancer. Their whole life revolves around comics. They have a very narrow vision of what comics can be. They're like career politicians who go to law school, intern for a congressman, then become a congressman. They're totally removed from the real world."

In 1979, Lash found himself back at the drawing board drawing his own comics again. He made an immediate splash with "Wolff & Byrd, Counselors of the Macabre," which ran in *The Brooklyn Paper* until 1996 and in *The National Law Journal* from 1983 to 1997. Eisner was never far from his thoughts.

"When I started doing my own strip, I took *The Spirit* approach. I did each story differently than the one ahead of it," Lash said.

Since May 1994, Wolff & Byrd have held court in their own bimonthly comic book, now titled *Supernatural Law* and self-published by Lash and his wife Jackie Estrada's company, Exhibit A Press. The same year that Lash began *Supernatural Law,* he also wrote one of the most bizarre comic book stories in the medium's history, *Archie Meets The Punisher,* a crossover between Archie Comics and Marvel Comics.

One of the greatest examples of how far Batton Lash traveled from Eisner telling him in 1974 that maybe he should think about a career outside of comics was his two Eisner nominations for his work on the comic book version of *Wolff & Byrd, Counselors of the Macabre.* (It was an anomaly that Lash was even nominated, actually, because his wife Jackie Estrada is not only the administrator of the awards but the co-publisher, editor, and letterer of the comic. "That would be a conflict of interest," she said. "That one year, the judges overruled me and decided that Batton deserved nominations in two categories: Writer/Artist-Humor and Talent Deserving of Wider Recognition. These were nominations specifically for him, and not the book.")

"When my first collection came out," Lash said, "I was a little nervous, but I sent it to Will and he sent me a really nice note and a blurb to help sell the book. He said, 'I am so pleased for you—and that you didn't give up.' Since then, he's been a major, major supporter of mine. I'm always pumped up when he says, 'I like what you're doing.' I feel I'm still in his class, showing him the new assignment."

⸻

John Holmstrom's life was never the same after meeting Will Eisner, either.

After his second semester with Eisner and Kurtzman, Holmstrom had financial issues and decided to leave SVA. Kurtzman, believing that Holmstrom was ready to be a professional cartoonist, even set him up with a job interview. "Nobody ever asks if you have a degree for cartoon jobs," Holmstrom said. "It was enough to say I was working with Will and Harvey."

As it turned out, Eisner hired his student as an office assistant.

"Will paid me the minimum wage," Holmstrom said. "He basically rescued me from being homeless. It wasn't much, but it enabled me to get an apartment in Brooklyn. I almost was homeless, in fact. I was about to take another job when he called me. I think he created work for me so I wouldn't be homeless. I swept the floors, took out the garbage. I converted a storage room into shipping. If I put together a package, he would tell me how to do it and he would criticize me for doing it wrong. That came in handy because how you present stuff in the mail is important."

It was an exciting place to be, Holmstrom said.

"I made friends with his receptionist. She looked out for me," he said. "Once while I was there she was all excited because Pete Hamill was interviewing Will. And one day, William Friedkin was there, talking about making a movie of *The Spirit*."

As important as Eisner became in Holmstrom's life, he remained an enigma despite being with Eisner day after day. "I didn't know anything about his family," Holmstrom said. "The conversation was always about technique and storytelling with Will. It was all business with Will. That and tennis. He was a fanatical tennis player."

After a year, it was time for Holmstrom to move on. His skill set dramatically grew under Will's continued tutelage. He thought his growth would come as an artist; in fact, he was one of the few people to cross paths with the legendary artist and come away enhanced and inspired by the man's business skills. Holmstrom took the summer off and hung out with friends from Cheshire, Ged Dunn and Legs McNeil. That detour, encouraged by Eisner, inadvertently led to the creation of *Punk Magazine*.

"So Will Eisner is like the founder of punk!" Holmstrom said.

"The Spirit is like the Iggy Pop of the cartoon world," said McNeil, whose career includes brilliant investigative reporting at *Spin* magazine and the book *Please Kill Me: The Uncensored Oral History of Punk Rock*. "And we were all very much into comics. Everyone was then. Chris Stein had his *Plastic Man* collection. Everybody had a favorite comic book back then. I had never seen *The Spirit;* John turned me on to Eisner, as he did Lenny Bruce and other things. He also taught me to write."

McNeil supports Holmstrom's contention that in some ways, Will Eisner was an inspiration to the punk scene.

"(Eisner) didn't think like the Establishment," McNeil said. "Punk used rock 'n' roll to talk about themes; Will used comics to talk about adult themes. It was like what we were doing."

Around the time *Punk Magazine* began, Eisner closed down the American Visuals office and stunned his former assistant by giving him his own desk as an office-warming present. Eisner said, "If you're going to start a magazine, you're going to need a solid desk."

"John was really, really proud of that. And I think we used Will's lawyer, too," McNeil said.

Punk had a distribution deal with *High Times* magazine, which, in turn, was distributed by Larry Flynt, publisher of *Hustler*. Those were different times, of course. "*Punk* was a way to get laid, get chicks, and get free beers," McNeil said. "I lived with Joey Ramone. Or stayed over all the time. We used to have Thanksgiving at the Kurtzmans. And Liz Kurtzman was a waitress at CBGBs."

(Later in his career, McNeil was assigned to interview Eisner for *High Times*. "I don't think I ever finished it because I got drunk," he said in typical McNeil fashion. "It was a very good interview. I'm sorry. I feel like an asshole.")

Holmstrom envisioned his new publication as something as different from *Rolling Stone* as punk itself was different from the Beatles. "I was trying to do a hybrid magazine, a new direction for the underground, something about music, comics, and photos," he said. "Will was always encouraging us. One of his favorite sayings was, 'You can't copyright an idea. And if you only have one idea, you'll go broke.' And Harvey said, 'The real money was in new ideas.' They were really happy with *Punk* and that I got off to a good start."

Holmstrom covered the punk scene and was a part of it. He designed the back cover and inside sleeve for The Ramones' *Rocket to Russia* album, and the front cover for their *Road to Ruin* LP. "They hired some expensive photographer to shoot the cover of their first album and didn't like it," Holmstrom said. "We did a magazine session with photographer Roberta Bailey and Legs McNeil and I set up the shot. That was the picture they used for the cover of the first Ramones record. *That* set the image of punk records.

"We defined what punk was," he continued. "We actually named it 'punk rock' and that stuck to it. That altered the way the world looked at the scene. People thought The Ramones were a novelty act. It wasn't until we started the magazine that people thought they innovated a whole new sound."

Punk Magazine was out of business four years after it began, publishing its last issue in 1979.

"It was a sad day years later when I called Will and said we were closing down the magazine," Holmstrom said. "He found someone for me to give the desk to. He also gave me a small bookcase that went with it. I still have that in my kitchen."

Holmstrom went through hard times after the magazine folded, but by 1987 his career was back on track. He became managing editor, then executive editor, at *High Times*.

"There are a lot of people out there who know who Will Eisner is, so I like to give my pedigree to people as often as possible. It's one of my proudest accomplishments, going to school with Eisner and Harvey Kurtzman and working for both of them," Holmstrom said. "Harvey got me the job at Scholastic that kept me alive for ten years. He also recommended me to draw a Woody Allen comic strip when it started, but the first issue of *Punk* had just come out. They offered a lot of money; it really would have helped *Punk* because we were always so broke.

"Eisner was like a football coach, like Bill Parcells," he continued. "After his team won, he was at his most critical. When the team lost, he gave it a light touch. Batton and I got more criticism because he knew we wanted to do this. And *working* for him wasn't any easier. He was a tough guy. He would drill his troops to be the absolute best. Yet I never saw him lose his temper or be overly harsh. He was never unprofessional or mean. He was never out of line. I learned more from Will and Harvey about how to act like a professional and deal with people. I did not come to this game with the best people skills, believe me."

━━━━━━━━

Geoffrey Notkin was born in New York City but grew up in South London, where he attended "a horrible, Dickensian place, a Church of England school" called Whitgift, where the students wore military uniforms. In 1972, when he was eleven, Notkin befriended one of the only other boys he met at the school who was a fellow comic book fan—Neil Gaiman.

"Neil was into DC, *Creepy,* and everything else. I was into Marvel Comics. I thought (Jack) Kirby was the best and I wanted to be a cartoonist. Neil and I became really close friends," Notkin said.

The duo even looked somewhat alike—same height, build, and similarly dark hair. People thought they were cousins. They sat together in the back of shared classes, Gaiman writing comic book stories and Notkin drawing the pictures. In art class, instructors assigned watercolor work; Notkin and Gaiman aped comic book artist Jim Steranko (*Nick Fury: Agent of S.H.I.E.L.D.*).

"You two will never amount to anything!" their art teachers said, frustrated. "Comic books are rubbish!"

Notkin remembered his friend as perpetually ahead of the curve, always reading. While Notkin focused on the *Fantastic Four* and *X-Men,* Gaiman dragged him into science fiction by Robert Heinlein. "Geoff, you've gotta check this out! Look at Will Eisner's *Spirit*! At Esteban Maroto!" In a woodworking class, the teacher caught Gaiman reading *Howard the Duck* issue number two and tore it up. That horrified the boys, because not only was it valuable, but Marvel Comics weren't easy—or cheap—to come by in England.

The Spirit issues (reprinted by Warren) reminded Notkin of *Tales of the Unexpected,* Roald Dahl, and Edgar Allan Poe stories: There was always a twist. The Warren reprints moved the young readers away from superheroes and into the underground world of Harvey Kurtzman and Art Spiegelman.

As often as they dared, the friends skipped class and went to the SoHo part of London where they'd get a fresh fix of American comics from a store called "Dark They Were and Golden-Eyed." It was behind the Berwick Street market in London's SoHo, a rough area with a lot of tough, working-class guys selling vegetables on carts. A "working girl" made eyes at Gaiman and Notkin one evening from a doorway as they were walking back to the subway station. They were fifteen or sixteen and wearing their school uniforms. She winked and said, "Come on darlings, 'ow 'bout some fun?"

In 1976, Gaiman and Notkin started a punk rock band with Gaiman as the singer. It began as "Chaos" and later morphed into "The Ex-Execs." Gaiman left after a couple years and the name changed again, this time to "Phazers on Stun." Gaiman continued to write songs for bands including "The Flash Girls" and "Folk Underground." With time, the once close friends drifted away from one another. Notkin moved back to the States in 1980 and briefly attended art school in Boston. He moved to New York, played in punk bands, and dated a girl who was a student at the School of Visual Arts.

"I went to see a show she was in," he said. "I walked into this place and said, 'This is for me!' I looked at the faculty list. It was Will Eisner, Harvey Kurtzman, and Art Spiegelman. Can you imagine, all of them teaching at the same place at the same time? In their own way, they pulled comics out of the gutter. With Harvey it was satire, with Art it was intellectual brilliance, and Will made them this movielike art form."

Everything Notkin did was geared toward getting into Eisner's class. Admission to the class required passing a portfolio review and an interview. Early in his freshman year at SVA, Notkin gathered his courage and walked up to Eisner's class. "I'd like to take your class," Notkin said. "Could I make an appointment for a portfolio review?"

"Let's look at your portfolio now," Eisner said, opening Notkin's portfolio in front of his class.

Some students turned their noses up at the contents, but Eisner went through every piece. Finally he said, "I agree to take you next year but you need to work on your anatomy." As virtually every student whose portfolio was ever reviewed by Eisner heard, he pointed Notkin to George B. Bridgman's book, *Constructive Anatomy*.

It was that fall of 1983 that Eisner moved to Florida and became a commuter, flying to New York every other week so he could continue teaching his Thursday classes. (He did this for eight years.) In the morning it was the Comics & Sequential Art class; in the afternoon he taught a three-hour portfolio class for seniors in the cartooning department. (On the alternative Thursdays, Andre LeBlanc, an old friend of Eisner's who then worked on "The Phantom" comic strip, filled in for Eisner.)

The Comics & Sequential Art class that fall was all male—twenty-two guys—half of them interested in superheroes, the others interest in satire, caricature, or alternative/underground comix. Only a handful—as it was every semester—knew the significance of the man in the tie and colored shirt teaching them. It was a lecture and demonstration setting, not a workshop.

"If you want to be a great cartoonist, you have to be a great storyteller," Eisner told his charges. "If you grow up reading only comic books and watching TV you'll have no stories of your own." He encouraged them to read O. Henry and Edgar Allan Poe.

Their first assignment was blocking out a four-page comics story in pencil. Then Eisner sat with each student, one-by-one, and offered suggestions such as, "This would work better if you changed the angle." (Notkin, tipped off to Eisner's manner, put tracing paper over his pages. Eisner drew on the tracing paper, giving Notkin not only direction but one-of-a-kind souvenirs that he still possesses.)

"One week, he looked at my pages and said, 'You're making great strides, my boy.' Great strides! I felt ten feet tall," Notkin recalled.

Eisner put so much of himself—and so much real beauty—into his work that he tried to make his students want to accomplish the same thing. In addition to giving his students a technical education, he also emphasized telling a story in pictures. "Look at Spider-Man," he might say. "He's chasing the Green Goblin down the street, saying, 'I'm going to catch you, Green Goblin!' The words and pictures both say the same thing. Show and elaborate on the action, don't repeat it." One of his assignments would be the creation of a one-page story in which two people meet but there is no dialogue.

Sometimes he surprised his students, like the day he took his cartoonists to the film department where SVA instructor and documentary filmmaker Roy Frumkes (*Street Trash, Document of the Dead*) was screening an early Charlie Chaplin feature. When it was over, Eisner stood up in front of both classes and gave an impromptu talk. "This," he said, "is where you see the similarity between comics and film. Look how great the action is—we all know what happened and there was no sound! Imagine if you could tell a comic book story as well as Chaplin did *and* you can put word balloons on top of the action!"

As it was every year, Eisner told the class that it would pull together to write, draw, and produce its own best-of comic book by the end of the semester. When he asked if anyone already possessed publishing experience, the only hand that rose was Notkin's. As a teen in England, he and Gaiman started a punk rock fanzine called *Metro*.

"Okay, Geoff, you're the editor," Eisner said. "Now you need to pick an assistant editor and a staff."

The only person Notkin knew in the class was Florian Bachleda, who sat next to him. And their knowledge of each other was limited to first names.

"Flo, why don't *you* be the assistant editor?" Notkin asked.

"No," Bachleda said.

"C'mon, it'll be fun!" Notkin said.

Bachleda was dubious. But Notkin thought he was a nice guy, liked similar music, and was calm.

Eisner said, "Here's how it works. The school pays for the printing. You put together the concept, negotiate with the printers and for delivery. I'll illustrate the cover and pick the art in it so there is no favoritism." The students had to do everything. He wanted them to learn every aspect of the business.

It was an intense class from that point forward, emphasizing the mechanics of the four-color printing process and why it was used to make comics. "You must understand the process of making comic books if you're going to be successful," Eisner said. He didn't just teach them how to draw cartoon panels. He taught them to prepare their work properly for print. They learned about stat cameras and proportion wheels, the two most important pre-computer tools an art director was given.

"A lot of artists and cartoonists get upset when they make a mistake," Eisner told his class. "God made black ink, but he made white ink, too, to correct your pages."

The day Notkin and Bachleda took their finished pages to the printer and they watched one thousand copies fly off the press still ranks as one of the most exciting days in Notkin's life. "It was the most brilliant practical exercise that a teacher could design for art students," he said. "We made a lot of mistakes—I called Will in Florida many times— but when we were done we knew how to make pages for a magazine, make a magazine, and do promotion."

It was such a great experience that Notkin and Bachleda took the class again. Only this time, producing the comic would mean taking on greater responsibilities because SVA could no longer afford to underwrite its publication.

Bachleda and Notkin wrote a serious business letter to SVA's president, David Rhodes, and arranged a meeting with him and Marshall Arisman, famed illustrator and chairman of the school's master of fine arts program.

"We had Will's permission to do this, but it was all off our own bat," Notkin said. "Will felt *Gallery* was over and there was no point in fighting SVA over it, which wasn't fair because Will had a deal with SVA that as part of his payment for teaching there, he'd have his own student magazine."

Notkin and Bachleda strongly believed that creating the magazine each year was one of the most important elements of Eisner's class, and they weren't about to let it die without a fight.

"This is a really important thing that the school does," Notkin told Rhodes and Arisman. "It educates us in the mysteries of a print magazine. What if we can drastically cut costs?"

Rhodes and Marshall were sympathetic to their proposal—and quite surprised at their passion.

"If you can keep our cost under $1,000," the administrators answered, "we'll keep doing it." SVA agreed to continue with reduced funding—less than half the original budget.

Notkin and Bachleda met the challenge, taking the 1986 edition of *Will Eisner's Gallery of New Comics* from a full-color glossy cover to two-color newsprint stock. Even with the reduced budget, they added more pages, so more students saw their work in print.

For most young student cartoonists, when *Will Eisner's Gallery of New Comics* came out, it was the very first time they'd seen their own work in print. "I'd had some of my work published in fanzines, and I'd done a lot of rock 'n' roll posters and record album covers for my bands, and so on, but I can remember how completely and utterly thrilled I was to see my comics in a book with Will Eisner's name on the front. It was a really big deal for me, too," Notkin said.

Notkin's experiences with Eisner landed him a job editing Harvey Kurtzman's student magazine, *Kartunz*.

Kurtzman's students had to raise all the money for his magazine on their own, through selling advertising to local stores and businesses. Because the funding did not come from the school, students had complete editorial control over the content, distribution, and print run. *Kartunz* traditionally had more pages than Eisner's *Gallery of New Comics*, but it was all newsprint with a two-color cover.

"It seems kind of silly now," Notkin said, "but at the time, I guess we all thought of *Gallery* as the 'official' SVA student comic art mag, and *Kartunz* was our underground/alternative book. The content of Kartunz was usually a lot racier, too. Will was so classy that he wouldn't have any inappropriate material appear in *Gallery*. I don't want that to sound square—Will was right to exercise editorial control because there was some really offensive and tacky work being done by a few of the students at SVA, and you didn't see any of that in *Gallery*."

And when another SVA instructor, Art Spiegelman, needed an administrative and production assistant on his new magazine, *RAW,* Kurtzman recommended Notkin, who became Spiegelman's assistant for two years while the artist worked on his landmark graphic novel, *Maus*.

Notkin and Bachleda worked together for two years producing the class magazine. The experience literally changed their lives. Bachleda went on to an extraordinary career as an art director for the *Village Voice,* *Entertainment Weekly,* and *Vibe.* Bachleda also ended up teaching an evening cartooning class at SVA himself.

After graduation, and after his time at *RAW,* Notkin worked as a studio manager for American Express. In 1989 he formed his own design firm, Stanegate Studios, where he did print design, web development, photography, and science writing.

"Flo and I had the same experience," Notkin said. "We wanted to be cartoonists and wound up being in design. To our amazement, we discovered we liked designing magazines better than drawing comics. I never intended to be an art director. I was going to be a cartoonist. Will's class set me down this road and I'm very happy it did."

The next time Gaiman and Notkin met up, it was 1987 and Gaiman was a young journalist. Notkin, then the editor of *Will Eisner's Gallery of New Comics,* showed off a cover sketch of the Spirit specially drawn for the magazine by his SVA instructor.

"I was *incredibly* jealous!" Gaiman said. "And he mentioned to me what an incredible person Will was."

Not long after that, Gaiman met Eisner himself at a comic book convention in England and gave his idol a copy of his own book, *Violent Cases.* "It was one of those things where I was astonished when talking to him that he knew who I was, and had read some of what I did and liked it," Gaiman said. "It was an amazing feeling that possibly I am doing something good."

One of the first things Gaiman said to Eisner was, "One of my best friends was one of your students."

"I find it hysterical that these two English school kids not only went into the business but both became friends of Will Eisner," Notkin said.

One graduate of Eisner's SVA class who went on to work in comic books (and asked for anonymity) remembered taking the class with celebrated caricaturist Drew Friedman.

"Drew's dad was writer Bruce Jay Friedman," author of *The Dick*, "so he came into the class with a little privilege and proceeded to wield it," the former classmate said. "He was literally mean to some of the other students. It was funny to me at the time, because at least he wasn't picking on *me*. Drew's the guy who thinks me and a few other guys in class are sellouts because we do superheroes."

Friedman is now a well-known illustrator for such publications as the *New York Times, MAD, The Weekly Standard,* and *Time,* but back then, Eisner had doubts about whether his mouth or his talent would lead his life.

"He was a cantankerous, nasty kid," Eisner said. "He did a lot of black jokes.

"One day he was supposed to drive a bunch of the guys in his car up to the Cartoon Museum in Rye, New York, but he never showed up. I spoke to his father when he didn't show. I said, 'Do you know where he is?' And he said, 'No, I don't; I've been on his case for weeks!'

"Drew drove Harvey Kurtzman to tears one day. Harvey walked out of class. Drew started pulling that stuff in my class, and I told him, 'Get out! There are a bunch of fine guys here who paid good money to take this course, and you are screwing everything up. You are a wise guy; get the hell out.' He didn't like me very much; I never liked him either."

(Friedman declined comment on his time in Eisner's class at SVA.)

═══════════

The first paying work former student Mike Carlin ever got in comics was from Eisner. Eisner was producing joke-books for Scholastic, drawing many of the illustrations himself but buying the jokes from his class. "If he liked the joke, he paid $1 a joke," Carlin said. "I sold him three hundred jokes. I used to be funny."

Eisner's books for Scholastic (and sometimes credited to Poorhouse Press or Stanowill Pub. Co.)—including *Star Jaws, 101 Outer Space Jokes* (1979), *Superhero Jokes* (1980), *Spaced Out Jokes* (1979), *Funny Jokes and Foxy Riddles* (1979), *Star Nuts* (1980), *300 Horrible Monster Jokes* (1980),

Bringing Up Your Parents (1980), *Dates & Other Disasters* (1980), *Classroom Crack-ups & School Disasters* (1980), and *TV Jokes* (1980) (many edited and/or written by Keith Diazun, with credited contributions by Carlin, Joey Cavalieri, You Noon Chow, Robert Pizzo, and Barry Caldwell)—were not his most memorable, but schoolchildren of that era ate them up. And, for his students, they were golden opportunities for resume entries.

"It felt good to get something published," Carlin said. "It was crummy stuff but Will paid in cash. I went to Blimpie right away and bought a sandwich whenever I got paid. But I didn't care about the money. I wanted a copy of the book. A 'written by' credit was very cool."

(Years later, when Carlin won an Eisner Award, he thanked his former teacher and said, "My price is now $2 a joke.")

For his contribution to *Will Eisner's Gallery of New Comics,* Carlin collaborated with Drew Friedman.

"Drew was great. He was definitely already there while the rest of us were figuring it out," Carlin said. "He used to draw all these weird faces. There was a husband and wife gardening team on TV in New York back then, Stan and Floss Dworkin. I did a weird drawing of them. Drew took it and did his own faces. He did, 'Find Stan and Floss.' My drawing stood out because it was so awful."

Eisner recognized Carlin's storytelling quite early on. "I also know he thought my draftsmanship needed a shitload of work," Carlin said, laughing at the memory. "He was cool about how he said things that were critical. Harvey Kurtzman was more blunt.

"Will was literally publishing *A Contract with God* as he was teaching the class that year," Carlin recalled. "It was an amazing time."

═══════════

While most of the artists who went through Eisner's class were interested in comic books and superheroes, the 1975 class contained two future daily cartoonists, Ray Billingsley ("Curtis") and Patrick McDonnell ("Mutts").

Even though only seventeen years old, by the time Billingsley entered Eisner's class at SVA in 1975, he was already an established artist in New

York City. He also had a cartoony look—giant afro, mustache, and goatee. In his own words, he looked like the meanest member of the Jackson 5.

Billingsley started drawing professionally at eleven when he was spotted and hired by the editor of *Kids* magazine. "I was born in the South and grew up in Harlem," he explained. "I was considered an oddball because I wasn't into anything anyone else was into." He went to SVA because of its cartooning program and even received special permission to take Eisner's class—normally reserved for sophomores— in his freshman year. (He actually took Eisner's class several times from 1975-79.)

Eisner, however, briefly slowed him down.

"Is this all you can do?" the teacher asked his new student during a portfolio review.

Billingsley didn't know anything about Eisner at that point. After looking up the man's work and background in the SVA library, he was impressed enough to set his ego aside and see what he could learn.

"He put me to task," Billingsley said. "I started improving just to show him that I could do better. Starting as young as I did, it's hard to show people you're capable. Will really challenged me. I knew people who dropped Will's class because he was too hard on them. A lot of people fell to the wayside. It was a hard act. And then Will went one step further: he published his graphic novel, *Will Eisner's New York: The Big City*. That inspired me. 'Curtis' is set in the city. And I always liked doing street scenes. I looked to him for inspiration."

A sketch that Eisner sent former student Ray Billingsley ("Curtis")
(Courtesy Ray Billingsley)

Billingsley said that most students in his class were already at their desks and drawing by the time Eisner arrived, and they all continued to draw quietly when he lectured.

"Will looked at projects objectively and asked what market we were interested in reaching. He was looking to create professionals," Billingsley said. "It didn't matter if you were underground or drew with markers, just as long as you were successful conveying an idea. He wanted us to create a good picture. And each picture should stand alone and push a picture forward. Will wanted us to know what it would be like in the real world where they would have no sympathy and we wouldn't get a second try. 'If a gag isn't working, discard it.' That's hard for a lot of artists. His class was hard work."

In 2000, Billingsley received the President's Award from the American Lung Association for the way Curtis kept pushing his father to quit smoking. He was surprised to see Eisner and Mort Walker come onstage and present the award to him.

"I fell out! I had tears in my eyes!" Billingsley said. "The two guys who inspired me presented *me* an award. It was a momentous moment. I thanked them so much."

Patrick McDonnell—whose "Mutts" comic strip appears daily in more than five hundred newspapers—was also influenced by his time in Eisner's SVA class.

"When I went to SVA, I took advantage; I wanted to try a little of everything," McDonnell said. "Will's was the only cartooning class I took. The thing I remember best was Will's enthusiasm, which was contagious. He loved the medium. I loved it too. Will's class was mostly people interested in comic books. I was leaning toward comic strips or the underground."

Will Eisner and Mort Walker were surprise presenters in 2000 when former Eisner student Ray Billingsley ("Curtis") won the President's Award from the American Lung Association
(Courtesy Ray Billingsley)

Eisner often brought European comics in and shared them with his students. The one that caught McDonnell's eye was a Swedish reprint of old "Krazy Kat" cartoons. McDonnell had only seen "Krazy Kat" once before, when he was thirteen.

"It was mind-expanding," he said.

So when Eisner brought in the Swedish *Kat,* he saw McDonnell's eyes light up. "He let me keep it, so I have a great foreign *Krazy Kat* book from Will."

McDonnell also learned about Japanese woodcuts from Eisner, who used them to demonstrate the roots of comic art.

"He saw so much potential in comics," McDonnell said. "I think he felt the medium was in its infancy. In class, he talked a lot about his education comics for the Army. I thought it was wonderful, the way he put together education and entertainment."

Those were heady days for SVA students. Although McDonnell didn't take Kurtzman's class, he did sneak in one day when Robert Crumb was a guest speaker. He even came away from it with a small Crumb sketch as a souvenir.

And when he developed a friendship with classmate Joe Coleman, an underground cartoonist who went on to be a painter, they formed a "fairly notorious" punk band called Steel Tips: F.T.D. (as in "for the dick"). The band even opened a show for The Ramones.

"SVA back in the '70s was pretty loose," McDonnell said.

McDonnell was a favorite of Eisner's. How could he not be? In his popular daily strip *Mutts,* McDonnell often channels one of Eisner's own early influences, "Krazy Kat." And he frequently brings Japanese wood-cut styles to his Sunday strips.

In 1998, McDonnell and Will were both up for the Reuben. The teacher and his student met as equals. Sort of.

"Of course, Will won," McDonnell said with a laugh. "I went over to him and said, 'You didn't teach me well enough!' That I was up against Will Eisner, for God's sake!"

McDonnell won the award in 1999.

━━━━━━━━

Not all of Will Eisner's students were successes right out of the class-room. In fact, some didn't even pass his class.

"He failed me," said Joe Quesada, who took over Marvel Comics as editor in chief in August 2000. Quesada rose to prominence as the guiding force (with Jimmy Palmiotti) of the Marvel Knights line featuring dark stories of Daredevil, The Punisher, and others.

"I wasn't in art school to be in comics," Quesada said. "I read comics as a kid; I dropped them as most kids do when they discover girls."

When he was at SVA, Quesada dabbled in many artistic fields. He had heard of Will Eisner, but didn't see him with the same reverence that Lash, Holmstrom, Notkin, Bachleda, Billingsley, and McDonnell did. It was just another class for a kid who wasn't particularly motivated.

"Will always came across as an incredibly knowledgeable person," Quesada said. "I took away many, many lessons on storytelling. I always tell people the one thing I walked away with from SVA was the business of art. I do a bunch of things okay. The one thing I can brag about is that I've managed my art career well. Will was one of the people who was influential in that manner. I think Will was preparing us for the world of work-for-hire and studio work. I do a lecture series at art schools now myself. I tell students that they can learn the technical stuff. But what's not out there is the business aspect and being businesslike in your approach."

Quesada's work did not appear in *Will Eisner's Gallery of New Comics* that semester; he did get published in Harvey Kurtzman's *Kartunz*.

"I failed because of lack of effort. I didn't show up often enough, didn't do the projects, so Will did the right thing and failed my ass. And just for the record, I failed Harvey Kurtzman's class that same semester!"

Quesada eventually began freelancing as a comic book artist. One of his first jobs was coloring a *Super Mario Bros.* comic for editor Jim Shooter at Valiant Comics.

"If I knew Joe was an Eisner kid, I would have been startled," Shooter said. "Eisner sent some students to Marvel looking for work when I was the editor there. But they were far from ready even when we were desperate. And when I was at Valiant, I had no money to pursue top talent, so I used a lot of guys from Joe Kubert's school. I got a steady stream from students from Will, too. But the problem with learning under a genius is they all thought *they* were geniuses! I would tell them, 'Do six-panel grid story pages. We're working Jack Kirby style.' But they wouldn't follow instructions. They told me, 'I studied under Will Eisner, what do you know?' And I said, 'I know I have a checkbook.' They came in with huge egos. We never had an Eisner kid work out. I think Will needed to take a two-by-four to class and teach those kids to be professionals."

Years later, Quesada—by then Marvel's editor in chief—reintroduced himself to Eisner at a comic book convention. During the course of the conversation, Quesada said, "By the way, I took your course and failed."

"And," Eisner said, "here you are!"

EIGHTEEN
God, Will Eisner, and the Birth
of the Graphic Novel

Will Eisner was born into a God-fearing family. His mother referred to God constantly, promising that if Eisner did the right things, God would reward him.

Personally, though, Eisner had a dim view of religion as an institution. This feeling grew during the Great Depression years.

"One Rosh Hashanah Eve, my father wanted to hear *Yizkor*—the Jewish memorial service for the dead—but we didn't have enough money to pay for the holiday tickets to the *shul*," Eisner said. "We went anyway and stood outside on the steps—the doors were open—and we listened from outside.

"The humiliation of that experience—being too poor to participate inside with the rest of the Jewish community—stayed with me. In fact, I became so angry that I never went into a *shul* again until I got married.

"I began thinking that the institution—not the fundamentals of Judaism itself—was what was wrong. It wasn't a philosophical or cultural problem. I was disillusioned by the institution, the realization that it is conducted like a business. Here is an institution that is sustaining myths that may or may not be true, and in order to do that, the leadership does the same things a dictatorial country does. Look at the Catholic Church's problems. It is defending an institution that operates on a concept that is essentially predicated on myths. Church leaders conduct themselves in a way that retains for them absolute power. And, as you know and I know, absolute power breeds absolute corruption."

When they met, Eisner's wife Ann was a member of a Reform temple, Temple Emanuel in Manhattan. After they were married in 1950, they moved to White Plains and joined another Reform temple. They didn't attend temple regularly, but they remained members because of their two children. When the Eisners moved to Florida in 1978, they looked into joining a *shul*. They attended Shabbat services one Friday evening, liked it, but never did anything more about it.

"I would like to believe that there is a supreme intelligence that is concerned with our lives and who guides us," Eisner said. "As a result, we have A Contract with God that we ourselves created. The problem with the contract is that neither party has lived up to his obligation. So I don't know. I'd like there to be a God, really.

"My wife Ann is a firm believer," he continued. "She believes strongly in God or in the existence of God. I am not as sure. I can't attribute the pattern of my life to the hand of God, although I would like to because it would seem that somewhere there is a hand that is guiding it. That would be of great comfort. But I can't find any reason to it."

All of which set the table —as far as the public knew until now—for the creation of Eisner's groundbreaking 1978 graphic novel, *A Contract with God and Other Tenement Stories*. Eisner was now sixty-one.

———

American Visuals was going broke by the early 1970s—one of its divisions was bleeding it dry—and Eisner got out in 1972. But there was the question of what to do next. He had money in the bank, and he took the bold step of giving up his Army contract on *PS Magazine*. Over the next few years, inspired by the underground comix scene, he invested his time and money in a full-time return to the drawing board. It was, in fact, a comment made by Ann that focused him. She said, "Why don't you finally do what you always wanted to do?"

They talked about this quite often, actually, so Eisner finally sat down and gave it some serious thought. Did he want to return to comic books?

The solid, rapidly growing base of fan market and the Kitchen Sink Press reprints of *The Spirit* generated a growing interest in his old work. Eisner had already turned down Stan Lee's offer of the editorship at Marvel Comics. Would the average mainstream or underground comic book reader be interested in anything more challenging from Will Eisner than this month's issue of *Daredevil*?

"I was struck by the obvious," Eisner said, "that readership was changing and a new approach to comics content was needed. Most obvious to me was that the time was now. The young preteen comic book reader of the 1940s was now close to forty years old. He grew up on the medium but what was there for a mature person to read in this format? It was an enormous opportunity."

Eisner reasoned that there might, in fact, be a new audience of adult comic book readers that no one had yet addressed directly. He decided he would only return to the medium if he could find a subject that would appeal to an adult readership. He found that subject in God.

"Everybody is concerned about his or her relationship with God in one way or another," Eisner said. "I created a series of short stories that emulated the famous movie, *Grand Hotel*."

Seeking a more mature expression of the comics' form, he spent two years creating four short stories of "sequential art." With the stories' 1930s Bronx tenements and slice-of-life moral tales, he returned to his roots and discovered new potential for the comics form—the graphic novel.

The book was originally called "A Tenement in the Bronx." A salesman with Eisner's original publisher, Baronet, said, "You will never sell this west of the Mississippi; no one west of the Mississippi knows what a tenement is." So they picked the title of the first short story—*A Contract with God*—as the title of the whole book.

"A Contract with God" was the most important element in that book as far as Eisner was concerned. It was based, again, on his underlying philosophy about God. All our lives, people are promised that if they live up to the so-called agreement they have with God, God will reward them. Eisner built *Contract* around that theme.

"When I'm working on something very emotional, as I did in *Contract*, when this fellow talks with God, I had to feel it," Eisner said. "I sat there at the board and acted it out in my head, with genuine feeling. I played the role internally."

═══════════

When his daughter Alice was dying, Eisner struggled with what to do with himself.

"I used to go upstairs where I had a studio, and I would sit there until three in the morning when I couldn't sleep, sometimes four, sometimes all night, and just draw, draw figures," he said. "It was the only way I could just keep going."

After she died, he immediately went back to work. No downtime, no time to mourn; he wouldn't have known what to do with himself. More recently, when his brother Pete died, he fell into the same pattern. He and Ann attended the funeral then went back to Pete's home for the wake and to support Pete's wife, Leila, her children, and grandchildren. But when the opportunity presented itself, Eisner excused himself— with Ann's blessing—and went to the office to work.

"My tendency is to try to get a hold of life and go on," he said. "I remember my wife being extremely distraught after Alice passed. As a matter of fact, she said *she* wanted to die, and I would say, 'No, we are not going to die, we are going to live through this.' But drawing has been a great savior for me emotionally. I have been able to use it as a way of living through very difficult times. With Pete, it was a different kind of thing. My reaction to Pete's death wasn't as traumatic as Alice's death, obviously, but just continuing work is a way of handling and dealing with a great loss, but a different kind of loss.

"With Alice, you know, I looked up at God and said, '*Why me?*'" he said. "*A Contract with God* is essentially a result of Alice's death. I was a very angry man when she died. I was enraged. She died in the flower of her youth, sixteen years old. There were heart-wrenching moments to watch this poor little girl die. The material I chose was all emotional— it was from my life."

Ann knew that *A Contract with God* was about Alice, "but we never discussed it," she said. "A friend would say, 'If it hurts, don't rub salt in it.'"

The Eisners experienced their friends' children marrying and having grandchildren, always happy for their friends, but hurt by the emptiness in their own lives.

"We did a lot of substituting. But it's not the same," Ann said.

———————

Eisner's general practice was to write a graphic novel in "dummy" form, which is the rendering of the book in rough pencil with the dialogue in place. Once he completed the *Contract* dummy, he thought about where he might sell it. He didn't want to approach a comic book house because he felt that his potential readers long ago stopped going to comic book stores and were now going into bookstores.

Eisner called Oscar Dystel, then president of Bantam Books, and pitched the concept. Dystel not only knew Eisner but was said to be a fan of his work on *The Spirit*. Dystel remembered him, but he was a busy man, as publishers usually are, and he was impatient. He wanted to know what it was that Eisner had, exactly. Eisner looked down at the dummy, and an instinct told him, *Don't tell Dystel it's a comic book or he will hang up on you.*

So Eisner thought for a moment, and said, "It's a graphic novel."

"Oh," Dystel said, "that sounds interesting; I've never heard of that before."

At Dystel's invitation, Eisner brought the dummy up to his office. Dystel looked at the dummy, looked at Eisner in disbelief, and then looked back at the dummy. Then Dystel shook his head.

"Call it what you will," he said sadly, "but this is still a comic book! *We* don't sell comic books at Bantam. I'm surprised at you, Will. Go find a small publisher."

So much for hitting the big time.

Despite his close relationship in 1978 with Kitchen Sink Press, Eisner felt that his first real book needed a New York City publishing house. "This one needs a Park Avenue address, not No. 2 Swamp Road," he told Kitchen.

Eisner called Stan Budner, the son of Max Budner, owner of Independent News Distributors in Wilmington, Delaware, who once distributed *The Spirit* and actually read it, too. Budner knew a publisher who might be interested in the book.

Budner introduced Eisner to Norman Goldfine, the publisher of a small start-up press called Baronet Books in New York City. He published adventure titles, and took a chance on *A Contract with God*.

Goldfine later encountered financial problems and Eisner loaned his company $25,000. At the same time, Eisner suggested he find more profitable, more mainstream titles to publish.

"The hottest thing at the time was the movie *Jaws*," Eisner recalled. "The other was *Star Wars*. I said, let's do a book called *Star Jaws*."

Star Jaws—the antithesis of *A Contract with God* and virtually everything else Eisner ever produced—became a joke-book that Scholastic Books bought and made into a big seller. It led to a successful series of such books that Eisner pumped out of his own Poorhouse Press imprint during the 1970s.

With just a few thousand sales of *Contract* in its first year, it wasn't apparent that a publishing revolution was in the air. In fact, producing a second graphic novel might have seemed a strange idea, but Eisner believed he was on to something fresh.

Two weeks after *Contract* was published, Goldfine called Eisner and said, "You'll be happy to know that Brentano's on 5th Avenue ordered copies."

"Oh, gee, that's terrific!" Eisner said. "That is exactly what I hoped would happen. I am now in a *legitimate* bookstore!"

Eisner waited two more weeks. Finally, he couldn't resist any longer and went to Brentano's to see for himself. For him, being on the shelves of Brentano's in and of itself was a "Wow!" Eisner felt that he was on the right track, that if this one didn't make it, maybe another book would.

Eisner introduced himself to the manager and said he was the author of *A Contract with God*, which the store carried, and he wanted to know how it was doing. He was concerned because he didn't actually see it on display.

"It did very well the first week," the manager said. "I put it on a card table out in front of the store. Then I had to put out another book, the new James Michener novel, and I put yours on the religious bookshelf."

The manager said that an elderly lady came over to him, the usual old woman in tennis shoes and blue hair, and she complained, "This is terrible, you have this in the religious section. This is *not* a religious book, it's a cartoon book!"

He thought about it and figured that maybe she was right.

This time, he put *Contract* in with the cartoon books, the *Peanuts Treasuries,* the collected *Garfield,* and Stan Lee's *How to Draw Comics the Marvel Way.*

But even that decision was problematic.

A father, pulling his kid along behind him by the wrist, was the next person to approach the manager. "You have a comic book that shows a naked lady in with the *Beetle Bailey* books!"

"That's terrible," the manager agreed.

"I don't want my kid being exposed to that kind of stuff," the father huffed, and stalked out.

So the manager removed his copies of *A Contract with God* from the shelf and put them in a cardboard box.

"Where is it now?" Eisner asked.

"It's in the cellar," the manager said. "I don't know *where* to put it."

Still, basement or not, Eisner was encouraged.

His book was in Brentano's—*somewhere*—and *Contract* even earned some good initial reviews. Eisner felt there was no other way for him to go, anyway. He wasn't about to go back into doing *The Spirit* again. He was financially independent thanks to several decades of hard work and successful investments.

Confident that he was onto something, he began work on a second graphic novel, *Signal from Space* (later published as *Life on Another Planet*). He would eventually publish eighteen more by 2005.

———

When Eisner wrote a new graphic novel, he treated it like a state secret. Even Denis Kitchen was out of the loop about the nature of new books until they were substantially plotted and dummied.

Their typical conversation went:

"I'm working on a new graphic novel," Eisner would say.

And Kitchen would ask, "What's it about, Will?"

"New York in the Depression; I don't want to say any more."

"Uh, okay."

A month might pass and Eisner would casually mention to Kitchen that he was still working on the mysterious project.

"Can you tell me anything more about it?"

"Well, it's about New York in the 1930s. I'd rather not talk about it."

Eisner believed it would interrupt his creative process if he talked about a project too early in the process. "I want to really think it through thoroughly and have the characters and plot well established," he said. "Once I get to the point where the story is in rough form with a beginning, middle, and an end, then I eagerly send it to Denis and ask for his candid advice. I also get an early read from my wife Ann, who has the perspective of a new reader."

Asking for candid advice and receiving it are two different things. At least that was true in the beginning of his relationship with Kitchen. And that applied to both Kitchen and the man who edited most of Eisner's books, the late Dave Schreiner. Schreiner was Kitchen Sink Press editor in chief for years, and Eisner eventually hired him directly as a freelance editor even though he always dealt with another editor on a publisher's payroll.

"I valued his insight and he understood me well," Eisner said. "I encouraged criticism."

But early on, both men viewed Eisner with a certain amount of awe, and Eisner discovered that if there was something they didn't like, they didn't want to tell him out of misguided respect.

"I can't remember which book it was—probably *The Dreamer*—but Denis and Dave privately agreed that there were significant flaws in this book," Eisner said. "They just didn't know how to tell me. One of them called me and pussyfooted around the issue. I could sense that they were holding back."

"Look," Eisner said firmly, "I want my publisher to be critical; I want my editor to be critical. Be completely honest with me; I expect nothing less of you. You are the reader's surrogate."

From that point on, they were. Eisner thanked them, made the appropriate changes in the book, and their relationship grew. They realized that while they obviously had a great deal of respect for Eisner, it was their job and their responsibility to give him honest feedback.

───────────

When Eisner began doing new work such as *Contract,* he became a role model for a new generation of outsiders.

"Oh, one can go beyond superheroes!" underground cartoonist Howard Cruse (*Stuck Rubber Baby, Gay Comix, Wendel*) remembered thinking. "The fact that he was interested in taking stories more connected with the real world interested me. Underground comix were also expanding my sense of what the medium could do. The fact that he didn't consider himself slumming to work in underground comix made an impression on me."

That Will Eisner, the dean of comic book innovation, licensed his *Spirit* work to Kitchen Sink Press and even drew a cover for *Snarf* (which literally placed the Spirit in a cesspool office filled with underground cartoonists) made an indelible impression upon Cruse and his generation.

───────────

Ann Eisner's involvement and interest in her husband's work developed during the last thirty years, starting from the point at which she admitted little familiarity with *The Spirit.*

A few years after that, Denis Kitchen was at their dinner table again. Eisner had recently sent him the final pages of *A Sunset in Sunshine City,* which was to run in the next issue of *Will Eisner's Quarterly.*

"I really liked the latest story," Kitchen said.

"*I'm* responsible for the first part of that," Ann said, enjoying the surprised look on Kitchen's face. "I read the story and I told Will it needed something to come before it so that I cared about the lead character in the story."

"That's great, Ann! That was my favorite part," Kitchen said.

Ann had gone from not reading her husband's work to contributing a great idea. Then Kitchen became mischievous.

"Maybe we should change the name to *Will and* Ann *Eisner's Quarterly,*" he said.

Eisner raised his brow until he realized Kitchen was kidding.

Ann was also responsible for censoring one of Eisner's panels in *Life on Another Planet*. There was a character named "Blood" and on page eighty-one, Eisner drew a scene of heavy rain—an *Eisenshpritz*. In the bottom-middle panel, "Blood" could be seen urinating. It became part of the *Eisenshpritz*. Ann saw it and said, "Will, that isn't like you!" He changed it.

The first person to look at the dummy for any new Eisner graphic novel wasn't Kitchen—it was Ann. Eisner trusted her judgment because she didn't think like a comic book person and she didn't read like a comic book person. She read the text first then looked at the pictures. Comic book people look at the pictures first.

"Batton Lash saw a dummy of *Minor Miracles*," Eisner said, "and he was so complimentary of the expressions and the body postures, but he never said a *word* about the story. I'm confident about the art; tell me about the story! Ann gives good criticisms. She's also learned good editing. She won't tell how to do something; she'll tell me what doesn't work, then she lets me figure out how to make it work."

———

Many writers since 1978 have saluted Will Eisner as the father of the graphic novel. Several arguments have ensued about whether or not he was the first person to apply the term "graphic novel."

Eisner, for his part, never claimed ownership of the term or staked a claim on being first. Critics, historians, and artists credited him because he was the person who popularized the form, even if he was not the first to apply it. That honor is most appropriately applied to the little known *Beyond Time and Again,* by George Metzger.

Comics historian—and Eisner friend—R. C. "Bob" Harvey said that Eisner deserves credit for many things in the history of comics, but this is not one of them.

"His 'pioneering' with the graphic novel has been overblown," Harvey said. "He's always been called the inventor and it's been said that he created the term. But *Contract* is not a novel; it's a series of short stories. It doesn't meet the criteria. Will took the idea that a comic book could be a great source of literature. And he explored it with great skill. When I call him a 'pioneer,' it's a term I invest with great significance and meaning. But he didn't invent the graphic novel and he didn't invent the term. His reputation isn't overblown. He has done so many things it would be difficult to overblow it. But his connection to the graphic novel as it is commonly represented is only vaguely true. It is sometimes skewed to where it is not historically accurate to nitpickers like me."

Eisner himself cringed when somebody said that he pioneered something. "I tend to look over my shoulder, and I suspect other people were doing it, too," he said. "Every time I think I have been there first, I discover that somebody else was there, too."

The term "A Graphic Novel by Will Eisner" does appear on the cover of Baronet's first edition of *A Contract with God*. And in a September 10, 1968, interview that John Benson conducted with Eisner for his fanzine, *Witzend*, Eisner gives the first hint of the work that lay a decade ahead of him:

> *WILL EISNER: You know, every once in a while I try to read ...* Graphic Story Magazine. *I'll tell you, if I were to go back (it isn't a question of going back, it would be going forward), if I had the time to devote myself fully, that would be the direction in which I would probably go.*
>
> *JOHN BENSON: Which direction?*
>
> *EISNER: In the so-called "graphic story," because this has been something that I believe the comic strip technique had all along ... But I don't think the media itself, right now, unless I misread the public, can stand an extreme acceleration into that area. It has to come somewhat from the public. I think that the public is a very impatient reader today. You see, if you refine the technique far enough, you'll come to film, and you'll be a film.*

Chris Browne, the artist behind daily comic strips "Hagar the Horrible" and "Raising Duncan," met Will Eisner at the original International Museum of Cartoon Art in Greenwich, Connecticut. He was eighteen and accompanying his father, Dik Browne (cofounder of the museum, creator of "Hagar," and cocreator of "Hi and Lois"). Eisner was there with Cat Yronwode.

The quartet was in the mansion's kitchen, eating a simple lunch on paper plates.

"I couldn't get over the fact that I was having sandwiches with *Will Eisner* at the Cartoon Museum!" Browne said. "I asked him, 'Will there ever be a *Spirit* movie?' And he chortled! He said that every few years somebody would show up and want to do a movie of the Spirit. They would option the rights and then somebody would cut him a check. That option would run for a certain period of time. They would scramble and try to put a deal together. Then that option would run out. There would be a lull and somebody else would show up with a check."

Over the years, a number of well-known Hollywood figures have taken a run at making a *Spirit* movie, including producers William Friedkin (*The Exorcist*), Gary Kurtz (*Star Wars, The Dark Crystal*), and, in 1994, Michael Uslan and Ben Melniker through their company, Batfilm Productions Inc. (*Batman, Batman & Robin, Catwoman, Batman Begins, Swamp Thing*). During Friedkin's option, he assigned and rejected scripts by Jules Feiffer (*Popeye, Carnal Knowledge*), newspaper columnist Pete Hamill, writer Harlan Ellison (*The Man From U.N.C.L.E., Star Trek, Outer Limits, The Twilight Zone*), and Eisner himself.

"Will always had this attitude that he could care less if somebody made a *Spirit* movie," said Denis Kitchen. "He didn't mind collecting the option checks. He said, 'They're going to do a movie; it might help you sell some books and magazines.' I remember being more excited than he was."

One producer succeeded in getting a *Spirit* movie made, but few people ever saw it.

━━━━━━━━

Paul Aratow knew Will Eisner through his 1984 experience as producer of another Eisner creation adapted for film, *Sheena*. Although Eisner passed all rights to the character to Jerry Iger when they split up in 1941, the rights subsequently passed through several studios by the time Aratow acquired an option in 1975 and released it to Columbia five years later. When he turned to Eisner for help unraveling the history, the two became friendly.

"I knew the *Spirit* property and thought it was wonderful," Aratow said. "I made the introduction between Will's attorney and Warner Bros. because I talked Warner Bros. into acquiring the rights for a deal that involved me. That was in '86. I fantasized about making a *Spirit* movie. But like many projects, it takes years to find the path to production."

Comic book-based movies were virtually unheard of at the time.

"I thought *The Spirit* was a classic film noir subject," Aratow said. "And Will's graphics are very Orson Wellesian. Or was it the other way around? But he's in the Caravaggio school, with strong patches of color. *The Spirit* had a mysterious air and it was a detective story."

"I had been a fan of Will Eisner's work for quite a while," said Frank Von Zerneck, producer of TV movies ranging from *Policewoman Centerfold* and *The Elizabeth Smart Story* to *Reversible Errors*. "We thought it might make a good series for ABC; they agreed."

Steven E. de Souza was commissioned to write the script for a ninety-minute series pilot that was coproduced by Warner Bros. Television. A lifelong comics fan, de Souza has brought his share of four-color fantasies to life. His credentials include blockbusters such as *48 Hours* (1982), *Commando* (1985), *The Running Man* (1987), and *Die Hard* (1988), as well as genre films such as *Judge Dredd* (1995), *The Flintstones* (1994), *Vault of Horror I* (1994), *Street Fighter* (1994), *Lara Croft Tomb Raider: The Cradle of Life* (2003), and unproduced screenplays for *The Phantom* and *Flash Gordon*. In television, he was a producer on *Knight Rider* (1982), and a writer on *The Six Million Dollar Man* (1974), *The Bionic Woman* (1976), *"V"* (1984), and the animated series *Cadillacs and Dinosaurs* (1993).

On paper, de Souza—a lifelong fan of cartoonist Alex Raymond ("Flash Gordon," "Secret Agent X-9," "Rip Kirby") and Silver Age comics—was the natural person to bring *The Spirit* to life in 1987.

"My whole background in TV and movies was hard, hard action," de Souza said. "They came to me because they wanted an action-adventure piece. It was a bonus for them when they found I knew the comics. It stunned Paul Aratow when he came to my office to meet me and I had Kitchen Sink's *Spirit* reprints already in my office."

"He's a wonderful writer and if you scratch him," Von Zerneck said, "he's an Eisner fan. So he was well suited to it. The script was excellent."

The three-million-dollar film was shot on the Warner Bros. lot in Los Angeles and directed by Michael Schulz, who was in a wheelchair following a skiing accident. The production was full of color-coordinated wardrobes and sets. The producers attempted to capture the mood of Eisner's strip through lighting effects because CGI (computer generated) images weren't terribly sophisticated or cost-effective yet.

The approach de Souza used in his comic book-to-film adaptations was to read the original and to be as true as possible for a modern-day experience.

"We had the Kitchen Sink Press comics on the set for *The Spirit* movie and I think it's very, very true to the look," he said. "We took our cues for art direction from Will Eisner's work. As they say in comics, we did some swipes. Camera angle after angle, scene by scene, it's a swipe. When Denny Colt goes to the police, when he first becomes the Spirit, it's very true. It was challenging because we were trying to play it as straight as possible. This was before comic book movies got respect.

I said, '"comic book" doesn't mean funny.' There was a certain kind of sincerity and naiveté, not to be confused with camp."

Sam Jones, who starred in the critically panned 1980 theatrical adaptation of *Flash Gordon*, won the dual role of "Denny Colt" and "The Spirit." Nana Visitor, who many years later rose to TV fame on *Star Trek: Deep Space Nine*, played "Ellen Dolan." Garry Walberg played "Commissioner Dolan," and Daniel Davis (the butler on TV's *The Nanny*) was "Simon Teasdale." Robert Pastorelli, who a year later joined the *Murphy Brown* series as the recurring character of "Eldin the Painter" also had a small role. The Spirit's controversial print sidekick, the big-lipped, jive-talking Ebony, was replaced in the movie by a more restrained child character named "Eubie." He was played by Bumper Robinson.

"We *had* to change the name," de Souza said. "The name 'Ebony' for a black kid was so inflammatory! It's such a mid-century relic. 'Eubie' talked like a kid today. But nonetheless, I think we created an authentic persona for him, that he could be not just a sidekick but a goad. 'C'mon Spirit, you can do it!' And he challenged the Spirit, who could be too trusting."

Aratow recalled that Sam Jones was a "regular guy," a jock—just not an inspired choice.

"He was sweet. I liked him," Aratow said. "It's just that acting is an intense occupation. And he's handsome. But that doesn't make you an accomplished actor. We showed Sam all the stuff and we had a drama coach on the set. We were getting it a line at a time. It was a *job*. In order to carry a picture, to be a star, you have to have charisma. Sam didn't have that level of intensity."

Von Zerneck, however, was enthusiastic about his leading man.

"Very, very, very good looking," the producer said. "And very adept at, in some ways, concealing that. You tried to get someone who could carry a series. In those days, it was all about who is in the center. It wasn't a multi-character environment. It was just this guy."

"The ABC administration insisted we use Sam," de Souza said. "It was non-negotiable. For whatever reason, ABC wanted him. If you saw him in *Flash*, he just cannot walk the line of playing it sincerely but honestly. He was inclined to play it campy. He looked great, but at the end of the day, I thought that was our weakest link."

Although many fans who have seen *The Spirit* movie rank it close to Roger Corman's unreleased *Fantastic Four* as one of the biggest clunkers in comics-to-film history, de Souza makes no apologies for the final product.

"It has a big look for the modest budget we had," de Souza said. "We wanted to set it in the 1940s but we couldn't afford the budget. Instead, we set it in a fuzzy no-period. *Batman* (1989) was later done in the same period. And the same art department that did *The Spirit* worked on *Batman* a few years later. It was a timeless, 1940s look we went for. If we had a phone, it was a dial. All the men wore hats. We deliberately didn't have any new cars. We created a timeless, vague car. We created a vague, mid-century America. And that blue—we had to get a special fabric to capture it. Eisner put the Spirit in a lot of fights. We had all these breakaway suits for the Spirit. If you looked at these suits sideways, they tore."

The movie stuck with a limited color palette much as Warren Beatty did later in the *Dick Tracy* movie (1990). There's only one red, for example. "It was interesting in the next decade, as other people made the same choices, but we were there first," de Souza said.

There were also obstacles that were beyond the crew's control. For one thing, ABC Television was sold in the middle of the shoot.

"When we went back to them with the finished movie, everybody had been fired and it was all new people," de Souza said.

One of Hollywood's cherished traditions is that when new management takes over a studio or television network, it jettisons virtually everything put in place by its predecessors, costs be damned. The new leaders of ABC, who had no emotional or financial connection with *The Spirit*, put it on in the summer without any advertising or promotion, guaranteeing it the smallest possible audience and leaving the pilot zero chance of a pickup as a weekly series.

"It was very frustrating," de Souza said. "In all honesty, it is just as much work to write a TV movie as a 'movie' movie. And yet it's far less rewarding. I was also a supervising producer. I was on set and was in the editing room. This was all I did for five months. This was my day job. Once the network was sold and the people we dealt with were gone, we knew we were in trouble. The new people said, 'We don't want to develop this now.' This was really a labor of love because I'm a fan of this and a fan of comics."

Like a lot of people, Aratow wasn't pleased with the end result.

"I thought it would make a better story than we ended up making," he said. "It's very frustrating. It took years to put it together. It may have looked fast, but it wasn't. It took a long time. I thought it was excellent from a script and production design view. But the casting left something to be desired. If we had had a different actor, I think the show would have been more successful. ABC said, 'Use him or it's no show.' The guy running ABC was in love with Sam or something. It's hard to say why people make these decisions. We had a great director and executives. Maybe it was simply executives exercising their power. And you have to follow their suggestions to prove their power. It was certainly not a reasoned decision.

"That's what went wrong with the product," Aratow continued. "Steve de Souza did a great job. He knew all the comics. He had a vast knowledge. And Warner Bros. gave us classy, elegant production design. They looked at all the Eisner graphics. The design of the show was stylish. It was particularly avant-garde for television at the time. We built a cemetery! We put every dollar on the screen. It just lacked that one element—the intensity of the star."

The Spirit was a labor of love for Von Zerneck, who had high hopes for its success when it aired on July 31, 1987.

"You work on something so long, you get real excited," he said. "Then you wonder if you've done it right. Will the fans like it?"

The answer was a resounding *NO*.

So what went wrong?

"Eisner's work required a particular edge and darkness," Von Zerneck said. "What was tricky was trying to remain true to his vision in terms of the depiction of the characters—without doing a cartoon. That's hard to do with sets and wardrobe. You must spend a lot of time refining that so the piece has a distinctive look. The Spirit wasn't Batman, but a very interesting character nonetheless. Television just wasn't ready for him. Personally, it was disappointing. I thought the material was unique. When you're passionate about something, you get it made, you lick your wounds, and move on."

After its initial broadcast, *The Spirit* pilot was never aired again or even released to the home video market.

Why?

"Odd length," Von Zerneck said. "It was a ninety-minute pilot. And pilots, if they don't sell a series, they rarely release them."

What was Eisner's reaction upon screening the final cut?

"It made my toes curl," he said. "Just awful. It's cardboard."

(Like Roger Corman's unreleased *Fantastic Four* movie, *The Spirit* can often be found in bootleg editions on eBay and at comic book conventions.)

TWENTY
The New Adventures

Denis Kitchen badgered Will Eisner for years to bring back *The Spirit*.

"The fan in me was curious," Kitchen said. "*The Spirit* dropped off in 1952. It didn't end as gracefully as people who loved it hoped it would. I said, 'You have to have a concluding chapter. Where is he now?' What Frank Miller did with *The Dark Knight Returns,* the landmark 1980s story detailing the possible last days of the Batman character, I was trying to get Will to do earlier with *The Spirit.* I said, 'How about one last hurrah?' He always resisted it."

It was not just that Kitchen thought it was a fun idea, he thought it would sell well, too.

"I know why *you* want to do it," Eisner told him, "but it's behind me. There is no personal need for me to do it."

Reviving the character became a running joke; if Kitchen didn't bring it up at least once a year, Eisner would be disappointed in him.

After years of goading, Eisner said, "Well, okay, but my heart is not in it."

The story he wrote was called "The Spirit: The Last Hero."

But maybe Eisner didn't have one more Spirit story to tell. The passage of time, and Eisner's growing interest in more personal work like the graphic novels, left him unable to recapture the character's magic. And it was Kitchen's unfortunate duty to tell his friend so.

"This is uninspired," he told Eisner. "It looks like something you *have* to do versus something you *want* to do."

"Right. Then don't publish it," Eisner said.

"No," Kitchen said glumly. "I didn't think I'd ever say this, but it's not your best work."

Once more, the idea of reviving the character was shelved.

In 1997, Kitchen Sink Press was struggling and in search of pragmatic medicine for what ailed it. This time, Eisner—who was on the board of directors—was receptive. He knew what his friend's situation was. "And it wasn't just me asking," Kitchen said. "It was other professionals. It was Neil Gaiman, Frank Miller, and Alan Moore. They'd say, 'Why don't you give us a new *Spirit*?'"

This time Kitchen suggested a different approach to Eisner.

"Will," he said, "*The Spirit* ended in 1952, the height of the McCarthy era, with all the Communist witch hunts."

"What are you getting at?"

"Maybe he was blackballed?" Kitchen said. "Maybe he was forced to retire?"

"You're starting to get my attention," Eisner said.

Kitchen talked about vigilantism, and about crime and justice. But at the end of the day, Eisner had other topics he wanted to explore. He was bored with the whole comic book genre. The graphic novel form was more important. Kitchen just couldn't bring Eisner to go down old roads again.

But Eisner's own intransigence opened the door for another approach. What if some of the greatest modern comic book creators were interested in tackling *The Spirit*?

This—and the possibility of helping Kitchen Sink Press out of a financial hole—interested him.

Eisner let Kitchen commission a new generation of creators to follow in the footsteps of Lou Fine, Jack Cole, Wally Wood, Jules Feiffer, and himself to produce a fresh series of *Spirit* stories. He even let the majority of the royalty income flow to Kitchen Sink Press, keeping ownership and only a token for himself.

Eisner laid down two cardinal rules to Kitchen and editor Katy Garnier: "The Spirit can't get married and he can't get killed."

The choice of a writer/artist team for the first issue of *Will Eisner's The Spirit: The New Adventures* was both inspired and completely unlikely.

Alan Moore and artist Dave Gibbons were on top of the world following publication of *Watchmen* in 1986, one of the most heralded comic book stories in the medium's history.

So it was somewhat of a surprise when Moore and Gibbons announced that their next collaboration would be the first issue of *Will Eisner's The Spirit: The New Adventures*.

Will Eisner's The Spirit: The New Adventures No. 1

"It was very nice to be working with Dave again," Moore said. "I am sure it was significant for anybody who enjoyed *Watchmen;* it must have been a lot of fun seeing me and Dave do something again. And it was certainly a lot of fun for us to work together. We enjoy working together. It was fortuitous. I was sure that Denis would find a good artist. When I heard it was Dave, I was overjoyed. Me and Dave, we are different people. He was a mod, I was a hippie. But we have a great deal of respect for each other's tastes, and our tastes are similar when it comes to comics. We both know what it is, the intangible things, that we like about this or that, and when it came to *The Spirit,* we both had a good idea of what it was that really made *The Spirit* tick for us, so we could make sure that we kind of infused the strip with that ... Me and Dave are both immense fans of *The Spirit* and of Will's work in general."

Behind the scenes, Moore came aboard because he owed Kitchen and Kevin Eastman work as part of a non-specific advance he had previously received. "This was on the understanding that I would do a certain number of pages of *something*. Kevin wanted me to do something with (artist) Simon Bisley, which at the time could have ended up being *The League of Extraordinary Gentlemen*. It's probably fortunate that didn't come about then. I am sure Simon would have done a very good job, but Kevin O'Neill is the only artist that I can imagine doing that one. Kitchen decided that some of the advance would be better spent upon me doing these three Spirit stories for the magazine."

To kick off the new series—they would be followed by a who's who of the industry's best and brightest over *The New Adventures'* eight-issue run—Moore and Gibbons started at the beginning with a retelling of the Spirit's origin.

Confronted with variant origins, they chose the elements that remained consistent through the series' history, and developed ways in which their three stories could capture different facets of the character.

"We did manage to kind of loosely connect them," Moore said. "It was immense fun going through all of the Eisner riffs—'How are we going to do the title lettering in this story?' 'What Eisner references are we going to make?' We were trying to get as much of what we had learned at Will's feet into the whole thing as possible. It was fanboy fun, but fun nonetheless."

Eisner met Gibbons more than twenty years before Gibbons was invited on board for *New Adventures*. Eisner was in England as a guest of the Society of Strip Illustration (now defunct) around 1975. Gibbons was just beginning his career, and his work had not yet appeared in the U.S. He found Eisner in a pub, killing time, waiting to be introduced to the Society, and said hello.

"You don't know who I am," the young artist said, "but I wanted to thank you for all your good work."

Not one to linger over his own importance, Eisner steered the conversation right to business.

"Do you have any of your work I can look at?"

"Uh, yeah," Gibbons said.

Eisner spent the next thirty minutes concentrating on Gibbons as if Gibbons were the only person in the pub. He gave criticism and he gave praise. He treated the future comics prince as if they knew each other for years. "I found that so encouraging," Gibbons said. "My opinion of him as a man equaled my opinion of him as an artist. It would have made my day just to shake his hand. But he gave me such good criticism about how I could break my work down differently. It was an impromptu master class. But he didn't pull his punches. He's got a good-natured way of doing it, but he wouldn't hold out false hope."

The next time they met was around the time that Gibbons and Moore's *Watchmen* was published and they were the toast of the comics world. "I remember being interviewed on stage at a convention and seeing Will and Ann in the audience. The first time I met him, I was unknown; the second time, I was gathering a bit of a reputation myself. Afterward, I reminded him of his encouragement. He couldn't be more proud of the success I'd had."

As Gibbons' star rose, they saw each other more frequently, at conventions in England, in Grenoble, France, and at the industry's biggest event, Comic-Con International in San Diego.

One year, Gibbons and Frank Miller—alongside several other pros and a contingent of fans with their bags full of comics—were trudging up a San Diego hill, the only thing on their minds the cold beer they would find at the top. Suddenly, they heard footsteps overtaking them on the hill.

It was Eisner.

"Hi, guys!" he said enthusiastically. "Can't stop to talk; got a meeting in five minutes." And he promptly left the much younger men in his dust.

Gibbons and Miller were suitably impressed. "If we could do that at a convention in thirty or forty years, won't that be something?" Gibbons asked. It was just business for Eisner. He had an appointment, and he wasn't going to be late.

The *New Adventures* job was presented to Gibbons after Moore agreed to it. Gibbons, a huge Spirit fan, couldn't possibly say no, describing the opportunity as "beyond the realm of any dreams I had as a kid, anything that could really happen. I always go back to his stuff if I'm feeling uninspired."

So while much of the industry was surprised that the first reteaming of Gibbons and Moore was on a character who last appeared regularly in new stories some forty-five years earlier and was never a comic book staple, the creative team couldn't wait to get started.

"Alan's scripts were so wonderful," Gibbons said. "He really got to the heart—in those three stories—of what's so great about the Spirit. Page for page, there is a lot of work in there. Alan and I get on so well together, personally. And as a team, something happens when we get together. We were offered many things. We could tell DC we wanted to do *Watchmen 2*. But the Spirit was different. It was a character we loved and we had such personal regard for Will. It was an opportunity to tick off another entry on the fanboy dream list.

"To me, the words and pictures and characters in an Eisner story are indivisible," Gibbons continued. "It's the way that Will tells a *Spirit* story that's important, not necessarily the character of the Spirit. We wanted to pay homage to Will's skill as a storyteller, the words and pictures working together. Alan said, 'I want to tell the first story so each page is framed by a different thing—pipes, flowers, smoke, and blood. The opening picture of the first story was a picture of a breakfast and we worked the word 'Spirit' into it with salt and pepper. In the second story, we kept coming back to the guy on the park bench. And in the third, the device was a notebook. The flavor was Alan: the mad genius in the first, the man in the street in the second, and the quasi-science-fiction in the third. We wanted to do the kind of stories that fascinated us the most that Will himself would do."

Moore never spoke with Eisner while he worked on *The New Adventures*, but Gibbons did. In fact, Eisner asked the artist to convey a greeting on his behalf to his partner.

At the San Diego Comic-Con that followed Gibbons and Moore getting the *New Adventures* assignment but before work actually began, Gibbons and Eisner met over morning coffee.

"I'm really pleased you and Alan are doing this," Eisner said. "Just one caution, and please pass this on to Alan: 'Please don't make the Spirit a drug addict.'"

Gibbons couldn't help himself; he laughed.

"I promise!" he said.

"I probably didn't need telling that," Moore said. "I know that I have done some grim things with characters. Actually, I am childishly respectful of the characters that I grew up reading. My Superman stories were a kind of homage to [former *Superman* editor] Mort Weisinger. *The Killing Joke*—I didn't really like that anyway apart from Brian Bolland's beautiful artwork. I thought that was too nasty, and we should never have done it. But other than that, I think I have taken other peoples' characters and tried to treat them with as much love and respect as possible. The thought of showing Denny Colt whacking up heroin never crossed my mind."

Moore wrote a second story for the third issue of *The New Adventures*. Titled "Last Night I Dreamed of Dr. Cobra ..." (and illustrated by Daniel Torres) it was typical Moore—rule-breaking, authority challenging, and pitch-perfect.

"It was a posthumous story about the Spirit," Kitchen recalled. "I said, 'Uh, oh! The Spirit is not supposed to die!' We sent it to Will, knowing it violated one of his cardinal rules. But he loved it. It was what you'd expect Alan to do, something very creative, a completely different take than his first story. When Will liked it, I thought we could probably violate *all* those rules if it's done right."

——————————

Denis Kitchen asked Neil Gaiman to write a story for *The New Adventures*, but Gaiman said no.

A short time later, Gaiman and Eisner were both guests at a comic book convention in Gijon, Spain. "Neil," Eisner said, "I want you to write a Spirit story."

And again, Gaiman declined.

"I am not going to write a Spirit story," he demurred, "because the best thing I will ever come up with is a second-rate Spirit story."

But Eisner wouldn't give up that easily. He invited Gaiman for a long walk along the beach. Mile after mile, Eisner listened carefully to all of Gaiman's reasons why he wouldn't write a Spirit story. When they finally stopped walking—and Gaiman stopped talking—they stepped into a café and Eisner gently explained why he wanted Gaiman to write a story.

"Because," he said, "I would really like to read it."

Gaiman knew when he was beaten.

"Okay, okay," he said.

"I hope that the story I did for *The New Adventures* ("The Return of Mink Stole") was Eisner-ish on two levels," Gaiman said. "Level one is the idea that somewhere in the background there is a Spirit story going on that keeps intersecting with our story, with all the classic Spirit motifs, including him being tied up. So there's that, and that wonderful final page. And one of the things I loved about a good Spirit story is that you would meet somebody on page one and care about them by page two."

———

Eisner, now eighty, pencilled most of the covers for *The New Adventures,* which were then inked by other artists. It was a way for him to collaborate with the new kids on the block. Some of the artists who worked with him reportedly photocopied his pencils and inked over the copies so they could keep the Will Eisner pencil originals.

———

What killed *The New Adventures* was not the project or its craftsmanship but the implosion of its publisher, Kitchen Sink Press. Little that the company published by that time was a raging success.

Moore regrets that he and Gibbons couldn't take *The New Adventures* through its entire run—perhaps keeping the enterprise afloat—but demand for their services was such that they couldn't possibly give *The Spirit* their full attention.

"When Will was doing *The Spirit,* I know he was doing other stuff as well all the time, but I think you get the impression that he could devote most of his energy to *The Spirit* at the times when he was working on it," Moore said. "You wouldn't want a half-hearted Spirit story;

that would be letting down Will, it would be letting down the character. But I think that if me and Dave could have kept on with it and had the time to devote all of our energy to it, yeah, we could have maybe carried it along."

But if he could only take responsibility for one *Spirit* issue in a lifetime, Moore said he's pretty proud of the one he and Gibbons did.

"I was always, personally, really, really happy to have done one, to my mind, near perfect for that one issue," he said. "If I had carried on doing that, I am not Will Eisner. It would only have been a pale imitation at best, and I think maybe that was the sort of the thing that undid the book. Me and Dave worked really, really, really, really hard to do those Spirit stories in exactly the way or as close to the way that we thought that Will would have done them, because that is the best way to do a Spirit story. There is something so inextricably bonded between Will Eisner and *The Spirit* that yeah, you will get some good stories by other people doing it, and it is a great deal of fun to do, but probably it was a wrong-headed venture, and it only got a certain amount of shelf life."

Fan response to the first issue of *The New Adventures* was strong; after the initial excitement, however, the booked slipped beneath the radar. But Gibbons didn't care. "The people who adored it and liked it *really, really* liked it," he said. "And we managed to do it without turning Denny Colt into a junkie!"

TWENTY-ONE
The Library

Will Eisner lived a long and productive life as a creative talent, and one day he found that his career's accumulated production was more than a single publisher could handle alone.

That's the position in which he found himself in 2000. DC Comics acquired selective rights to *The Spirit* and a majority of Eisner's graphic novels soon after Kitchen Sink Press closed. DC created a high-end reprint product, *The Spirit Archives,* which includes six months of in-continuity original stories in every deluxe $49.95 hardcover edition. DC also organized "The Will Eisner Library," an imprint for keeping all of the master's graphic novels in print. Kitchen Sink Press created the brand and logo; DC took the added step of an imprint.

Meanwhile, lifetime Spirit fan Mike Richardson, publisher of Dark Horse Comics, wanted in on the Eisner game. He had been on a quest to be the publisher of record for everything DC did not have, leading to an eclectic slate of books that included everything from *Last Day in Vietnam, Shop Talk, Eisner/Miller,* and *The Will Eisner Sketchbook* to this biography.

Other current Eisner publishers include NBM (*Moby Dick, The Last Knight, The Princess and the Frog, Sundiata: A Legend of Africa*), Doubleday (*Fagin the Jew*), and W. W. Norton (*The Plot*).

Comics & Sequential Art (1985) and *Graphic Storytelling & Visual Narrative* (1996), both published by Eisner's own Poorhouse Press imprint, bore drab textbook covers until given dramatic facelifts in 2004.

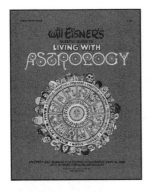

A gallery of Will Eisner's lesser-known books
(Courtesy Will Eisner)

"I originally kept them austere because they were textbooks," Eisner said. "Austerity conveys authority. They shouldn't have had flying figures."

But the very austerity that once established them as central texts in cartooning and illustrating classes around the world also discouraged hobbyists and comic book collectors from purchasing them, so Eisner compromised on covers that were more graphically pleasing.

But Eisner's biggest bestsellers are books rarely even credited to him. These include such incongruous titles as *The Complete World Bartender's Guide* and *Robert's Rules of Order: The Standard Guide to Parliamentary Procedure* (Bantam Books). *The Complete World Bartender's Guide* alone has earned its illustrator more than half a million dollars in royalties to date. And although *Robert's Rules of Order* was in the public domain when Eisner got hold of it, he hit pay dirt with a new edition because nobody had ever illustrated it before. While its sales don't approach *The*

Complete World Bartender's Guide's, it still produces a reliable royalty every year. Another book he packaged, *What's in What You Eat* (Bantam Books, 1983), also followed the recipe of adding illustrations to public-domain information. Produced with the help of Cat Yronwode and Robert Pizzo, it was quickly surpassed in the marketplace by books with more detailed, current data.

Perhaps the only Eisner books no longer in print may be his children's joke-books for Scholastic, the *Gleeful Guides,* and his ordnance books (*A Pictorial Arsenal of America's Combat Weapons* [1962]; *America's Space Vehicles: A Pictorial Review* [1962]; *The M16A1 Rifle Operation and Preventive Maintenance* [1969]; *Freedom's Edge: The Computer Threat to Society* [1974]).

Paul Levitz, president and publisher of DC Comics since 1989, first met Will Eisner when Jim Warren published *The Spirit* magazine in the early 1970s.

It was Levitz who, in 2000, first took Eisner from his status as an industry standard and put corporate muscle behind him, with DC taking over publication of Eisner's graphic novel collection. When Kitchen Sink Press had it, it went under a brand name, "The Will Eisner Library." The inherent challenge for DC was in standardizing the Library, because many of the books were published by KSP in different formats.

"But it was nice to have a landmark book like *A Contract with God* on our list, and then do what we could with the whole group," Levitz said. "They sold some copies every year."

As the guiding force behind the publisher's adventurous, edgy Vertigo line, Karen Berger was on the front lines of high profile works by creators such as Eduardo Risso (*100 Bullets*), Neil Gaiman (*The Sandman*), Brian Azzarello (*100 Bullets* and *Hellblazer*), and Bill Willingham (*Fables*). But she was still nervous about overseeing her first Eisner graphic novel, *Minor Miracles,* and adding a final touch after Eisner's longtime personal editor, Dave Schreiner.

"Absolutely," she said. "Will's status speaks for itself. I was a little intimidated. But I got over it pretty fast because he made you feel so at ease."

After finishing *Miracles,* Berger was at the San Diego Comic-Con and met the Eisners for breakfast. She asked what he wanted to do next and Eisner described *The Name of the Game,* but said he had set it aside. Berger said she'd like to see it.

"Let me think about it," he said.

A week later, Eisner called her back.

"I'm glad we talked about it," he said. "I'd like to go back and finish it."

Editing *Name* was a much easier experience than *Miracles* for Berger.

"The first time, I talked to Denis Kitchen for guidance. He was like, 'Just talk to Will.' In *The Name of the Game,* I had a few story questions," Berger said. "I was concerned with how Will dealt with southern Jews. I questioned a non-Kosher menu at a wedding dinner. Will explained to me that southern Jews were more liberal. Will tells the stories that he wants to tell. My job in working with him is to make sure that that vision is clear. If something didn't ring true, or the logic didn't follow or felt wrong, I brought it up."

One area in which Berger and Eisner experienced a great deal of back and forth was the cover of *The Name of the Game.* "We wanted a hardcover look that was more of a bookstore approach," Berger said. "We came up with a photographic look. Old. Will liked the approach but thought people would think the photos were associated with him, so we didn't go that way."

Berger said that Eisner was "an amazing force of nature," adding that he was always young at heart. "Each book, he was still nervous about whether it was any good or not. Which I thought was very humble considering how much he's achieved. His attitude, his approach to creativity, his work ethic, his professionalism—he's such a pleasure to work with, such a wonderful human being."

When Levitz announced that DC would publish a library-quality edition of every weekly newspaper installment of *The Spirit* from 1940 to 1952, it elevated the Spirit to corporate icon status, alongside DC's better-known superheroes, Batman and Superman.

"The *Archives* represent the lively intersection of commerce and art," Levitz said. "We've found in our *Archives* program, by learning to manage our inventory, and finding the right economic model, that it's possible to make a reasonable profit, pay a reasonable royalty, and make these books work to a small audience."

When Kitchen Sink Press shut down, Levitz found the potential availability of Eisner's body of work irresistible.

"Our VP of sales and marketing, Bob Wayne, and I were at Diamond Comics Distributors that week," Levitz recalled. "We were just two comic books fans at that moment, sitting around BS-ing—'Wouldn't it be fun to have *The Spirit* in Russ Cochran's EC Comics hardcover reprint form?' We were interested in bringing it into our line and bringing some of the most important comics into continuous availability for the scholars and fans who want access to it."

Levitz discovered *The Spirit* in the 1960s the same way a lot of comics fans did, in the pages of Jules Feiffer's book, *The Great Comic Book Heroes*. A few years later, Mark Hanerfeld, editor of *The Comic Reader* fanzine, sold Levitz a set of duplicates from his collection of *Spirit* weekly sections. That gave him about half the run. Then he began filling them in with purchases from collectors Steve Geppi and Walter Wang. But in the end, he couldn't complete the entire run, which left Levitz frustrated.

"I'm the anal retentive kind of fan who isn't happy having half," he said. "So I sold my half because I wasn't happy with half. So when we introduced *The Spirit Archives* line to retailers, I was on a retailers panel at the San Diego Comic-Con and I told them, 'This is my chance to finish off something I've been working on for thirty years."

The Spirit Archives are in a format that Eisner never imagined when he did the original work more than half a century ago. He began at a time when all comics were transient, although he had the good sense to keep his rights and the bulk of the source material—art and photostats—as well. Detective/National Comics itself didn't do that, allowing thousands of its original artworks to be destroyed, given away, or stolen.

As prestigious as *The Spirit Archives* promised to be, and as successful as the series would be in cementing Eisner's legacy for the ages, he approached the opportunity with the same outsider trepidation that always governed his decision making.

"Will had a set of concerns," Levitz said, "reasonably based on the fact that he had never had his most precious creative child with a large corporate publisher. He had a lot of unique considerations in looking at a contract. He's always taken the long view of what he did. That may be the fundamental difference between him and most cartoonists: he always bet on himself."

Eisner always negotiated realistically. His issues over *The Spirit Archives* were less financial and more creative, just as they were with Kitchen and Warren before DC.

Eisner was extremely proud to have his work collected in DC Comics' *Archives* editions
(Photograph by Bob Andelman)

He found that Levitz, who personally oversaw *The Spirit Archives*, was the right man for the job.

"They were books that were important to me as a reader," Levitz said. "They were books that didn't quite fit with the rest of our lines. If something is a logical Vertigo book or DC Universe title, it's natural to turn it over to the person heading up that line. We had never acquired anything for the *Archives* from anywhere else; there wasn't a clear model for it. I knew Will, knew Denis, knew the material, so it was easier, and fun, to do myself."

DC staffers were especially tickled by the success of *The Spirit Archives*. "They were a real artistic feather in our cap," said Dale Crain, senior editor of collected editions for DC. "Everybody was thrilled when the deal went through. It's all totally classic, beautiful, and important material."

Crain, who designed and edited comic strip reprint books for Kitchen Sink Press before joining DC, was responsible for working with Eisner on the look of *The Spirit Archives* books and on an important detail: how the books would be colored. Up until volume twelve, every strip was reconstructed from original published strips. Crain and Eisner went through several iterations of coloring approaches in search of the right one.

"Fortunately, we were on the same wavelength," Crain said. "We wanted to add as much fidelity as possible to the original. To try and get the meter set correctly, we would digitally scan the pages. The problem, when you scan it, is that your end product is only as good as the original. It takes quite a bit of handwork. We took color newspaper pages and made them black and white, then re-colored them by computer, just as the computer removed the original color. It's a fairly convoluted process. You take it back down to what it was originally and recreate it. Often a black line becomes chewed up, requiring a lot of smoothing and cleaning. The first eleven volumes were done that way. With the twelfth volume (the first featuring Eisner's post-war return to the strip), we started working from Will's own first- or second-generation originals." A few months after the first *Archive* appeared, Eisner got a call from Levitz, who told him that the first edition of *The Spirit Archives* outsold the first issues of the *Superman Archives* and the *Batman Archives*—despite a ten-year head start for *Batman* and *Superman*.

"It's one of the most successful we've done," Levitz said. "We may have cumulatively sold more *Superman,* but that may not be true. A lot of people wanted to have the whole run of *The Spirit* to watch the evolution than wanted to watch *Superman* evolve. Most had seen this imperfect reprinting. There was a lot of pent-up demand."

"This was the first time The Spirit met these venerable characters (Superman and Batman) on equal terms," Eisner said. "I am quite proud of that."

━━━━━━━━

When Dark Horse Comics Publisher Mike Richardson first entered the comics industry, he and Denis Kitchen were introduced at a San Diego Comic-Con party. Richardson made his name as a force in the industry in many ways, but particularly with his success in licensing comics characters such as The Mask, Barb Wire, Mystery Men, and Hellboy to the movies. But for Kitchen, the new guy was most memorable for being the first to challenge Kitchen's traditional height advantage over the industry.

Kitchen was six-foot-six, but at six-foot-eight, Richardson towered over him.

The two publishers were on opposite sides of the room when Eisner approached Kitchen.

"You're taller than that Richardson fellow, aren't you?" Eisner asked.

"No way," Kitchen said. "Why?"

"Because I bet $5 on *you*," Eisner said.

Kitchen knew Eisner didn't like to lose money, but a fact was a fact.

"You lost five bucks," he informed his longtime friend and mentor, as he watched Eisner's brow furrow deeply.

———

Before Dark Horse Comics editor Diana Schutz ever worked with Will Eisner, she met him in 1999 in front of several thousand people at a ballroom at the San Diego Comic-Con. Eisner was on stage, handing out the annual industry awards bearing his name, and Dark Horse was enjoying a pretty good run.

Frank Miller's *300* had been published that year and won three Eisner Awards. Other Dark Horse award winners included Stan Sakai's *Usagi Yojimbo* and Matt Wagner's *Grendel: Black, White, and Red*, a four-issue anthology series edited by Schutz. When *Grendel: Black, White, and Red* won the award for best anthology, Miller pushed a terrified Schutz toward the stage to accept.

"I really *was* terrified," Schutz admitted, "but I had a vague little something in the back of my head to say at the mic. But when Will handed me the award on stage, he leaned in and kissed me on the cheek—and at that moment everything blew out of my head. All I could say to the audience was, 'Oh, my God, Will Eisner just kissed me!' That's the effect he had on me."

Within months, a kiss blossomed into a full-fledged, accidental working relationship. Kitchen Sink Press imploded during that time and Denis Kitchen, as Eisner's literary representative, shopped rights to his library of graphic novels and *The Spirit* reprints. DC Comics jumped at the opportunity and grabbed his entire back catalog in the spring of 2000.

But Eisner's most recently completed graphic novel, *Last Day in Vietnam*, was not part of the deal. The project was done, but unpublished, and Eisner wanted it to be published in time for the upcoming

San Diego Comic-Con that July. The comic book publishing industry is incapable of working that fast; it relies on an ironclad schedule for announcing new products to retailers and consumers in the Diamond *Previews* magazine. A comic book intended for sale in July must be listed in the May issue of *Previews;* a graphic novel needs to be announced a month earlier than that.

DC passed on its right of first refusal, unable to meet Eisner's publishing schedule, and gave permission for Kitchen & Hansen to offer it to other publishers. Their first stop was with Dark Horse and Richardson.

Richardson told Kitchen that his company would not only publish *Last Day in Vietnam* but would get it solicited in *Previews* in time for San Diego, even though Dark Horse had already sent its solicitation for that month to Diamond.

"We'll do the impossible," Richardson claimed.

"It was insane," Schutz said later. "We had to pull favors from Diamond, from everyone. I was running to army bases to get photos to run between the stories. That cemented my relationship with Will, because we pulled it off and the book was out for San Diego. It was one of Mike's proudest moments: to publish Will Eisner. And I figured *I* could retire! I mean, it just doesn't get any better than being *Will Eisner's* editor!"

Since then, Dark Horse has published "The Will Eisner Collection"—an imprint akin to DC's "Will Eisner Library"—which includes everything from reprints of the complete run of his 1930s adventure strip, *Hawks of the Seas,* to *The Will Eisner Sketchbook,* a deluxe coffee-table book showing the artist's raw pencils and blue lines from *The Spirit* and many of Eisner's graphic novels. It also has the right to republish Kitchen Sink's *Will Eisner's The Spirit: The New Adventures.*

━━━━━━

In 2000, the Comic Book Legal Defense Fund sponsored a fundraising cruise during which fans could mingle and socialize with some of the comic book industry's greatest and most successful talent. Among those in attendance were Neil Gaiman, Frank Miller, Neal Adams, comic book writer Kurt Busiek, graphic novelist Chris Ware, and Will Eisner.

During a lull, Miller and Charles Brownstein suggested it would be interesting if Miller and Eisner engaged in a detailed discussion about the history and philosophy of comic books. They agreed that the conversation should be captured in book form and shared with the industry. Intrigued, Eisner said he would consider the project. Brownstein wrote a formal proposal, which Eisner then countered. Dark Horse committed to the book as publisher and the project seemed well on its way.

"We all agreed in September 2000 to do this," Brownstein said. "But then a whole lot of personal turmoil took place in Frank's life. He went AWOL for a long time. Will and I were on track to get it done in '01, but Frank disappeared for the entire year, working on *The Dark Knight Strikes Again*."

Miller finished the graphic novel in 2002; by then, Eisner had grown impatient.

"I'm fighting a losing battle with time," he complained to Brownstein.

At Eisner's insistence, the trio scheduled their first common window of time, a weekend in May 2002. But it was probably a mistake, in retrospect.

"Frank was mentally exhausted and Will didn't do his homework," Brownstein said. "We agreed to talk about the medium in a contrast between a graphic novel of Frank's (*Sin City*) and one of Will's (*A Contract with God*), and Will clearly hadn't read Frank's book. That led to less than we expected. Frank and I hoped to get an Alfred Hitchcock/François Truffaut discussion. Instead, Will was very contrary. Will started by insulting Frank's work. He said Frank's reader is concerned with pursuit and vengeance. Whereas Will's reader, he said, is someone interested in the institution of marriage. Will said, 'Your reader doesn't have time for the institution of marriage.' Will waved the red flag in front of the bull."

Here is an excerpt from what came next in the conversation:

> *EISNER: We separate there, because you are more connected to what's going on. I'm still reporting, telling stories about the past ...*
> *MILLER: I tell stories too, Will.*

EISNER: I know you do, I know you do [Miller laughs]. *But I'm talking about—you're connected with the main flow. I talk about yesterday.*

MILLER: I think I probably fit more street theater in my stories. I jump all over what's currently going on. I don't know. I think there are central questions we're all facing as to what our intent is.

EISNER: Well, for instance, I talk to people about the institution of marriage. You've got no time for that, because the people you're talking to are not dealing with it. You're involved in the mainstream. You're right in there with the excitement of it, and you're aware of it. I'm talking about, in A Contract with God, *man's relationship to God. The guy who's reading your stuff doesn't give a shit about man's relationship to God. He wants to see whether Marvin kills that son of a bitch or doesn't kill that son of a bitch or whatever it is he's adopted to assassinate or kill or beat up. We're talking to different people. You're aware of it.*

MILLER: Really, that was an unfair characterization. My stuff deals with that too. It's more than pandering. My stuff is just more operatic than what you're currently doing. I'm not going to go into a lengthy defense of the complexity of my work, but my stories aren't just about people killing each other.

"It was downhill from there," Brownstein said. "It was a very contentious exchange between Will and Frank. Neither one of them, speaking candidly, was in top form that weekend. Will was aggravated because starting the book took longer than scheduled, so he was aggravated with Frank. And Frank had literally just finished *DK2*, so he was fatigued. It led to a very contentious exchange."

Even Denis Kitchen acknowledged it wasn't one of his friend's best moments.

"Will didn't show Frank respect," Kitchen said. "He didn't do his homework. If he read *Sin City*, he would have seen it was very different than what Todd MacFarlane (*Spawn*) was doing. Frank does what Will does; he thinks about his panels, his layouts. He's a serious auteur. And Will didn't acknowledge that."

Eisner, an impressive a judge of human nature, immediately recognized his *faux pas*.

"The natural result of a conversation between two guys like this is a comparison of their work and who their audience is," he said. "I thought his audiences were a bunch of guys who were waiting to see Marvin, his main character, beat the hell out of the next villain. Frank thought that was much too shallow a comment, and he was upset. I softened it up later on."

Although he transcribed the final manuscript (published in 2005), Brownstein's role over the weekend was as mediator between the two great artists. He provided questions that provoked them both and he kept them on track when they veered off topic. It was an eye-opening experience for Brownstein, who had known both men for several years.

"What I learned about Will from that is that there are two Wills," Brownstein said. "There is Will the Schemer, and Will the Dreamer. The dreamer is the grandfatherly founder of our industry who made great strides for graphic novels and comics and believed through his whole career that this is worth pursuing.

"Then there is the other Will, the businessman," Brownstein continued. "He revels in business. He's very good at business. And he's very cunning. He doesn't really let that side of him out. And he doesn't reveal how that has played in his career. One of the frustrations that Frank and I had was that we wanted to get into the political business of the field. But Will is more interested in the form and his contribution and what other people have built on. The guy was shrewd enough in his twenties to secure his rights to *The Spirit*. *The Spirit* wouldn't have meant as much as it did if he didn't own it. He later sold comic books to the Army and General Motors. That is a mind we admire but don't have much access to. That is something I saw that weekend, but it's something Will doesn't want to get into."

As they sat out on the pool patio at the Eisner's home with the tape recorder running, Brownstein and Miller tried cajoling Will into revealing more of himself.

"Diana Schutz is always saying I should reveal myself more," Will said.

"You've got nothing to hide, Will," Ann said.

But that's just not the way Eisner played the game. He could talk for hours at conventions, in interviews, or at parties about the importance of art and story, textures and layers, and capturing a character's humanity in words and pictures, but when it comes to the non-creative side of the business, he just doesn't see why anyone cares. Ironically, that's the part of the business that comes more naturally to him than the stress of creation. But it doesn't interest him in the least as a topic of public discussion.

"It should be known, though," Brownstein said. "Will is that important."

In late 2004, W. W. Norton acquired DC's rights to The Will Eisner Library, a major coup for Eisner and his agents, Denis Kitchen and Judith Hansen, who long believed that a mainstream book publisher could get Eisner's work in front of a mature, new audience that a comic book publisher couldn't access.

Eisner's final books brought the prestige that Eisner—a former resident of what he called "the comic book ghetto"—sought all his life. He took great pride in mainstream publishers, such as Doubleday (*Fagin the Jew*) and W. W. Norton (*The Plot*), acquiring his work.

"It's an affirmation," he said. "I'm with the folks on the hill. It's where I've always felt I should be. I *know* that sounds egotistic. It's something one doesn't say. It's something one shouldn't say. But I'm writing to their audience. I'm not writing to the eighteen-year-old kid who reads superheroes. It's a way of saying that I'm allowed in the company of the people who we regard as the cultural aristocracy."

W. W. Norton publishes many of America's greatest writers, including Faulkner, e. e. cummings, Arthur Schlesinger, Henry Roth, Primo Levy, and David Mamet.

"I think Will belongs in the same group," said Robert Weil, the Norton editor who acquired *The Plot*. "We were very honored to work with Will."

TWENTY-TWO
The Amazing Adventures of
Kavalier & Eisner

Michael Chabon knows that one of the hardest things in the world is composing a letter that asks a favor from a personal hero. In the case of the letter Chabon wrote to Eisner, the rising young novelist entrusted the delivery of it to a middleman. Chabon chose his words and structured his prose even more carefully than usual.

October 19, 1995
Dear Mr. Eisner,

Please pardon this intrusion on your time and your privacy, particularly as I write in the hope of persuading you to spare me a little more of both. I am the author of two novels, The Mysteries of Pittsburgh *(Morrow, 1988), and* Wonder Boys *(Villard, 1995), and a story collection,* A Model World *(Morrow, 1991). Most of my stories have also been published over the last eight years in* The New Yorker. *I plaster this paragraph thus with my credentials not in an effort to impress you, but simply to establish that I am, at least in theory, a serious person, and that by this letter I attempt to reach out to you, if I may take the liberty of so designating myself, as one artist to another.*

*I have been an admirer and a fan of yours since com-
ing across Jules Feiffer's* Great Comic Book Heroes,
*at the age of eleven, in the public library in my home-
town. As the title of my first book indicates, my work is
deeply connected in a mysterious way to the city of
Pittsburgh, and one of my proudest possessions is an
original copy of the Spirit adventure that ran in the*
Pittsburgh Post-Gazette *on April 17, 1949.*

*To come to the point of this letter without further
boasting or flattery: I have recently begun work on my
third novel. Tentatively entitled* The Golden Age, *it is
set in New York City just after the Second World War,
and concerns the adventures of a couple of fictitious
comic book writers and artists and their doubly fictitious
costumed creations. I have a number of excellent books—
histories and encyclopedias—detailing the facts and
general chronologies of that era in the history of the
comic book, as well as fine books about New York in the
same period. But when it comes to matters of texture—
of how it* felt *to be alive then and working in that lost
city, in that strange business—I have only my imagination to rely on. I would hate to get it all wrong.*

*Which brings me to this: I would love to be able to
talk to you, to correspond with you, at the very least to
pose you a few questions about your memories of that
time and place and trade. I want to understand the
marketing and production side of the business in those
days; I want to know where you all lived, what you ate,
if you took the subway, what music you listened to, etc.
Sure, I could make all that up, but I think my book, for
all its eventual flights of fancy, will be great only insofar
as it is rooted in* the way things really were.

*Mr. (Marv) Wolfman has been very protective of your
privacy, and so I don't even know the ultimate destina-
tion of this letter, but if you are in the continental United
States and by some remote chance are agreeable to our*

meeting, I would be more than willing to travel any dis-
tance, at any time, to effect this. If you prefer to limit
our interaction to the mails, I will of course be grateful
for that much. I know this is a huge imposition on my
part, and I will certainly understand if you have no
interest in wasting any of your valuable time on me and
my project.

In any case, even if I never hear from you again, I'm
grateful for this opportunity simply to tell you, once
more, the hours and years of delight I have derived
from reading and looking at your incredible work.
Thank you.

Regards,
Michael Chabon

"I had very limited resources when it came to contacts and connec-
tions in the comic book world when I started," explained Chabon, author
of the novel that began life as "The Golden Age" but eventually was
published and became the 2001 Pulitzer Prize winner for fiction under
the title *The Amazing Adventures of Kavalier & Clay*.

At the time Chabon reached out to Eisner, his *Wonder Boys* had
been well received but had not yet become a feature film with Michael
Douglas and future "Spider-Man" Tobey Maguire. Chabon was not
especially well known outside of certain hip literary circles.

"In the opening paragraph in my letter to him, I was trying to per-
suade him that I was not Joe Schmo," Chabon said. "I felt there was a
good likelihood that he was going to just say, 'I don't know what this is
about, but no thank you.' I would not have been at all surprised if he had
turned me down. And that was true of Stan Lee and Gil Kane, too, but
on the contrary, all three of them were really gracious. Gil Kane talked
to me for three hours, and Stan gave me an hour over the telephone. He
was too busy to get together face to face, but still, he was very expansive
when we spoke over the phone. I was expecting to get shot down, *boom,*
boom, boom, and instead, they all three said sure."

If he started writing the same book today, Chabon would be able to
talk to just about anybody he wanted to for background on the project.

But in 1995, he was a complete outsider to the comic book industry. His only connection going in was as a fan who grew up reading and loving comic books.

"I didn't know anybody," Chabon said, "but I knew a couple of people who knew some people, and I had a friend, Cy Voris, who was a screenwriter, and he knew Marv Wolfman. My friend asked Wolfman, 'Do you know any old-timers that this guy who's got a stupid idea for a novel could talk to?' and he said, 'Yeah, I know Will Eisner.'"

Eisner, who was living in Florida, responded to Chabon by mail and said he was planning an upcoming trip to Oakland, where he was to be a guest of honor at the annual Wondercon comics convention. He would be delighted to give the young writer an hour of his time, Eisner wrote, and whatever else he needed.

For Eisner, it was another interview in a lifetime of answering questions about his craft and career, as well as one of a thousand times in which he put someone else's career ahead of his own. With Ann at his side, he spent an hour answering all of Chabon's questions.

"I filled up several pages in my notebook with the things that he told me," Chabon said. "It was a crucial meeting for me, because not only was I thrilled at the chance to meet the great Will Eisner and talk to him, but he really helped solidify certain ideas I had that were maybe a little shaky before this."

Eisner turned to Ann for confirmation sometimes, or she would amplify something her husband had said. One of the more arcane details that went into Chabon's research was a chart he developed of every Manhattan and Brooklyn telephone exchange that he came across. "As soon as I found one, I would write it down," he recalled. "Sometimes I would just come across a two-letter abbreviation, you know, AL-6, and sometimes in ads they would write them out. But I still had a bunch of blanks, so I sat with Will and Ann and started pitching them these two-letter phone exchanges. They would look at each other and say, 'Yes, that was Gramercy or Butterfield.' She remembered a lot of them."

There were many more questions, most of them unrelated to the comic book business. What kind of music did Eisner listen to? Did he listen to it on the radio or on records? Did he listen to music while he worked? Did he smoke? And, if he did, what brand did he smoke?

Did the guys in the bullpen smoke while they were working? If the room became really smoky, did he open the window? Where did he have lunch? Did he go to a lunch counter, have lunch in a restaurant, or have food delivered? Why did he think so many of the original creators were Jewish? Was there anything specifically Jewish about comic books?

"I wanted the particulars, the details of not just the business itself, although I definitely wanted those too, but I also wanted the details of just everyday life," Chabon said. "There was this one wonderful moment where he brought up the idea of the Golem, the Golem of Prague, in particular, and sort of cited it as an example of the kind of traditional figures that might have been somewhere buried in the mix that led to the creation of the superhero, and Superman in particular. And when he mentioned the Golem, I had just started to write the Golem into my book. Gadzooks! To hear him mention it—to cite it in that way! Then he went on to say this wonderful thing that I wrote down, and that then became the epigraph for the whole novel, which is, 'We have this history of impossible solutions to insoluble problems.' I wanted this book to be about that very thing. It was definitely a signal moment for me."

Eisner's attitude toward Chabon's inquisition was one of tolerance. "He was nothing but courtly and polite and cordial," Chabon said. "Honestly, I don't remember now whether he actually expressed a certain amount of skepticism, like, 'What is this crazy thing you are going to be doing?' or whether it was just some vibes that I picked up."

Chabon wasn't wrong. At one point in the interview, when Chabon looked down at his notepad, he missed Eisner silently mouthing the word "Fanboy" to his wife.

That was their only contact until after *Kavalier & Clay* was published. But the importance of that contact is clear, not only in Chabon's words here, but in the Author's Note in the back of the novel, which begins, "I am indebted to Will Eisner ... " After Eisner comes everyone else. (Chabon said his acknowledgments were alphabetical, but after Eisner came Stan Lee, then Gil Kane.)

"I saw to it that he was sent a copy," Chabon said, "and then, as I recall, I did not hear from him. I think I did not hear that the copy I had requested be sent was actually sent, so I did not have that certainty that he got it. Then, somebody I know who knew him said, 'Oh yes. He got it. He read it. He loved it. He was very excited about it.'"

Chabon's quest to interview Eisner came from a strong desire for historical accuracy. And there is a significant difference between a book of acts and an oral history. "My dream was that someone who was alive back then and remembered New York during that period would say, 'There are no major errors here,'" Chabon said. "Then, secondarily, anybody that was actually in the comic book business who read it would know that I had not gotten too many things wrong, either, so just to have him even factually approve of it, that was sort of the most I could hope for."

Many people recognized shades of Will Eisner in the character of Joe Kavalier in Chabon's book, although the creator of the Spirit was nowhere near as tortured a soul as the cocreator of "The Escapist."

But only in two places in the novel does Chabon acknowledge that his art imitated life, or imitated Eisner.

"I had just barely started when I met with Will," he said. "When it came time in the writing to sort of figure out what Joe's attitude toward comic books was going be and how he was going to feel about his work as a comic book artist, I pretty consciously decided to bestow on him what I imagined was Will Eisner's attitude toward it, and the impression was confirmed by my having read a 1941 *Philadelphia Record* article ("The 'Spirit' of '41" by Norman Abbott). It clearly documented his belief—startlingly early on—that comic books were art, or at least that they had the potential to be art eventually. That idea is what I decided to give to Joe Kavalier.

"And then later—much later—in the book, when it came time to describe the sprawling two-thousand-page comic book that Joe had drawn about the Golem, there is a very conscious, very deliberate borrowing from Will Eisner's art in the way that I describe how each chapter of this huge gothic novel opens with this splash panel on which the letters of the words 'Der Golem' become all kinds of different things. That is obviously borrowing from the classic Eisner trick with splash panels."

A couple of years passed before Chabon saw Eisner again. When they finally were reunited at the San Diego Comic-Con in 2000, there was no silent use of the term "fanboy."

Will Eisner and Michael Chabon at San Diego Comic-Con International
(Courtesy Jackie Estrada)

"Will was just extremely warm and affectionate, patting me on the shoulder and calling me 'my boy,'" Chabon said. "He was almost at least acting as if he were unworthy of the compliment that I had paid him by quoting him in the epigraph in the novel and so on. I told him that (longtime *Incredible Hulk* artist) Herb Trimpe sent me a fabulous re-creation of the cover of *Amazing Midget Radio Comics* #1 passing it off that he had bought it at a yard sale! Will got this funny look on his face, and he said, 'I feel bad; I should have done something for you. I never told you how much I liked the book. I should have sent you something.' Within a few weeks, I received this lovely painting of the Spirit sitting with his reading glasses on his nose and *Kavalier & Clay* in front of him. Below, it said, 'Thanks, Michael, you really captured how it was.' So that was lovely, and I have it framed in my office."

TWENTY-THREE
The Will Eisner
Comic Industry Awards

Will Eisner received the news of the nomination with mixed emotions. Being recognized by your peers is one thing. But how would you feel about competing for your industry's highest honor ... if it was named for you?

That was Eisner's dilemma in 2002—again. At the age of eighty-five, in the fourteenth year of the comic book industry's Eisner Awards, an independent, blue-ribbon panel nominated Eisner for his own award for the tenth time.

History shows that in Eisner's case, these nominations are more than just a nod to comics' grand old man. During the 2002 awards, Eisner had won four of nine catagories. His influence on the industry not only remained constant over a sixty-year career but actually increased from 1978 onward.

One of the biggest developments that brought Eisner's name to the forefront of the comic book industry, and to the attention of a new generation of artists and readers, was the decision in 1988 to name one of the industry's two major awards after him—the Will Eisner Awards. Eisner was a little uncomfortable with the honor, but knowing that the industry's other major award, The Harveys, was named for his old friend

Harvey Kurtzman was a great comfort.

In 1985, there was a single industry award called the Kirby Award, named after Jack "King" Kirby. Kirby, from his beginnings in the Eisner & Iger Studio, had risen to the pinnacle of his profession by cocreating the Marvel Comics characters Captain America, The Fantastic Four, The Hulk, and the Silver Surfer, as well as inventing numerous characters for DC Comics, including Kamandi, The Last Boy on Earth, and The New Gods.

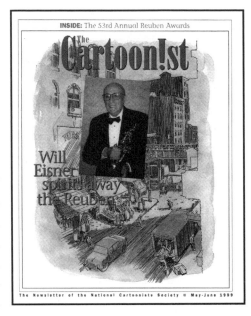

The Cartoon!st magazine announced Eisner winning the coveted Reuben Award in its May/June 1999 issue
(Courtesy Will and Ann Eisner)

The Kirby Awards were started by Gary Groth's company, Fantagraphics (publisher of *The Comics Journal*), and administered by employee Dave Olbrich. After Olbrich had a falling out with his employer and quit in 1987, he thought he could take the awards with him. Fantagraphics strongly objected. The situation unraveled into an ugly struggle for control, accompanied by plenty of bad publicity for all sides. And Kirby himself, who was alive at the time, got caught in the middle. He and his wife, Roz, were fond of Olbrich, but they also understood Fantagraphics' position. According to Eisner, they said, "We don't want to be torn apart, so just forget about it."

That's when Olbrich came to Eisner.

"Look," he said, "I have this award ceremony in place; Jack doesn't want it in his name anymore for political reasons. May we name it after you?"

Eisner didn't have to think about it long.

He said yes without hesitation.

"A respected industry award raises the standard of the medium," Eisner said. "I certainly want to be a part of that."

Meanwhile, Fantagraphics went to Harvey Kurtzman and asked him the same thing—"Can we name our award after you?" Kurtzman's career in many ways paralleled Eisner's, spanning many decades and including stops at EC Comics, where he created *MAD* magazine, then *Trump* for Hugh Hefner at *Playboy,* and *Humbug,* as part of an artist-owned group. While working with Jim Warren, he published another landmark magazine, *Help!* The "Public Gallery," section of that magazine introduced the new breed of underground cartoonists like Jay Lynch, Robert Crumb, Skip Williamson, and Gilbert Shelton. While there, with Will Elder illustrating, Kurtzman created, wrote, and laid out "Goodman Beaver," which evolved into "Little Annie Fanny," and became a *Playboy* fixture. Kurtzman said yes to Fantagraphics, and that is how the Eisners and the Harveys started at the same time.

The Harveys adopted "The Kirby" as an award within the Harveys. For many years, they presented the Jack Kirby Hall of Fame Award—which Eisner himself won early on. (The award has not been given for the last several years.)

Meanwhile, the Eisners became associated with the annual Comic-Con International in San Diego.

"Olbrich dropped the ball with the awards in 1990, which is why no awards were given that year," according to Awards Administrator Jackie Estrada. "It all had to do with errors in the nominating process and the fact that Dave was trying to run the awards in his spare time. It was at the 1990 San Diego Con that Will and Denis approached Fae Desmond (executive director of Comic-Con) and me about taking over the awards. Will and Denis felt that it would be a good fit, since Comic-Con is a nonprofit and since the Kirby Awards and then the new Eisner awards had been given out at San Diego, albeit in daytime programming rooms. Will specifically asked me if I would take on the administration. Soon after I took over, I switched the nominations process from the open ballot—which the Harveys use—to the judging panel approach. This, along with different criteria for the award categories, is the main distinction between the process for selecting the nominees.

"Over the years," she continued, "I have turned the awards into a gala nighttime event rather than a daytime program, and have introduced a number of elements, including an interactive slide show, a keynote speaker, etc. Today's Eisners bear little resemblance to the Olbrich-created version."

For many reasons, the Eisners and Harveys have long been intertwined. Eisner, for example, has won awards from both groups. In 2001, he was nominated for both awards twice, once each for a new work, *The Name of the Game,* and once each for volume one of *The Spirit Archives,* reprinting work from 1940. Eisner lost both Eisners but won both Harveys. "So much for the fix being in!" Eisner said.

The Harveys were given out in Pittsburgh that year. Eisner was not present, but Denis Kitchen accepted the second award as a stand-in.

"I am accepting this on behalf of Will Eisner, who I am sure will be very pleased to receive this award named after his good friend Harvey Kurtzman," Kitchen said. "Isn't it remarkable that Will has won awards for works that are ..." he paused, " ... *sixty* years apart?"

―――――――

When Howard Cruse's *Stuck Rubber Baby* (Paradox Press/DC) won an Eisner Award in 1996 in the best new graphic novel category, he beat out Eisner himself, whose book *Dropsie Avenue: The Neighborhood* had been nominated for the same award category.

"I was so flustered on the podium," Cruse recalled. "I made a joke about how weird it was to beat Eisner for an Eisner. I was supposed to follow it up with an appreciation of Will but I completely forgot."

―――――――

Will Eisner and Al Feldstein at San Diego Comic-Con International
(Courtesy Al Feldstein)

Al Feldstein, best known for his work as an artist and writer for EC Comics and *MAD* magazine, where he was editor for nearly thirty years, went to work as a teenager at Eisner & Iger Studio just before he was drafted and just after Eisner left the company. "He was a myth and a legend even then," Feldstein said.

The shadow cast by the studio's departed founder only grew thanks to one of Jerry Iger's unshakeable traits. "The only reason it was still called 'Eisner & Iger Studio,'" Feldstein said, "was that Jerry was too cheap to throw out all the pre-printed Strathmore boards, so we worked on 'Eisner & Iger' boards."

Some thirty-five years later, in 1977, Feldstein was surprised at the San Diego Comic-Con with an Inkpot Award. Earlier in the evening, Eisner recounted for the audience the famous story of his former partner's cheapness when it came to towels.

When that year's award winners were announced, Feldstein walked to the stage, dumbstruck. He didn't know what to say.

"Then I thought of Will," he recalled. "I said, 'I owe my career to Will Eisner. I wasn't good enough to get a job drawing so I got a job at the Eisner & Iger Studio erasing fingerprints from finished comic book pages. And the reason I got the job—for $3 a week after school—was that nobody had any towels to wash their fingers. Jerry wouldn't spend the money."

In 2003, Feldstein and Eisner were reunited in San Diego when Feldstein was voted into the Will Eisner Hall of Fame.

"Will," he said in his acceptance speech, "I made a full circle. I started in your shop and now I'm in your Hall of Fame."

———

Demand for Eisner's time at the August 2002 San Diego Comic-Con was extraordinary. Even though Eisner had turned eighty-five that year, his schedule was packed.

"He sends me a schedule every year, and we compare," said Denis Kitchen. "We always have certain meetings that we attend together, so we look for holes in our schedules to conduct business, which, when you are getting closer to the show, are far and few between."

Kitchen spotted a two-hour open block on Eisner's schedule just before the Eisner Awards were scheduled to begin.

"That's right before your awards, so you don't want to do anything then," Kitchen said.

"Well, why not?" Eisner replied.

338 **WILL EISNER: A Spirited Life**

"Aren't you a little nervous? Don't you want a little time ..."

It didn't matter to Eisner, just one more thing on his schedule. "He had a schedule that would have exhausted a forty-year-old," Kitchen said. "He did confess to me after that year for the first time that he thought he would have to cut back next year. He was finally pushing the limit. But he says yes to almost everybody."

Eisner scheduled himself from early morning breakfasts with publishers and well-wishers through late night dinners and parties with fellow creators. In between, there were panel discussions for fans and retailers and autograph sessions.

Young fans wanted to meet the man behind *John Law,* the Will Eisner character Gary Chaloner had revived, after fifty-four years on the shelf, just that year.

There was also an organizer of a comic book convention who invited Eisner to be a guest in 2003. Eisner demurred due to previous commitments, but promised to come in 2004—when he'd be eighty-seven.

And, of course, there was the annual Will Eisner Comic Industry Awards ceremony on Friday night, August 2, 2002.

For comic book professionals, the highest honor in the industry is either an Eisner Award or a Harvey Award. Kurtzman, who discovered talents as diverse as Robert Crumb and Gloria Steinem, passed away in 1993, making Eisner the last man standing.

Literally.

Every year that there had been an Eisner Awards ceremony (no awards were given in 1990) through 2004, every recipient was handed his or her award by the man himself.

In 2000, a big red velvet chair was put on stage for Eisner.

"Jeff Smith called me," Estrada recalled, "and suggested that we come up with a way to get Will to sit during at least some of the ceremony. Before the Con, I arranged with a Comic-Con worker who is also involved with the San Diego Opera to borrow a throne from their props room. At the beginning of the Eisner ceremony, Jeff and Kurt Busiek grabbed the throne from where we had it hidden, and brought it onto the stage, much to the delight of the audience."

Eisner sat on it briefly, got a laugh out of it, but then he stood up again, and stayed on his feet the rest of the night. Eisner demonstrated his strength of character and enduring physical wherewithal by standing on stage throughout the entire presentation, shaking hands and personally congratulating the winners. Although each presenter gives out three awards, no one else stood for as long as Eisner.

"You know," said *Amazing Spider-Man* writer J. Michael Straczynski, during his acceptance speech at the 2002 Eisner Awards, "you get the Emmy, you don't get it from 'Emmy.' You win the Oscar, you don't get it from 'Oscar.' How freakin' cool is this?"

"Will was the elder statesman in our field," said Maggie Thompson, editor of the *Comics Buyer's Guide*. "I don't know another case where the best-of-an-industry award was named for a living person. In comics, we were smart enough to realize this was richly deserved."

Thompson noted that no matter how high a pedestal Eisner's fans and fellow professionals in the business built for him, it only took a cockeyed look from the artist's wife to bring him back to earth.

"He routinely received standing ovations wherever he appeared," she said. "But at the Eisners, Ann sat there with that expression that said, 'He's only Will.' They were a fascinating couple. I don't know if he could have managed it without her. There is a strength and support there—although sardonic—that I think benefited our industry."

MAD magazine artist Jack Davis expressed his appreciation to Eisner
(Courtesy Will and Ann Eisner)

"He was absolutely an artist's artist," Neil Gaiman said. "It's why we take pride in having an award named after Will."

The buildup to the award for the best new graphic novel that year was already pretty satisfying to Eisner. His friend, Art Spiegelman—who a month earlier (June 3, 2002) made a speech in Manhattan's Plaza Hotel introducing Eisner as recipient of the National Foundation for Jewish Culture's Lifetime Achievement Award—was nominated for three awards. His former School of Visual Arts student, Batton Lash, shared honors for Best Humor Publication (*Radioactive Man*). Jon B. Cooke, the scriptwriter of his brother Andrew D.

Cooke's documentary on Eisner's career (*Will Eisner: The Spirit of an Artistic Pioneer*), was nominated for and won an Eisner for Best Comics Related Periodical (*Comic Book Artist Magazine*). And Eisner's good friend, writer Max Allan Collins was on hand as a presenter, riding a wave of publicity from the movie adaptation of his graphic novel, *Road to Perdition*.

The three hundred comic book VIPS (presenters, nominees, Comic-Con guests, and Eisner sponsors) invited to the event were seated at thirty tables close to the ballroom stage. Behind them sat 1,200 comic book fans, the largest turnout in the history of the Eisner Awards. Eisner took his place on stage with awards administrator Jackie Estrada. Ann Eisner was seated in the audience with Denis and Stacey Kitchen, as well as Eisner Awards Hall of Fame honoree Sergio Aragonés (whose ticklish contributions to pop culture extend from *MAD* magazine, *Plop*, and *Groo the Wanderer* to the TV show *Laugh-In*).

When Aragonés climbed to the stage to read the nominees for the best new graphic novel category, a mixture of excitement and dread came over Eisner. He picked up the award without peeking at the name underneath and prepared to hand it to the winner.

The nominees:

The Book of Leviathan, by Peter Blegvad (Overlook Press)

Fallout, by Jim Ottaviani, Janine Johnston, Steve Lieber, Vince Locke, Bernie Mireault, and Jeff Parker (GT Labs)

The Golem's Mighty Swing, by James Sturm (Drawn & Quarterly)

Hey, Wait . . ., by Jason (Fantagraphics)

Mail Order Bride, by Mark Kalesniko (Fantagraphics)

The Name of the Game, by Will Eisner (DC)

Pictures That [Tick], by Dave McKean (Hourglass/Allen Spiegel Fine Arts)

The competitor in Eisner wanted to win. The realist in him wondered if this wouldn't be the year that someone else's star would rise and his would finally set. How should he react when someone else's name was called? Smile, naturally, extend a hearty handshake, and step aside. If he won? Well, the odds were against that happening again at his age.

"And the award goes to ..." Aragonés paused for effect. "*The Name of the Game,* by Will Eisner!"

For the fifth time in ten years, Will Eisner passed the award trophy from one hand to the other, stepped up to the microphone, shook his head, smiled, and admonished the cheering audience. He was proud, but somewhat embarrassed.

"*Aww* ... you guys just need to cut it out," he said, laughing and blushing. "It used to be funny. Now it's getting tough to answer this ... Thank you very much."

━━━━━━━━━

The Will Eisner Awards gave their namesake a sense of great achievement, as did the creation of another prize in his honor, the Will Eisner Spirit of Comics Retailing Award, which was his idea and has been given out annually since 1993.

"It's a pleasurable thing, emotionally and personally, to know that the industry would be willing to give an award in my name," Eisner said. "Seeing it happen was more important than anything else. Seeing it happen and watching people getting the awards, hearing somebody say, 'I am an Eisner Award winner.' It is a badge of his accomplishment. That gives me a sense of satisfaction. It feeds my ego. It is almost like being at a wedding. I stand there throughout the whole procedure and shake the hand of the award winners. After it is over, a lot of them now have been asking me to sign the back of the award that they get, so that is kind of neat.

"I guess if Pulitzer were alive today," he added, "he would probably feel the same way."

TWENTY-FOUR
Epilogue

At eighty-five years old, Will Eisner's right shoulder finally betrayed him. The rest of the artist and writer's body might have been in denial, but by early 2002, the shoulder on his drawing arm could no longer be a party to the lie.

Eisner, it whispered, *you're old! Give up playing tennis!*

And for the next three years, although he bitterly missed his daily game, he replaced it with a vigorous thirty-minute daily swim and time on the treadmill. Ann, his wife of fifty-four years, even bought him a recliner with a built-in heating pad to soothe that aching shoulder.

"At the end of the day, it hurts. I couldn't do an oil painting or murals anymore. But working on a drawing board, that I can do," he said. "One of my problems is I've always used my whole arm. Once I start inking, I only use my wrist."

By spring 2004, the pain returned.

Eisner, his shoulder demanded, *you're eighty-seven years old! Stop hand-lettering your books. Use the computer!*

For the next year, Eisner and his shoulder reached détente. He kept telling his stories in the form he popularized. And his tired right shoulder throbbed in agony if he pushed it past quittin' time at 4 P.M.

Will Eisner at work on *The Plot*, May 2004
(Photograph by Bob Andelman)

The last day I saw Eisner in person was an exciting day in May 2004. The final unedited page of what would be his last completed book, *The Plot: The Secret Story of the Protocols of the Elders of Zion,* was on his drawing board, and he was excited about getting it to the publisher and into print.

"There will be a lot of challenges to this book," he said, anticipating the debate.

The Plot represented a new dimension in Eisner's storytelling. Where his previous book, *Fagin the Jew,* took a supporting character from Charles Dickens' *Oliver Twist* and gave him a life and legend of his own, *The Plot* represented his first head-on, non-fiction attack on real-life anti-Semitism. It stemmed from his research into the origins of a book called *The Protocols of the Learned Elders of Zion,* which Amazon.com categorized as "controversial" and listed it alongside books on UFOs and conspiracies. *Zion* is an inflammatory, untrue representation of Judaism that has nonetheless circulated in the Arab world for decades, inflaming contempt for Jews and Israel. The "plot," as referred to in the title of Eisner's work, is the perpetration of this hoax as truth.

"I think it really remarkable that Will was ready to tackle some of the most pernicious and monstrous propaganda directly and accessibly," said Eisner's friend, author Neil Gaiman. "*The Plot* is what the Spirit might have done, if he could draw."

After the *New York Times* profiled his work in progress in February 2004, Eisner was contacted by an executive of the Anti-Defamation League, who expressed interest in helping him with his dream of getting a special edition of *The Plot* published—in Arabic.

"The people who I want to read this are the people for whom *Protocols of Zion* is being published," Eisner said. "The whole purpose of *The Plot,* the only justification for doing it, is that this medium has the chance of being read by the people for whom *Protocols* was written. There are ten books condemning *Protocols,* all by academics for sophisticated readers. Those are not the people who need to be told this book is a fraud. But in a graphic novel, I have a chance of capturing readers who never heard of this before. The chance of them reading something with illustrations, a picture book, is greater than of them reading a condemnation written in text by an academician."

A book of this sort would probably stand a better chance of acceptance by an Arabic audience if a Gentile produced it. But Eisner—who started his career in the 1930s by producing comic books under five different names—never considered disguising his identity for this work.

"I start my foreword by saying, 'I am Jewish,'" he said. "It would be nice if it were done by a guy with a non-Jewish name, I suppose."

A Contract with God was the first time that Eisner consciously produced work that identified him as a Jew. And once he opened the floodgates, there was to be no turning back. *To the Heart of the Storm* was an autobiographical look at not only his life but also that of his immigrant parents as they struggled against prejudice and anti-Semitism in America during the early part of the twentieth century. And in *The Name of the Game,* he told the multi-generational story of one Jewish family—modeled in part on his wife Ann's family—as it struggled through assimilation and rose through the social ranks of New York.

Benjamin Herzberg worked with Eisner as both a researcher and sounding board on both *Fagin the Jew* and *The Plot.* He secured the bona fides of both books, moonlighting from his day job as a private sector development specialist for the World Bank in Washington, D.C. and publisher of Gasp! Editions.

"*The Plot,* in its final form, is quite different than where it started," Herzberg said. "I was the one who told Will to put himself in the book. He didn't want to, but I convinced him. The latter part of the book otherwise lacked a device to advance the narrative.

"Will started at the beginning not knowing where he was going at the end," he continued. "It originally started with white supremacists in the United States and how they were using the *Protocols* to fuel stereotypes. But that was in contradiction to what *I* perceived he wanted to do. We had this relationship where we could talk and clarify what he wanted to do.

"By focusing his initial introduction on white supremacists, he obviously would miss addressing the wide spread of the *Protocols* in the Middle East. He had an instinct about what he wanted to do and we reframed that toward something more constructive. At the same time, events were happening in Europe, especially in France, where a lot of anti-Semitic acts were happening."

They refocused the introduction and conclusion of the book—which give the book its moral resonance—as well as some chapters on being able to affect a larger audience, including people subject to the propaganda of fundamentalism in the U.S., silent witnesses of Old World anti-Semitism in Europe and last but not least, the population in the Arabic community.

Another issue that Eisner and Herzberg wrestled with was Eisner's desire to state the facts about the *Protocols* plainly and simply, putting emotion on the shelf.

"There was a need to convince people that the *Protocols* had caused tremendous pain," Herzberg says. "He didn't want to do a book that was going to be a pamphlet against anti-Semitism. He didn't want the book to be preachy. What he wanted to do was an educational comic. He wanted to communicate the truth about the *Protocols*, stay on the facts, and gain as much credibility as possible. Will was obsessed with credibility.

"He was in big trouble because he wanted to portray things without having been there. And, on the other hand, he wanted to be accurate."

As Eisner himself said, his primary goal in producing *The Plot* was putting it in front of the very people in the Middle East who believed the lies in the *Protocols*. Because the book was dispassionate, a verified and verifiable history of the *Protocols* and not a political pamphlet, he hoped it could have a deeper impact on the Arabic population, that it could be seen as historically correct and not bashing Arabs.

"Will felt that the people who believed in the story of the *Protocols* are not anti-Semitic by nature," Herzberg said. "The people who are anti-Semitic will always exist. You cannot change them with a movie or graphic novel or trial. However, the other eighty percent of the population doesn't know otherwise. The available information is not reaching them. That's why Will wanted to stay away from propaganda. It would not be accepted as a valid document. He did not want to answer propaganda with propaganda. He wanted to reach the mainstream."

When Eisner negotiated the deal for W. W. Norton to publish *The Plot,* he sold the company worldwide rights—except in Arabic countries. He retained those rights.

"The choice of Norton ensured respectability and trust in the content and a very efficient strategy with European publishers to ensure it would be published in other languages," Herzberg said. "France is the place where the truth of Mathieu Golovinski, a Russian exile living in France who wrote the *Protocols* in 1989, was discovered—by a *French* researcher. Éditions Grasset & Fasquelle is the publisher of *The Plot* in France. Grasset, in the 1920s, introduced the *Protocols* in France. It's a flip of history; Will loved that story."

In this final chapter of a remarkable, enduring career, Eisner emerged as a standard-bearer for Judaic life and existence. But he insisted that any resemblance to his becoming a crusader was strictly coincidental. This was a man whose last consistent attendance at *shul* came when he became a *bar mitzvah*.

"I am not in the business of promoting Jewish culture," he protested. "I write about the things I know. I know about Jews. I don't consider myself any different than Faulkner, who wrote about the things he knew. I write about Jewish life, Jewish culture. If I were Irish, I would write about Irish people and culture. I consider myself a Jewish Frank McCourt."

━━━━━━━━

Will and Ann Eisner were each other's greatest fans and their favorite company. More than half a century since he grudgingly gave Ann a ride from New York to Maine at the insistence of his best friend, the couple was still inseparable. In fact, since the December 2003 death of Eisner's brother and office manager Pete, Ann became a daily presence in her husband's business life for the first time. She and Eisner's secretary Florence Simpson oversaw the studio, and Ann personally typeset all the lettering for his final book, using a specially developed computer font that captured her husband's distinctive handwriting.

At home in Florida, during their final years together, they started their days taking turns swimming in the pool (he liked it quiet for his laps, while she preferred listening to books on tape). His breakfast preference, nurtured for decades, was a grapefruit, cereal, or Jewish soul food—bagel and lox. They raised delicate orchids in the lanai, but his prized possession in his last years was a small grapefruit tree. It didn't yield much fruit, but every day he hoped that there would be more.

Will and Ann Eisner, May 2004
(Photograph by Bob Andelman)

Saturdays and Sundays were Ann's to schedule as she pleased. He was not allowed to go to the office over the weekend—which was less than a mile from home—but he snuck work in anyway. Sometimes you could see it taking place in his eyes.

"I love my work," Eisner told me on that day in May. "In the beginning, this was a means to an end. Now it's an end in itself. One factor is, I can still do it. I'm still hungry for approval. And there's so much yet to do."

———

I was getting my daughter ready for school on January 4, 2005, when, at 7:30 A.M., the phone rang. For us, as most people, the phone doesn't usually ring at that time of day. And, if it does ring that early, it's never good news.

Checking the Caller I.D., I felt uneasy. The number was familiar and while the name flashed "Will Eisner," I knew that wasn't possible. It had to be Ann.

A few weeks earlier, Eisner went to his doctor complaining of short-ness of breath. The doctor sent him immediately to the hospital and the next morning he underwent quadruple cardiac bypass surgery. But it went smoothly—at nearly eighty-eight, this was a man in extraordinary physical and mental health—and plans were made for a return home the following week to begin recuperation and rehabilitation.

Unfortunately, he never left the hospital.

The following week, Eisner got out of bed and collapsed. He was taken back into surgery to relieve fluid around his heart. Again, the procedure was declared a success. But, late during the evening of January 3, on a routine bed check, Eisner's nurse discovered he had passed away in his sleep.

A lot of remarkable things happened in the days following Eisner's passing. The great love and respect he received in life was extended into death as the mainstream media treated his passing as a substantial loss to the world of arts and letters. Obituaries included a half-page in the *New York Times,* stories and photos in *Entertainment Weekly, Newsweek, Time, The Economist,* and a front-page mention in the *Wall Street Journal.* National Public Radio eulogized Will Eisner, as did ABC-TV's *This Week with George Stephanopoulos.*

And it wasn't just an American outpouring, either. Reverent stories of Eisner's life and work appeared around the globe, from *The Times of London* and *The Economist* to the *Jerusalem Post* and the *Manila Times,* which eulogized him on its editorial page.

Perhaps appropriately, the last weeks of Will Eisner's life were bookended by his work on two final projects, *The Plot* and an appearance by the Spirit in Michael Chabon's spinoff comic book from *The Amazing Adventures of Kavalier & Clay, The Escapist.*

"The last work he did was The Spirit/Escapist story," Dark Horse Comics editor Diana Schutz said. "He FedEx-ed the six-page story to me, and only after he finished it did he finally go to the doctor complaining about his shortness of breath."

Schutz spoke with Eisner by phone the night before his first surgery.

"Why did you wait?" she asked him. She was worried about him; he told her not to worry, although he admitted some anxiety himself. It was the first time Schutz ever heard vulnerability in the man's voice. He must have heard it, too, and quickly recovered his natural positivism, talking about how blessed he had been to have the life he had, to have worked at what he loved, and to have the wonderful wife and many friends he had.

"Did you get the Spirit/Escapist pages?" he asked, changing the subject. "You know, I didn't get to the doctor until after I finished those pages. And he told me to get back in the car and go straight to the emergency room."

"You shouldn't have waited," she said, but he didn't want to hear it.

"But that was Will; professional to the end," Schutz said later. "That's just the way he did things. And the pages were beautiful. It's just ironic that the last thing he did was the last Spirit story."

———————

Robert Weil, Eisner's editor at W. W. Norton on *The Plot* and the newly acquired Will Eisner Library, was the last editor to speak with Eisner.

"I spoke to Will twice the day that he died," Weil said. "Once, just before noon, to wish him a Happy New Year. I hadn't called earlier because I didn't want to disturb him. He literally sounded like he was on a sundeck. He was in great shape. We had an edit conversation. He was remarkably upbeat and cheery. He wasn't depressed in the slightest. This was a man planning to get out later the same week."

Late in the day, Weil called back with good news: the Spanish rights to *The Plot* were sold at auction to Grupo Editorial Norma. Ever the businessman, Eisner was interested in all the details of the deal. Weil, whose publishing house had an ambitious plan for Eisner to promote *The Plot* during the spring and summer of 2005, believed plans might get back on track based on the vibrancy he heard in his author's voice.

"I had just edited his thoughts in the introduction to the *A Contract with God* trilogy," Weil said. "The last words he said to me were, 'Run it by Denis.'"

When Weil received word of Eisner's death the next morning, he called in shock and relayed their last conversations.

"Will loved his work," Weil said. "He died doing his work, literally. He was the John Wayne of comics—he wanted to go out in the saddle."

———————

APPENDIX A
Jerry Iger: A Postscript

In 2001, more than a decade after his former partner Jerry Iger died, Will Eisner received a short letter that read in part:

> *Dear Mr. Eisner,*
>   *My name is Robert Iger. I am the president of the Walt Disney Company. I just read about you in the* Los Angeles Times *and was intrigued that you were a partner of my great-uncle, Jerry Iger.*
>   *Robert Iger*

Robert Iger indicated that his father was Jerry's nephew.

"It is very strange," Robert Iger said in his note, "that there is an Eisner and Iger now—Michael Eisner, chairman of Walt Disney, and myself—and there was an Eisner and Iger then. What an interesting coincidence."

Eisner—who was not related to Michael Eisner—was curious about the coincidence, too. He wrote back to the younger Iger and told him what he could about Jerry. Robert responded immediately.

When they eventually reached each other by telephone, Robert candidly told Eisner, "My family never thought much of Jerry because he was a blowhard."

"Well," Eisner said, "they weren't wrong. Jerry acted just like many little guys like that. We always had a problem because he kept saying to me sarcastically, 'You're trying to win an art director's award,' because I always talked about quality while he always insisted we were selling frankfurters here; 'Just get the stuff out!'"

"I had a few things to say about Jerry," Robert said. "I think we both agreed that Jerry was a bit of a bullshitter. And we felt he had an ability to embellish. I grew up in the 1950s and '60s. Jerry was slick. He was a bit of a dandy, pinstriped suits, always well dressed. Lived in New York, dated pretty women. He was smooth. He probably spent more money than he had. He created an aura about himself that he was a bit of a playboy. He loved women; you could see that in his art. You'd be more apt to see him in a nightclub than anywhere else, certainly not a ballgame."

Robert said that Jerry would come to his birthday parties and draw comics for his friends. He was disdainful of the 1985 book, *The Iger Comics Kingdom* published by Blackthorne Publishing, a biography of his great-uncle written by Jay Edward Disbrow. "It's an homage to Jerry; Jerry may have even funded it," he said. "Will and I both got a chuckle out of it."

He last saw his great-uncle when he was in his teens.

———————

Jerry Iger doesn't come off well in the story of his one-time partner's life.

Robert Iger agreed to be interviewed for this book. He also arranged for his father Arthur (Jerry's nephew and the inspiration for Jerry's comic book character "Bobby") to be interviewed. While neither Arthur nor Robert ever met Will Eisner, their willingness to reminisce about Jerry seemed an opportunity to inject balance into Jerry's portrayal of his partner. Or at least that was the general idea. Turns out that Jerry was everything that his former partner said that he was—and more.

Samuel Maxwell Iger—who later went by his nickname, Jerry—was born near a Choctaw Indian Reservation in Idabel, Oklahoma, in 1903, the youngest of four children. Jerry's father was an Australian peddler who owned a horse and wagon and lived by a creek, according to

Arthur. "Jerry had polio," he recalled. "My grandmother, Rosa, carried him everyday to the creek to bathe his leg, which was crippled."

The Igers were dirt poor. When Arthur's father, Joe, went into the Army, he saved his money and brought the family to New York, where he set his father up in the real estate business.

Arthur, who was born in 1926, was a favorite because he was the first grandchild in the family. "Jerry adopted me long before he became a father himself," Arthur said. "On Saturdays, I would take the subway into the city from Brooklyn where we lived, and I would go into Jerry's studio—the S. M. Iger Studio. It was a big brownstone, and I would spend the whole morning with the cartoonists who worked for Jerry. He would get me involved. He seemed proud of me; he acted paternal to me. He was wonderful to me in his own way. One of the artists had a sailboat that Jerry had access to whenever he wanted it. I learned to sail on Sheepshead Bay on that little boat. But when Jerry became a father, I had no further contact with him" as a child.

The Igers heard all the Jerry stories over the years. "Cheapskate, charmer—how many were true, who the hell knows?" Arthur said.

During the war, when Arthur came home on leave, the Iger family—including Jerry—would celebrate by going out to good restaurants. "Jerry would always be there and my dad would *always* pick up the tab," Arthur said. "The word for Jerry was that he was a *schnorrer*"—that's Yiddish for a beggar, panhandler, or a moocher. (It rhymes with "snorer.")

Once, Jerry got free tickets to a Broadway show from a friend, playwright Canada Lee, and he took Arthur as his guest. The one gift he gave Arthur that lasted a lifetime was music. "He strummed a banjo and taught me songs," Arthur said. "I thank him for that. Music became my passion." Arthur later wrote two well-received books about jazz.

In the early 1950s, Jerry called Arthur and said he was going to be drawing cartoons on an afternoon children's television program and that Arthur should tune in.

After drawing some cartoons, Jerry turned to the camera. "I would like to say 'Hello' to my nephew, little Artie Iger, who is recuperating from an auto accident and we wish him well."

Arthur was never so embarrassed in all his life.

"Thank you for wishing me well," Arthur told Jerry in a phone call later that day. "But I'm grown up, I'm married! I went through the war, for Pete's sake! Cut that out!"

Arthur spent his career in advertising and public rights, not far off from Jerry's own career.

"Jerry Iger was not very well liked in our family," Arthur said. "He was not a nice person. He was not nice to his two sisters. My father was well enough off to help them when they had financial problems. Jerry was well enough off to help them with money but he did it at big interest rates. My father didn't believe in that. My aunts' accusation was that Jerry was miserly, egotistical, phony, and pretentious."

Arthur and his mother, Ruth, were fond of Jerry's first wife, a lovely woman named Louise Hirsch. But when Jerry and Louise divorced, Arthur's father told Ruth that she could no longer be friends with Louise. Those sorts of things were disloyal to family.

Arthur recalled that Jerry's longest-lasting personal relationship was the one he had with his assistant, an attractive redhead named Ruth Roche. She had a son from a marriage that ended before she met Jerry, according to Arthur. "She loved Jerry," he said. "But he never married her."

In subsequent years, there were many wives that Jerry talked about—neither Arthur or Robert knew for sure how many—but whom he never introduced to his family.

Arthur's father was a natural host, and he and his wife frequently welcomed their extended family into their home for Sunday brunches. "Everybody brought something," Arthur recalled. "Jerry would bring chocolate and a showgirl. His braggadocio was laughable. He claimed to once go out with actress Bea Arthur. He was that way."

When Robert was born, he became Jerry's pet in much the way Arthur had. "When Bob was born, Jerry gave us a sterling silver rattle," Arthur said. "That, for Jerry, was far, far away from a chocolate bar."

But, over the years, Jerry became estranged from the family. "There was never anything criminal or horrible or terribly untoward that he did to us," Arthur said. Money problems contributed to the estrangement, but, in general, the rest of the Igers just found Jerry unpleasant to be around. "He would rail on the phone with my mother and say that his sisters did him bad," Arthur said. "I didn't love the guy. I *couldn't*. He wasn't lovable. He wasn't for real."

When Arthur's father died in 1962, Jerry attended the funeral and kept in touch with Arthur's mother for several years.

Arthur wasn't impressed with Jerry's autobiography any more than was his son. "It was so full of errors about the Iger family. I put it down with nausea," Arthur said.

The last time Arthur saw Jerry was in the early to mid-1970s in his office at Macmillan Publishing in New York City, where Arthur was vice president and publisher of the educational division. "Jerry was living in Sunnyside, Queens at the time," he said. "He came to visit me. I took him to my favorite restaurant. And, of course, I paid. That was my wife's first question when I got home that night—'Did Jerry go for the check?' Of course not!"

The next time any of the Igers heard news about Jerry was when they read his obituary in September 1990.

APPENDIX B
A World of Influence

ALAN MOORE
(writer, *Watchmen, From Hell, The League of Extraordinary Gentlemen*)

According to Will Eisner, the nicest thing anyone ever said about his work came from writer Alan Moore, who provided a complimentary blurb to a Scottish comic book-convention flyer that said, "Eisner is the single person most responsible for giving comics its *brains*."

Moore said he meant every word of it.

"The masters of the early twentieth-century American newspaper comic strips came up with wonderful storytelling devices, breathtaking work," he said. "The thing that Will Eisner brought to comics, in my opinion, is a kind of methodical intelligence. He didn't just think up a few visual tricks, a few storytelling devices, and exploit them marvelously as perhaps the early twentieth-century pioneers can be said to have done. Will came up with a complete philosophy of comics that applied to almost every detail of them, the drawing, the writing, and, most importantly, the storytelling, the kind that occurs between the drawing and the writing."

Moore's first exposure to Eisner came through the two Harvey *Spirit* reprints in the 1960s. Later, he was "blown away" by a feature in the *Will Eisner Quarterly* magazine called "Hamlet on a Rooftop."

"Will was experimenting and seeing if you could use the comic strip medium to adequately get across a Shakespearian soliloquy,"

Jay Lynch parodied *The Spirit* in this underground
comix featuring his characters Nard n' Pat,
originally published in *Bijou Funnies* No. 2, 1968
(© 1969 Jay Lynch. Renewed 1997)

Moore said. "This is something which works fine on stage if you have the physical presence of an actor, but was it possible to do it simply with the expressiveness of your drawing and your storytelling? That was something that I admired about Will, that his brain never stopped. He didn't just come up with a few really spectacular devices and let his reputation rest upon them. He came up with a method, a whole way of approaching comics, that opened up hitherto unsuspected dimensions for someone like me."

When Moore first entered the business of writing comics, Eisner's work was a benchmark that he sought to live up to. "Even if the benchmark is unreachable, then you can still stretch yourself a little bit in reaching for it, and I think that is one of the invaluable things that Will Eisner has given the comics medium. He set a high standard, which I am sure that most people working in it would have equally cursed him for and admired him for. I wouldn't have it any other way."

Moore said that the "Grayshirt" stories in his creator-owned America's Best Comics *Tomorrow Stories* were homage to Eisner's work and influence.

"I wasn't trying to reproduce his storytelling techniques or to simply have the word 'Grayshirt' spelled out in crumbling tenement buildings or make obvious Eisner references like that, but I was trying to fill the gap that I felt had been left in the wake of *The Spirit*," he said. "*The Spirit* was a perfect vehicle for doing incredibly tight little stories where the whole story could be built around a particular storytelling device. I wanted to do that with (*Grayshirt* artist) Rick Veitch."

In the second issue of *Tomorrow Stories,* there is a building, four panels to every page, and each page was a shot of the building in which there were four floors, so each panel was a shot of one of the floors of the building arranged in a stack. The complex narrative on the top floor of the building takes place in 1999. On the next floor down, it is 1979. On the next floor down, it is 1959, and on the lowest floor, at the bottom of the page, it is 1939. The narratives can be read either horizontally—reading one particular time stream at a time—or up, down, or any way the reader chooses.

"It wasn't like anything that Will himself has done, but he was the driving influence behind it," Moore said. "I was trying to be as smart as Eisner, which is generally a doomed venture. We were trying to come up with a tight, eight-page story based upon a storytelling device that was well turned and sort of could have been a *Spirit* story if Eisner had thought of it before I did or whatever. That was the pinnacle we were aiming for."

Moore said he and Veitch consciously discussed Eisner when they were concocting the Grayshirt character, "but at the same time, we didn't want it to look like Eisner, and we didn't even want it particularly to remind people of Eisner. We wanted it to have its own style and feel, but the engine for the strip, the thing that provided the inspiration, that was one-hundred percent Eisner."

CARMINE INFANTINO
(artist, *The Flash*; former publisher, DC Comics)

"When I was a kid, Bill Eisner and Lou Fine were my idols. I was about sixteen or seventeen years old and I was reading *The Ray*, *Black Condor*, all these things Busy Arnold put out. Bill and Lou were almost interchangeable for a while. The distinctive storytelling was Bill; Lou was a beautiful designer. Bill is and was one of the best storytellers in the world. Some of the covers I created at DC might bear an Eisner influence. There was one, a Batman cover—"The House of Joker." That was the kind of thing Will would do, mid-1950s. And I did one where this villain, Blockbuster, is busting through the lettering of 'Batman.' That's also the kind of thing Will would have done."

A variety of artists show their
appreciation for Eisner
(Courtesy Will and Ann Eisner)

DENNY O'NEIL

(writer, *Green Lantern*/*Green Arrow*; former *Batman* writer and editor)

"In my work, the Question was most heavily influenced by the Spirit. The Question is not far from the Spirit—a human scale, vulnerable character. It's not the appeal of Superman, a greater strength. I didn't create the Question, of course—Steve Ditko did. The general approach was a willingness to deal with adult themes. I remember Frank Miller was in my apartment in SoHo and I showed him a couple pages I had written for my first issue of *The Question*. It was very talky. I was seeking advice—should I put more action in it? Frank said no. But for a guy used to dealing with demi-God characters, that was a departure, to let the dialogue and human interest carry and predominate."

HOWARD CRUSE

(writer/artist, *Stuck Rubber Baby*, *Barefootz*)

"I did some teaching at the School of Visual Arts and Will's work was always touched on as an approach to page composition. You wouldn't detect obvious hints of Eisner in my page composition because he has a way of drawing pictures together and I'm more anal retentive or a formalist than him. I tend to stick to rectangles and only break out occasionally. But I can tell marvelous draftsmanship when I see it. I'm always challenged to be more adventurous by artists like Eisner.

"When a guy in my work bends his arms at the sleeve, the way the clothing hangs, I do my Eisner thing. Except I do it with stipples, where you create a shade with a lot of dots, instead of crosshatches. The way he shades within a fold of clothing was distinct from the Milton Caniff approach. Between Caniff and Neal Adams and a handful of others, you veer closest to realism in clothes. Eisner made it look simple; I always found that appealing."

JERRY CRAFT

("Mama's Boyz," *New Kids on the Block, Sweet 16*)

Craft never attended a class taught by Eisner or swept floors for him. But in the early 1980s, someone told him about a book Eisner wrote. It changed his life.

"I always heard *Comics & Sequential Art* was something that I should read," Craft said. "The only other similar book I saw at that time was *How to Draw Comics the Marvel Way*. I was ten.

"When I picked up Will's book, I was blown away that there was that much thought process behind comic books. As a kid you think it just comes out. Today, everything is so PC, writers don't let characters speak with accents. They're afraid to offend someone.

"With Eisner, everything was an element of design. The panel lines were thick, thin, some rounded. I read in his book about how thinner panels conveyed a sense of being cramped and stressed, or the open ones being laid back and having tempo. I started putting that stuff into my work. Bolding certain words, for example. If a sentence was dropping off, I would literally curve it downward. Eisner said that everything has life to it and that inspired me.

"When you learn new techniques you tend to go crazy with them," Craft said. "There is a chapter in the book that told me to slow down and not overdo it. It's page ninety-eight—the bottom eight panels. Before reading the book I would have done the stuff on page ninety-nine, trying to get the most exciting panel. Reading this, however, I realized that you need to do what's best for the story. This page was great because the art lulled you into thinking this is a regular guy ('The Story of Gerhard Shnobble'). When he flew out the window at the end of the story, that shocked me. The way I would have done it would not have told the story as well. That is something I remembered from the day I read the story till this moment."

Like all artists, Craft is often asked by young people how he started in cartooning and what tools would help them. He always recommends they buy a copy of *Comics & Sequential Art*.

Craft met Eisner for the first time on a panel on graphic novels at the University of Massachusetts at Amherst. At the end, Craft gave him a copy of his own book and Eisner later wrote him and said he liked the story. "People don't write stories anymore," Eisner wrote.

"I took that as one of the highest compliments I'd ever gotten," Craft said.

MIKE CARLIN
(writer/artist; editor, DC Comics)

"Will counts. I got my first real break in comics by dropping Will's name. I called *Crazy* magazine at Marvel. The editor was Larry Hama. I mentioned that I studied with Eisner and Kurtzman and it definitely opened a door."

JERRY ROBINSON
(writer/artist, *Batman*)

"When I started to do my own *Batman* stories, I recalled some of Will's splash pages on *The Spirit*. They were great. He always had different concepts and techniques. The first one I did, I was thinking of the things he did. I enjoyed doing symbolic covers and splash pages for *Batman*; maybe Will was the reason.

"I always enjoyed doing the Joker. One Joker story was called 'Slay 'em with Flowers.' The Joker operated a flower shop as a front. For the cover, symbolic of the Joker, I drew a flowerpot as big as Batman and Robin. Out of it came a flower, winding around, and bursting out was the Joker, who sprayed insecticide on Batman and Robin. It never appeared in the story, but the approach was inspired by *The Spirit*. I tried to do a poster cover. It was more interesting. And on the cover, it made a much more dramatic impact. There was a lot of competition on the newsstands in those days. Those are all things where I was inspired by Will."

JIM KEEFE
(former writer/artist, *Flash Gordon*)

"I keep the Warren *Spirit* magazines next to my desk for inspiration. For lighting, for setting the mood. It's film noir. As the artist on the 'Flash Gordon' Sunday comic strip, I did a sequence on July 30, 2000, that was essentially a *Spirit* story about a prison break. I actually did seven weeks of stories where Flash wasn't in it. Dale was transported back to Earth. She's in a top-secret prison. Secret Agent X-9 knows who she is and where she's come from. X-9 goes in to rescue her. It's the stuff Eisner is a master of, lighting a mood. My little homage to Eisner is in the last panel where Secret Agent X-9 escapes."

JOHN HOLMSTROM
(writer/artist/publisher, *Punk Magazine*)

"*Punk Magazine* number three was my tribute to Will. Lots of bricks. And number six had a lot of his influence as well. Legs McNeil was a huge Will Eisner fan. He wanted that issue to be a combination of Damon Runyan ("Guys & Dolls"), Will Eisner, and a James Cagney gangster movie."

MARK CHIARELLO
(art director, DC Comics)

As the art director for the comic books in the DC Universe, Mark Chiarello is charged with assigning the artists who draw the all-important covers.

"When I'm trying to tell a young artist what makes an effective cover, I always say, 'Look at Eisner's splash pages,'" Chiarello said. "It's a complete course. *The Spirit* was done so long ago, but it speaks to what comics should be about today. Comics have matured for both the good and the bad over the last fifteen years. The comics that are the most effective and the images that are most effective are rooted in what Eisner, Alex Toth (*Space Ghost, Josie and the Pussycats, Zorro, The Herculoids, Super Friends*), Jack Kirby, and Harvey Kurtzman did. I've taught at colleges about Milton Caniff. Kids say, 'I don't get Caniff.' I say, 'Backtrack from your favorite current artist, someone like Jim Lee, and you'll wind up at Caniff. Go to Frank Miller and take another step back and it will lead to (artist Jim) Steranko. Where it all ends is Will Eisner and the cinematic approach to storytelling.' That's how young fans can appreciate what Will Eisner is all about.

"One month I had the concept of doing just character faces on every DC Universe cover. The artists had to somehow integrate the name of the comic into the image. It was very Eisner-influenced. I would talk to an artist and if he didn't get it, I'd say, 'Look at Eisner splash pages and do that.' We called it 'Icons of the DC Universe.' It was a tip of the hat to him."

MARV WOLFMAN

(writer; former Editor in Chief, Marvel Comics, cocreator of *The New Teen Titans*)

"Mike Ploog and I did a tribute to Eisner in a *Werewolf by Night*. The splash page was right out of Eisner's work, a beautiful woman coming through a beaded curtain."

MIKE PLOOG

(artist, *PS Magazine, Man-Thing*; film designer)

"Neal Adams and I and a few other artists did satirical pieces for *Esquire* magazine. Mine had a Spirit-like character and Will wrote me a letter about it saying, 'I hope you are not going to pursue this character any further than this. If you do, I am afraid I will have to have my lawyer contact you.' It was a letter I carried around for the longest time. It was in my glove box in my old car. I wanted to hang onto it, but I sold the damn car, and the letter was in it."

PATRICK MCDONNELL

(writer/artist, *Mutts*)

"My opening panel on Sundays is always a tribute to someone. I haven't done a *Spirit* takeoff—yet. But there was a Sunday page (September 28, 1997) that was definitely Will Eisner-esque. It was about mysteries. Unfortunately for the title panel I went with the Shadow, but the rest was definitely Eisner-esque. It was definitely a tribute to Will. It's reprinted in the first Sunday *Mutts* book."

RAY BILLINGSLEY

(writer/artist, *Curtis*)

"I credit Will with a couple things in my strip that came from him. For example, every Kwanzaa, I do an original *Curtis* story with a moral. I usually draw it in a different style than *Curtis*. I attribute that to Will; he always said that we should show we could do things differently; it would make us more attractive in the field. When Kwanzaa first came up, I didn't embrace the idea right away. I thought it was a little dull the way I originally presented it: as fact, nothing more. Then I thought, *Instead of staying so rigid, why not make up my own*

African tales? Usually after those run, I get a lot of mail asking who the guest artist was.

"I also tried to make my strip grittier. And that went back to Will's influence.

"Of course, Will didn't tell me everything I needed to know about the business. For example, he didn't tell me that some ideas may catch on that you may not want to catch on."

TOM ARMSTRONG
(writer/artist, *Marvin*)

"I like the film noir look of Eisner's stuff. I love that look. I tried to do a mystery strip once called 'Hugh Donnit' that was Eisner-esque. I have a Will Eisner instructional book and I used it for some of the shadowing in the sample strips. But the syndicate didn't like it so I put it into 'Marvin.' When Marvin's dad is involved in a mystery, that's 'Hugh Donnit.'"

JACK JACKSON
(writer/artist, *Comanche Moon, The Secret of San Saba*)

"When I was a kiddo, Eisner's *Spirit* was an exciting weekly thrill. I made regular Sunday trips to a neighbor's house for the comics section of the San Antonio paper, as they were subscribers and my mom wasn't. Nobody could draw sexy women as good as Will and his page layouts always grabbed me."

NEIL GAIMAN
(writer, *Sandman, American Gods*)

"I am a story-driven animal. What fascinated me about comics was the idea that it was a medium in which you could tell stories that you could not tell with other media and that you could use storytelling in a different way. Without Will Eisner, I don't think I would ever have realized that. Without seeing what he could do, what he did with shape, what he did with form. Everything is about people and what happens to them. This is stuff nobody else was doing in comics. Not in a way that I could grasp and get hold of. To me, what Will did was and is timeless.

"Just as every *Spirit* story was not about the Spirit, every *Sandman* story that I wrote was not about the Sandman. Morpheus was a small part of many of the stories, and there were some in which he didn't even appear at all. On the other hand, it was his comic, and it was his place, and I wouldn't have dared do that if Will hadn't done it forty years earlier.

"Nothing Will has ever written feels like it could have been written by anybody else, which I love. I love the fact that you always know that it was Will who wrote it. There is never any attempt by Will to sound like someone else, to be someone else. But the first thing you learn from Will is brutal economies. And they are brutal. Watch what Will could do in seven pages, week in, week out, and then you look at what it takes some people, myself included, several hundred pages to do. I always wind up in awe at that point. It is astonishing what he can do best. So that's one thing. Easy, instant characterizations, a willingness to steal from theater, a willingness to steal from radio. It would be hard to make television shows of those classic *Spirits*. On the other hand, it would be easy to turn pretty much any of them into really good audio theater.

"What interests me about what Will does is he tries something different every time. The family saga of *The Name of the Game* is absolutely fascinating. Watching these characters age, watching them change— there is a level on which Will tends to work in a broad stroke because he feels like the tradition he came out of is almost theatrical rather than literary. You know quickly with Will's characters what kind of people they are or what kind of people they will show themselves to be. One of his enormous advantages is that he has been around and he has seen generations. I don't know that a twenty-year-old could have written *The Name of the Game* as convincingly. You need to have watched a couple of generations of people start out and age and breed and what happens in order to get where you can do it with conviction.

"I like to think of Will as being like the Velvet Underground. Brian Eno said, 'Only five thousand people ever bought a Velvet Underground album, but every single one of them started a band.' That is kind of how I feel about Will. If you found Will at the right age, and you knew what Will was doing, why would you want to do anything else?

"Then you have the people who will explain to you how Will is the father of the Underground comics movement. And mean it. And there is definitely an argument in which he is. And when you start to talk to

Will, you realize the level to which he was the father of everything else, as much by the things he didn't do as sometimes it is the things that he did. Which I think is hilarious.

"The strange thing about being an artist is that you encounter your heroes long before you meet them. I encountered Will in 1974 as a fifteen-year-old, buying a copy of the second of the two Harvey *Spirit* reprints, which I bought because I saw it hanging on a wall in Allen Austin's basement in Clapton (in London), which doubled as a comics shop two days a week. I had no idea what it was at all. It could have been anything, but it showed this guy in a mask being menaced by some beautiful women. I paid $10 for it and took it home. I didn't know these were reprints from the 1940s. As far as I was concerned, these were just incredibly amazing stories. I remember reading the "Plaster of Paris" story, and it was like an electric shock. I took this thing home and just fell in love.

"The only drawing I ever did and submitted to a British fanzine (*Fantasy Unlimited*, later renamed *Comics Unlimited*) was of the Spirit. And I got a pretty nice letter back from the editor, Allen Austin, who was also the guy who owned that basement comics store, explaining that he had real artists like John Daniel Breck drawing for him, telling me to fuck off.

"Over the years, one of the things I have loved about Will is having conversations with him about whatever we are doing or whatever is happening and he is probably the only person in comics who is capable of saying, 'Of course, they tried that in 1947, but they did it like this and it worked.'

Index

About the Author

Bob Andelman is the author of *Will Eisner: A Spirited Life* (October 2005). He is the author or co-author of ten books, including three business bestsellers (*Mean Business, The Profit Zone,* and *Built From Scratch*) and three sports books (*The Corporate Athlete, Stadium For Rent,* and *Why Men Watch Football*). A five-time Florida Magazine Association award winner for investigative reporting, Andelman wrote the syndicated "Mr. Media" column from 1994-98 for Universal Press Syndicate and currently co-authors the weekly column "Sports of the Weird" with Chuck Shepherd, also for Universal. He lives in St. Petersburg, Florida, with his wife, Mimi, daughter, Rachel, and two dogs. For more information, please visit http://www.andelman.com.

Will Eisner and Bob Andelman, August 2003
(Photograph by Pete Eisner)